Biography of a Businessman

HENRY W. SAGE, 1814-1897

Henry W. Sage (1814–1897)

Biography of a Businessman

HENRY W. SAGE, 1814-1897

By Anita Shafer Goodstein

Cornell University Press

ITHACA, NEW YORK

© 1962 by Cornell University

CORNELL UNIVERSITY PRESS

First published 1962

Library of Congress Catalog Card Number: 62-19172

PRINTED IN THE UNITED STATES OF AMERICA
BY VAIL-BALLOU PRESS, INC.

Preface

HENRY WILLIAMS SAGE was a successful businessman in that century which brought to successful businessmen power and prestige in all aspects of American life. It was not strange that Sage was both a lumber baron and a trustee of Cornell University and that he worked with equal vigor in each capacity. Cornell University needed the wealth and influence of "captains of industry" who accepted trusteeship as a tribute to their ability, as a duty owed their society, but rarely as a justification for lives dedicated to profit seeking. The businessman was proud not only of his success but also of his calling. He was the adviser as well as the patron of the university and the church.

Undoubtedly a primary reason for the dominance of the business personality in the nineteenth century was the immediacy of economic opportunity. Business enterprise was free, largely private, and often highly profitable. Few governmental restraints impeded the businessman's progress. The resources that made for business success were abundant and available. Expansion was the key word in American economic development just as optimism was the key word in American intellectual and religious experience. Ithaca, the town in which Sage grew up, and Bell Ewart and Wenona, the mill towns which Sage created, were communities which self-consciously applauded growth in population and appreciation of property values. Sage's secular and religious education had taught him that hard work and moral determination must result in success and salvation.

Yet the very fluidity of the economic order, the consciousness of omnipresent opportunity, created dangers. There were booms but there were also panics. The insecurity of the businessman was perhaps intensified because his philosophy of expansion and optimism did not adequately account for panic, depression, and failure. To keep from "breaking" became a moral as well as a business imperative. Success was achieved in an atmosphere of intense competition which placed a premium on gaining and maintaining ultimate control of any operation in which the businessman was interested, and this drive toward exclusive control was carried over into nonbusiness relationships.

As a biography of a businessman this study deals with the nature, development, and profitability of Henry Sage's business operations. As a biography it emphasizes the ideas, motives, and prejudices Henry Sage brought to and derived from his business experience.

I am very much indebted to three teachers and friends at Cornell. Working with and for Professor Paul W. Gates has been a stimulating experience. His advice, constructive criticism, and aid, including his notes on Henry Sage, were generously given. Professor John G. B. Hutchins of the Graduate School of Business and Public Administration provided a rich background in business history which helped me to see my subject in perspective. Mrs. Edith M. Fox, Curator of the Collection of Regional History and Cornell University Archivist, was a constant source of enthusiasm and gave invaluable aid in locating and obtaining access to manuscript materials.

Dr. Mary Elizabeth Young of the Ohio State University read and criticized the manuscript and generously helped with the maps.

I should like to thank also members of the Sage family, especially Mr. Olaf Holter, Mrs. Henry M. Sage, and Mrs. Henry W. Sage, for making available manuscripts and other sources of information. Miss Emma Speed and the late Miss Bessie Speed kindly permitted use of their photograph of Susan Linn Sage. The photograph of Henry W. Sage was provided through the courtesy of the Cornell University Archives. I sincerely appreciate the many services extended to me by staff members of the Bay City Public Library, the Cornell University Archives and Collection of Regional History, the Cornell University Library, the DeWitt Historical Society, and the Library of the University of the South.

Some of the material presented here, particularly in Chapters II and V, has been used previously in two articles published in the *Bulletin of the Business Historical Society:* "The Williams Brothers, Merchants and Shippers, 1825–1850," XXVI (1952), 73–94; and "Labor Relations in the Saginaw Valley Lumber Industry, 1865–1885," XXVII (1953), 193–221.

A fellowship from the Social Science Research Center of Cornell University and a Cornell University summer research scholarship enabled me to complete a great part of the research. A Gillmore Fellowship from the Department of History of Cornell University enabled me to revise the manuscript for publication.

For support, both financial and moral, I owe a great debt to my husband, Marvin.

ANITA SHAFER GOODSTEIN

Sewanee, Tennessee
March 1962

Contents

Illustrations

Maps

Abbreviations

Cornell University Archives

ADW, Andrew D. White Papers
GS, Goldwin Smith Papers
JGS, Jacob Gould Schurman Papers

Cornell University Collection of Regional History

HWS, Henry Williams Sage Papers
JBW, Josiah B. Williams Papers
WF, Williams Family Papers

DeWitt Historical Society

DeWitt, Miscellaneous papers relating to Henry W. Sage, especially a small collection consisting largely of the correspondence of Henry B. Schuyler and a small collection of the papers of John McGraw

Biography of a Businessman

HENRY W. SAGE, 1814-1897

Chapter I
The Young Man, 1814-1836

HENRY SAGE thought of himself as a self-made man. Neverthe-less, he did have the decided advantage of an industrious, pious, and literate Connecticut Yankee background. Henry Sage's family traces its ancestry in America to David Sage, a Welshman who settled in Middletown, Connecticut, about 1652.[1] The Williamses, the family of Henry Sage's mother, are descended from Thomas Williams, also a Welshman, who is known to have established his home in Wethersfield, Connecticut, at approximately the same time.[2] For at least five generations both families continued to farm or keep store in central Connecticut. Jehiel Williams, Henry Sage's great-grandfather, moved to Upper Middletown in the 1750's, and by 1813, when Sally Williams and Charles Sage were married, the local newspapers were recounting the activities of a number of Williamses and Sages.

Henry Sage was born on January 31, 1814, in the home of his grandfather, Josiah Williams, a farmer who worked also as a shoe-maker during the winter months. Josiah's large family apparently never suffered want or neglect in his household, although Josiah was far from wealthy. The Williamses were a close-knit family, and when one by one the sons made their way to western New York anxious letters followed them suggesting remedies for ailments, urging visits home, and above all warning against getting "too much entangled with things that perish with their rising." [3] Well

[1] Sage to Atlantic Publishing and Engraving Co., Dec. 3, 1884, HWS. Henry W. Sage will be referred to throughout the notes by his surname only.
[2] Murray E. Poole, *Williams Geneology* (Ithaca, N.Y., 1910), p. 9.
[3] J. E. Williams to J. B. Williams, Nov. 14, 1831, WF.

1

into the thirties their correspondence was deeply colored with evangelistic messages.

The Sages lived with Josiah Williams until 1816, when Charles Sage moved his family, now including a daughter, to Bristol. Charles was at this time about twenty-one. For some part of the eleven years he remained in Bristol he seems to have been moderately successful. In 1822 his young brother-in-law, Jehiel F. Williams, sent thanks for gifts from Sally and Charles and was glad to hear that business was "lively." [4] Charles maintained a pew in Bristol's Congregational Church and sent his son to Sunday school and to the Bristol Academy.[5] Evidently young Henry began to cherish hopes of attending Yale.

The family increased regularly; four more daughters and another son were born, but a girl and the boy died in infancy. Close contact was maintained with the Williamses, and in 1827 Charles Sage decided to follow Sally's brothers to Ithaca, New York, where abundant economic opportunities were expected to follow from the newly opened Erie Canal system.

Probably Sage's fortunes had already begun to deteriorate before the decision to move was made, for he seems to have brought very little capital with him. For a few months in 1828 he advertised himself as a merchant with "a small assortment of Dry Goods and Groceries, of a good quality, which he wishes to sell cheap for cash, lumber, or produce. . . . N.B. Shingles wanted for goods, or money if I have it." [6] This modest advertisement does not seem to have attracted many customers, and Charles Sage ceased advertising within a few months.

In the next few years Charles Sage became "a poor relation." Ague and fever dogged the family: "Sally has been sick. She is able to sit up now. Henry has not been able to do the least thing for months." [7] Resentment grew against the Williams brothers,

[4] April 29, WF.

[5] Eddy N. Smith et al., Bristol Connecticut (Hartford, Conn., 1907), pp. 180, 191.

[6] Ithaca Journal and General Advertiser, Nov. 26, 1828.

[7] Charles Sage to J. B. Williams, Oct. 20, 1829, WF.

Timothy and Manwell, who had by this time established themselves as merchants and shippers in Ithaca and Albany. Sally Sage complained bitterly, "It is no private thing that we are considered beneath the notice of our other brothers." [8]

Timothy Shaler Williams had introduced two of his brothers to his business, which in time was to absorb a third. Each of these men eventually assumed a full partnership through gift or purchase. Apparently the same opportunity was not extended to Charles Sage. Possibly the stock in trade which Sage offered to the public in 1828 had been provided by the Williamses. Sage's failure, whether with his own capital or theirs, would not have encouraged the Williamses to trust his ability or character. Theirs was a Calvinist training which linked failure with moral weakness; it is significant that young Henry Sage was later to offer his uncles as security his "business abilities and moral character." These formed a test by which Henry Sage, too, judged people throughout his life.

Charles Sage could not meet the test. After an attempt to support himself and his family by taking in boarders—the project failed, and he was left with a house whose rent was difficult to pay: "No income but the Old Cow. She lives on the Public & yields us a tolerable mess twice a day" [9]—Sage worked intermittently for his brothers-in-law. In the summer and fall of 1830 he captained one of the Williamses' canalboats on the Ithaca-Albany route. Even in this position, however, he did not inspire confidence in the Williamses.

Sage has made a poor trip I am almost afraid to trust him again for fear he will sell the whole load. You must not give him much money . . . if he has ever so much he will keep it. We never can get any back I dont see what he does with all the money.[10]

By November of 1830 Charles Sage had not yet found a permanent position; Sally's mother wrote anxiously, "I no not what

[8] To J. B. Williams, 1829, WF.

[9] Charles Sage to J. B. Williams, June 7, 1830, WF.

[10] Fragment of a letter of M. R. Williams, Aug. 23, 1830; see also J. B. Williams to T. S. Williams Co., Sept. 11, 1830, WF.

will become off his family. . . . I wish that he would try to get in to bee a clark for some store . . . and bee prudent that he might get along some." [11] In 1831 Timothy Williams commented, "I don't see how they [the Sages] are to live unless I help them— I feel willing to do all I ought but I don't want to be [curs'd] for it." [12]

Undoubtedly a central fact of Henry Sage's adolescence was this unhappy situation. The humiliation of having their furniture sold to pay the rent, the repeated forced moves from one to another rented house, the illnesses aggravated by cheap housing close to the Inlet of Cayuga Lake, the indignities and resentments of "poor relation" status must all have left their mark. Particularly in so small and competitive a community as Ithaca in the 1830's the success of the Williamses must have afforded a sharp contrast with the failure of Charles Sage. We cannot know exactly the effect upon the young boy of the existence of these two models so immediately a part of his life—one earning universal approval, the other sufferance or perhaps contempt. Certainly he became ambitious to secure a happier position for his family and himself. At seventeen he wrote, "I try to look up from the mist of poverty and obscurity which at present surrounds us and to hope—and be determined that at some future period we shall once more emerge from it and cut something of a figure in this world." [13] Worldly success became a goal which neither revivalists' sermons nor the excitement of intellectual pursuits could disparage.

As a boy Sage proved receptive to both evangelism and "science." His family migrated from Connecticut to western New York, from one fierce theater of evangelism to the very "burned-over district" in which Charles Grandison Finney's rousing, revivalist techniques achieved extraordinary results in the late twenties and early thirties. Again and again religious enthusiasm was experienced by pious New Englanders at home and in New York; Sage's

[11] Charity Williams to J. B. Williams, Nov. 13, WF.
[12] To J. B. Williams, April 28, WF.
[13] To J. B. Williams, April 22, 1831, WF.

family did not escape. Although religion was a constant feature of the Williamses' correspondence, this theme seems to have reached a peak in 1831 when announcements of conversions were coupled with admonitions to others in the family to hurry and become "real Christians." In April, Henry Sage and his oldest sister, Julia Ann, were "subjects" of a revival in Ithaca. At Middletown in May, Jehiel Williams "experienced religion" and Chauncey Williams appeared "to feel a great interest in the cause." [14] Yet it is doubtful that young Henry's conversion marked a more than average interest in revivalism. Indeed it may have left a fainter impress on him than on most. It would have been difficult for a boy of seventeen to withstand the emotional fervor of the occasion, and for one who had good reason to seek approval and prestige conversion may have had an extra if unconscious appeal. In the same month in which he underwent conversion, Henry Sage protested to his Uncle Josiah:

You may say that the things of this world are vain and transitory and that after death they sink into insignificance, and I shall certainly agree with you on that point. But through the short career which man has to run in this world I think that every one had ought to take as much enjoyment from it as he is capable of doing.[15]

Evangelism did not mean, then, an abandonment of ambition.

Sage's uncles were to participate largely in the movements that evangelistic fervor sponsored: temperance, Sunday schools, Bible distribution, and later, abolition; the Williams brothers sponsored an association which proposed to bring religious education to the canal laborers. Although he was listed as a contributor along with Ezra Cornell and other Ithacans to this Waterman's Association, Henry Sage does not seem to have taken a very active part in evangelistic drives. Perhaps he had not the time; by 1836 he was seriously involved in promoting a business career. Undoubtedly his commitment to religious enthusiasm was less complete and

14 J. E. Williams to J. B. Williams, April 30, 1831; copy of a letter of J. B. Williams to T. S. Williams, May 7, 1831, WF.

15 April 22, 1831, WF.

less rigid than his uncles'. In the late thirties Sage's extrabusiness energies were being devoted to self-culture and phrenology.

We know very little of Sage's formal education. The Bristol Academy and his own diligence did result in a very elegant handwriting replete with flourishes; in 1831 his writing was also full of grand verbiage, "According to agreement I now hasten to give you for leisure perusal a page or two of my ungrammatical effusions." [16] Luckily this style was discarded when he became a businessman. After the family's removal to Ithaca, Sage does not seem to have had formal schooling for about two years. Then, beginning in June of 1830, he studied for some months with Dr. Austin Church, a physician, who advertised that he would

attend to the instruction of Medical Students in the science of Botany. . . . The course of instruction will embrace—1. Systematick Botany; 2. Physiological Botany; 2. Economical Botany or Botany as applied to the practice of Medicine and the Arts generally.[17]

In later years Henry Sage explained that he was forced to leave Dr. Church's classes because of poor eyesight. It is true that he suffered from eye complaints during the whole of his life, but this did not prevent him from writing by hand innumerable letters each day or from attending to the ledgers and account books. Possibly his lessons with Dr. Church were undertaken in a period when his father had been engaged for the boating season and were abandoned at the end of this season.

In any case formal education at this juncture of his family's fortunes was less desirable than "getting into business." [18] The latter was the quickest and most obvious way of achieving status in Henry Sage's society. His attending a course of lectures may have reflected simply the lack of opportunity to begin a business apprenticeship. When in the spring of 1831 he failed to get a job as a clerk in a store, Henry wrote despairingly:

[16] To J. B. Williams, April 22, WF.
[17] *Journal and General Advertiser,* June 2, 1830.
[18] Sage to J. B. Williams, April 21, 1831, WF.

I am kicking about the streets and doing nothing or at home sullenly and silently thinking of the state and prospects of our family, and of some means of extricating them from it but no way seems to present itself at present unless we have something to do.[19]

It is significant that Henry Sage did not begin to work as a clerk in the Williams organization until 1832, when he was eighteen years old, despite the obvious financial needs of the Sages. His youth was not against him, for Josiah Williams was working for Timothy at fifteen and at nineteen was managing the Albany branch of the business while Maxwell Williams began to work for Timothy at seventeen and Chauncey Williams at least by the time he was sixteen. It may very well have been that his father's reputation placed considerable difficulties in young Sage's path.

His acceptance as a clerk was the all-important first step. A clerk had status; he was a recognized member of the striving class. Unlike the canal laborer with whom he often dealt, Henry now had practical alternatives, the ability to save, the opportunity for private trading or investing, the possibility of partnerships. He could take a place in "society" and in the numerous societies of the community.

In the first few years of his apprenticeship with the Williamses, Henry seems to have been on easy and familiar terms with his uncles as was fitting for a young man who was not only a relation but also a contemporary. A "P.S." to his "Dear Uncles" teased:

M.R. Esq. must recollect that I am in duty bound not *to tell tales*—He can *guess* & so can I *and I guess*—That somebody very frequently *sits up late with the ladies*—My room is at the head of the stairs and *as people pass*—I *sometimes hear*—*a thing or* two.

He also relayed business gossip with confidence bordering on boldness:

Wheat comes in pretty fast—and TS—is "going in" pretty deep (say $3000 to $4,000) . . . . It is *too much*—and you must lose money—M.R.

19 *Ibid.*, April 22.

7

Esq. is opposed to it—but TS—says he will bear the loss as to the storage business.

There are indications, however, of a certain insecurity in Sage, of the need constantly to prove his own worth to his uncles. On one occasion Sage wrote of a man with whom his uncles were associated in what was probably a joint venture:

He is not fit to do-business even for *himself*—much less for other people. . . . The accounts are so fixed that we shall know nothing about them—The freights are very often paid to him—and in two or three cases which I have found out *he has made no entree of the* money.

And again Sage wrote of a boat captain, "Every time he has been here—I have done more to unload & get him off—than himself and all his hands." The emphasis in these reports was on his own superior capacity. When another young boy was taken on by the firm on much the same basis as Henry, perhaps in pique, perhaps in fear of competition, Henry wrote: "Little Jim Nichols is here —J.B. has hired him for one year $96—& his board—hoping to make a man of him—But I fear he will not." [20] It was only two months earlier that J.B. had written of Henry, "I expect to make him not only a business boy, but to raise his moral standard to a man." [21]

From 1832 to 1837 Sage continued as an employee of the Williamses. He kept the books, made up the shipping bills, helped load and unload the canalboats, and in the process gained some grasp of the intricacies of mercantile capitalism with its numerous ventures and joint partnerships. In a day before the hired employee was common except for apprenticed clerks or laborers he learned the function and the difficulties of agencies and partnerships. He worked in both Ithaca and Albany and occasionally in

[20] To J. B. Williams, Aug. 24, 1833; to Dear Uncles [T. S. and M. R. Williams], July 9, 1834, WF. Dashes were Sage's form of punctuation throughout his life. The number of dashes varied from one to four. For the sake of convenience one dash will be used in the material quoted.
[21] Copy of a letter to T. S. Williams, May 1, 1834, WF.

8

New York City, where manufactured goods were purchased for the retail trade of the Williamses and lumber, grain, and shingles sold. The work was strenuous. Chauncey Williams noted while weighing a place in his brother's business against farming, "Piling shingles and lumber, by the way, lays as great a tax on the bodily powers as any operations in farming, though perhaps not quite so constant." [22] And life in the canal trade was rough, far removed from the church- and lyceum-oriented "society" to which these young clerks sought admission during "the season," after the close of navigation on the canals. Chauncey indeed tried to avoid the freighting aspect of the business "at any rate, if there was *fighting* to be done." [23] Young Henry Sage reported to his uncles as a matter of course and of business that when one of their boat captains had started out "himself and crew were drunk. I am afraid he will sell some of his cargo before he gets there." [24]

By 1836 Henry had assumed considerable responsibility in his uncles' organization. Sage was not satisfied with his progress, however. The diary he kept in 1836 and 1837 indicates his pressing ambition to become an independent businessman.

Perhaps the most striking aspect of Henry Sage's diary is the deep anxiety it reveals. At twenty-two Sage was confident of his ability but extraordinarily sensitive about his reputation. He thought he recognized enemies in Ithaca who spread malicious gossip about him; he was conscious of being snubbed. Sage was after all at the very bottom of the success ladder. He intended to climb high but he feared a fall and feared especially because there was no one to break the fall. He was growing up in an excited society, eager for wealth and progress. The Ithaca and Albany he knew in this period were fast-developing communities caught up in a speculative boom. The young men of Sage's circle seemed to live in an earnest and highly competitive milieu. One acquaintance of Sage, a law clerk, wrote a mutual friend:

22 To Mary Williams, Jan. 11, 1838, WF.
23 C. P. Williams to Williams & Bros., Jan. 11, 1838, WF.
24 To Williams & Bros., July 7, 1834, WF.

You were probably aware that my principal object in leaving Ithaca was the formation of business habits. The lax way which country lawyers have of doing business, and the many inducements which you know I had from attachment to society . . . finally satisfied me that the best thing I could do would be to clear out.[25]

Sage's concern with self-improvement and success was not peculiar, although it may be that his insecurity was somewhat more intense than that of his fellows. Perhaps as a means of defense he affected a kind of superiority.

I sat with Grant and *family* at Church yesterday afternoon . . . and other friends—as usual. No attentions—B—S—and other dm'd fools —as usual also. Poor devils, I wish they knew how heartily I despise them—but I won't think of them—they are unworthy.[26]

He was above these petty enemies; he would show them!

Undoubtedly Sage's central fear was the taint of his father's failure. The younger Sage's future depended largely upon his uncles' willingness to advance him capital on the security of his "business ability and moral principles." For Charles Sage had not managed to work his way out of that "poverty and obscurity" which his son resented. His latest scheme, to settle colonists in Texas and thereby earn land bounties from the Texan government, appeared to Henry doomed to collapse. Sage had given up hope of help from his father and rather sought to disassociate himself from the older man. Upon Charles Sage's return from his first Texas expedition his son found him still unprepared to assume his family's support. There was little rapport established between father and son; Henry reported that they rarely met except at mealtime and then they spoke little.

Yet his father was evidently very much in Henry's thoughts. Just before Charles Sage set off for Texas in the fall of 1836, he arrived in Albany, where Henry was working, to raise money for the expedition. His son commented:

[25] L. S. Eddy to J. E. Shaw, Oct. 26, 1835, JBW.
[26] Diary of Henry Williams Sage, Dec. 19, 1836, HWS.

He lacks prudence—and financial wisdom. He builds "baseless fabrics" and centers all his hopes upon them—they fail and he builds others . . . but, learning nothing from experience—they meet the same fate —they contain the elements of decay—and cannot stand.[27]

As he planned his future, Henry returned repeatedly to the theme of his father's failure, concluding that paternal experience and guidance must always be denied him. The intensity of Henry's feeling and the emotional conflict it aroused in him are perhaps best revealed in a dream which he described in detail.

As I entered the room I recognized my father's face sitting opposite me —it wore a stern and frigid aspect. He viewed me with a cool—sarcastic gaze—and arose. His stature seemed enlarged to gigantic dimensions. His head in the region of self-esteem and firmness was increased in size almost to a deformity—yet it served to heighten the effect and dignity of his bearing—and there he stood—the beau ideal of a proud, haughty overbearing spirit—the cold smile of scorn was playing on his lips—and the shafts of deadly malice gleaming in his eyes. "Father," I exclaimed, and in an instant his features were changed, they wore the same, bitter, sarcastic smile, but there was no malice, and he stood gazing on me rather as a thing of pity and contempt, than an object of revenge. "Father," I repeated—he turned to me and extended his hand—shuddering—as if he were about to grasp an adder. I felt injured, and wounded at this treatment—I know I had never deserved it—and speaking firmly I said—"NO! It is too great an effort—I *cannot* take your hand!" "CANNOT!" he repeated in a voice of Thunder. . . . His face became livid with rage—he drew a dirk from his bosom. . . .[28]

The dream ended as father and son murdered each other. Although Henry dismissed the dream with the casual notation, "Half an hour before going to bed I ate two broiled chickens," his uneasy relationship with his father haunted him. He had in fact usurped his father's position in the family, assuming the care of his mother and sisters since his father had "ceased to acknowledge" that burden. It was the only course and the only honorable

[27] *Ibid.*, Sept. 28. [28] *Ibid.*, Aug. 7, 1837.

course young Henry could take, yet the indignity to his father was apparent. Henry justified himself in terms of his father's conscious abdication of responsibility; he nevertheless recognized that it was not so much a matter of what his father would not as of what he could not do. It is significant that the attributes Sage's father assumed in the dream, "self-esteem," "firmness," "dignity," even haughtiness, were just those he lacked in his son's eyes. Still more significant is the clear memory of the expression in his father's face, and the immediate interpretation of that expression by the son. "Sarcasm," "scorn," "contempt," even "malice" toward his son were revealed. The younger Sage seemed to sense that if his father were a man of spirit he would respond to his son's evaluation of him in these ugly terms. For in the final summation the son had neither respect for the man nor sympathy for the failure. In a sense one can measure Sage's passion for success by his rejection of his father.

Sage over and over again asked himself why his father had failed. Of the New Englanders who migrated to New York in the twenties some succeeded brilliantly, others got on, still others lost all. But the fortunes of the game or the statistics of the situation were not sufficient explanation. And Sage, surprisingly, did not look to factors like insufficient capital. Rather he sought the explanation in character. In a gentler mood he attributed the difficulty to a certain generosity in his father which made him incapable of facing the harsh business world. More commonly in drawing up the final balance Henry Sage gave most weight to the item, moral weakness. One could not after all resent fate or generosity. Henry could write off all possibility of encouragement from his father because the latter had failed through "his own imprudence." This was of course not only his personal judgment; it was the judgment also of the respectable, Calvinist people about him, and these people could not have been dismissed lightly. Nevertheless for young Sage himself it was a troubling judgment.

Perhaps a close approximation of the dream wish was Henry's reflection after the first meeting of father and son upon the former's return from Texas, "He talks of returning to Texas again soon, I hope he will and I hope he will never return 'till he returns an altered man." [29] To be rid of this symbol of failure seemed the younger Sage's most profound wish despite the shame and guilt he experienced in acknowledging it. Subconsciously he may have feared that repudiation of his father deserved extreme punishment. But regardless of such fears and in the face of his own statement that it was a faulty standard which equated wisdom and virtue "in exact proportion" to a demonstrated ability to accumulate wealth, the pressure of his need for approbation and prestige was drawing Henry Sage to accept this rationale as a practical formula.

In 1837 on a return voyage from Texas, Charles Sage's ship was wrecked off the coast of Florida, and he and the other survivors of the wreck were massacred by Indians. Henry's diary ends before this news reached him; we have no record of his reaction. Undoubtedly, horror, guilt, and relief were mingled in that reaction. Henry was free now to attend to his own character building. From this time on his father's name rarely appeared in Henry's correspondence.

Henry Sage had turned early to the example of his uncles. These men had earned wealth, prestige, and influence. Nor were they venerable old men. Indeed their closeness in age and training to himself undoubtedly reinforced Sage's conviction that he too could repeat the pattern of success if he were given the chance to work for himself.

Yet in young Sage's mind a successful business career was not the sole and simple goal. His respect for his uncle Timothy, for example, was tempered by recognition of a flaw in his uncle's character, "the too constant concentration of all his powers to obtain" money.[30] Sage was drawn on the one hand by the rewards of business success both in material terms and in terms of the community's esteem; it was the way out of both poverty and obscurity. But he was attracted also by a less "worldly" ambition

[29] *Ibid.*, Aug. 11.   [30] *Ibid.*, Nov. 26, 1836.

which he considered opposed to business pursuits. Sage's understanding that although higher sentiments might direct the uses of wealth "they have little to do with obtaining it" [31] was hardly profound. Yet it represented the crux of his youthful dissatisfaction with business methods. This observation was the basis of his frequently repeated resolutions to quit business entirely and devote himself to study before he became thoroughly corrupted; or to set a time limit, six years perhaps, in which to amass a competency which would enable him to retire; or to devote six hours a day only to business and six to study. Such resolutions were daydreams rather than practical considerations, however. The alternatives were never equally weighed; while he toyed with one course, he was already acting out the other.

Sage's preoccupation with a "higher" life may have been part of his intense desire for admiration. In a world of businessmen, on which he had not yet made an impression, he may have needed to stress his independence of businessmen's judgments. By criticizing his uncle he maintained his own integrity. Sage recorded his resentment of a division made between the young men of his circle slated for business and those working toward professional status. When his own young business friends decided to exclude the students from their discussion club, Sage protested on the ground that they were thereby confessing an inferiority to the students which he for one was not ready to grant. Apparently he alone of the young businessmen joined the students' group as well.[32] To identify himself with "higher sentiments" perhaps enabled Sage to defend himself against the success of others. Yet this flirtation with the higher life was at most semiserious. At the same time he was observing:

Those who are born in the humbler ranks of life—who have no counsel or support but their own native energies, are forced to crush every nobler feeling—to paralyze every higher sentiment . . . to the God of gain. Yet this is necessary to become rich.[33]

[31] *Ibid.*, Sept. 26.   [32] *Ibid.*, Sept. 18, Oct. 7, 1837.
[33] *Ibid.*, Sept. 26, 1836.

14

Although the direction of "the higher life" was as vague as his aspirations its most persistent aspect was self-development.

I have often tried to analyze my own feelings with regard to my future destiny—to give a name to that *ideal* something for which I am ever ready to grasp—but I cannot. . . . Confident of the success in all well defined plans which I attempt to execute—and conscious of ability to excel in *many spheres* of action—I sometimes in anticipation enjoy the highest honors of all. When, upon reflection, I find myself incapacitated by want of education and mental improvement from attempting . . . the attainment of anything beyond the reach of ordinary capacities.[34]

Religious training contributed to Sage's enthusiasm for self-culture. The message of the evangelists in the thirties was optimistic. Along with their congregations they assumed progress.[35] The inconsistency between worldly goals and higher sentiments which Sage noted did not trouble him long. Moreover, there was nothing in the conservative social doctrine of the churches to disturb the conscience of a young man.[36] If the rich were castigated for their pride, the poor were charged with idleness and enviousness. On the other hand the crusades of the evangelists did not excite Sage's imagination. His living habits, indeed, had become somewhat worldly. We get a rare glimpse of the young man about town in the letter of a friend, "Lord Grener alias Cyrus Powers was here last night and Sage and three or four others and myself got him and ourselves a little drunk for old and new acquaintance sake." [37]

What Sage retained from his religious background was the optimism and a natural and sentimental religious impulse resembling neither profound piety nor superficial lip service. Religion provided a metaphysics, a moral code which may have operated more

[34] *Ibid.*, July 7, 1837.

[35] C. C. Cole, *The Social Ideas of the Northern Evangelists, 1826–1860* (New York, 1954), p. 232.

[36] *Ibid., passim;* Henry May, *Protestant Churches and Industrial America* (New York, 1949), pt. I.

[37] L. S. Eddy to J. E. Shaw, Oct. 26, 1835, JBW.

effectively in personal than in business relationships, a sincere feeling for charity. He seems not to have questioned religious dictates even where experience proved them to be inoperative. At the same time he did not undergo that emotional crisis common to many of his generation as a result of the substitution of love for damnation in popular theology. Religion did not disturb Sage. Instead it gave him an assurance of the solidarity of Christian men and a conviction of the essential validity of Christian doctrine which may have transcended business experience. He accustomed himself early to a division of experience; one area was reserved for "higher sentiments," the other for business activity. It was not a clear-cut division, however. Hazily, illogically at times, he imposed concepts of order and harmony borrowed from the first sphere onto the chaos of the business scene.

The moral code he espoused was simple and direct. Work and good works were its basis. At seventy-eight Sage wrote solemnly to an old employee, a lumberjack who had decided to reform his drunkard's habits:

Full forgiveness is promised by God to all who repent and forsake their sins—Claim this promise as your *right* from him—& none the less from man—In doing this avoid undue depression or arrogance—but modestly & warmly claim your right to manhood as long as your life is manly.[38]

"Manliness," the term in which Sage most often summed up all virtue, was linked in his mind with dignity and independence, the qualities he had found lacking in his father, with industry, which stood high in the roster of evangelist virtues, with the "Christian" way of life.

Throughout his life Sage was a regular churchgoer; in the thirties he listened enthusiastically to the words of Edward Norris Kirk, pastor of the Fourth Presbyterian Church of Albany. Kirk was popular and active, the leader of successive revivals and a disciple of the New School theology, which offered salvation to all men

[38] To David Hope, June 21, 1892, HWS.

rather than to only the elect. Like the younger and more famous
Henry Ward Beecher, whom also Sage was to hear in fervor and
friendship, Kirk was not concerned with "the logical discrimina-
tions and refinements" of theology. Again like Beecher, Kirk
evidently had an excellent stage presence: "Teachers of dancing,
gymnastics, or etiquette, may strive in vain to impart a style like
Mr. Kirk's." [30] The appeal of these men was at once to the emo-
tions and to what Sage would have called common sense, salvation
translated as hard work and self-improvement. Kirk's enthusiastic
biographer reports that the first sign of Kirk's influence on the
poor neighborhood in which his church had been built "was mani-
fest when people began to paint their homes and fences." He goes
on to report Stephen Van Rensselaer's reaction to Kirk's work in
Albany: "Mr. Kirk has doubled the value of my property in the
city." [40] Sage's response to Kirk was based on the "phrenological"
aspects of his sermons. "Kirk is a great man—his views of men
and things of the universe, and the relations we bear to it and to
futurity—are liberal, enlarged, and comprehensive. His sermon
this morning was, in many respects—decidedly phrenological." [41]

Virile self-culture was inculcated by secular as well as religious
teaching. Sage's almost compulsive attention to his intellectual
development resulted in his working out courses of reading largely
in phrenological works but including also geography, medical
jurisprudence, and even etiquette. There was in his reading lists
an almost excruciating burden of the anatomy, physiology, and
the pseudo psychology of the phrenologists, Gall, Spurzheim, and
Combe. The message which Sage sought and found in these unlikely sounding volumes was a type of nineteenth-century Strength
Through Knowledge.

This evening I have been reading "Combe on the Constitution of
Man." . . . His is a philosophy which appeals to the *common sense*
of man—to his interests as a physical, moral, and intellectual being—

[39] David O. Mears, *Life of David Norris Kink, D.D.* (Boston, 1877), p. 333
and p. 318, quoting "a critic."
[40] *Ibid.*, p. 70.   [41] Diary, Oct. 30, 1836.

How happily he has shown that our happiness on earth is chiefly dependent on our own acts—on our obedience to the natural laws of the different elements of our being. When these are more fully understood, their influence will be beyond all calculation. We can then look for the entire supremacy of our moral and intellectual natures and it requires no great stretch of the imagination to see a path opened for our eternal progression. . . . We are acting upon the combined expression of the whole world, and development of religion, of the principles of government, of industry in all its branches, literature, the arts and sciences—all are tending to exalt the nature of man . . . and ultimately to produce the highest degree of human perfection.[42]

The possibility of this secular millennium appeared real to Sage especially since common sense and self-interest would be the driving forces. The idea of the application of science to man as a moral as well as a physical creature, the great preoccupation of the nineteenth century, seemed to confirm the assumption of progress. Nor was "progress" subject to confusion. A hierarchy of values was understood and stated; logically external to science, derived essentially from Christian tradition, it constituted the rationale of science. In that hierarchy moral and intellectual values stood at the top.

Sage could have abstracted from innumerable cults and clubs the spirit of optimism and the impulse toward self-culture. That he happened upon phrenology was not completely fortuitous. In every city and town of size phrenological societies were organized in the thirties and lectures delivered on the subject. In Ithaca the Lyceum and the weekly discussion club were the sponsors of lectures on phrenology, and the young men of Sage's circle were avid lecture attenders. Phrenology offered a specific method to develop the characteristics one desired. It "inspired hope and courage in those depressed by the consciousness of some inability." [43] For a young man with Sage's fears and ambition the appeal was obvious.

[42] *Ibid.*, Oct. 6.

[43] Merle Curti, *The Growth of American Thought* (New York, 1943), p. 342, quoting James Freeman Clarke.

The phrenologist's working concept was natural law defined as a description of the constant relationships among natural phenomena. The discovery of natural law as related to human character was to make possible earthly happiness, for the phrenologist assumed also man's ability to control himself and his world once he understood them: "Intelligent beings exist, and are capable of modifying their actions." [44] It is very possible that phrenology served in the case of a man like Sage as a link between his early religious training in an area where Christian perfectionism was preached with vehemence and his later almost imperceptible absorption of popular social Darwinism. All three assumed an inherent capacity for progress, and as a corollary implied that failure was the outcome of weak character, of a lack of "manliness." Natural law became Sage's framework later for the interpretation of economic phenomena. Optimism based on natural law was a thoroughly happy philosophy for a man at the outset of his career in the thirties. It was only in the post–Civil War decades that such a philosophy espoused by a man at the height of success came to sound hollow and even callous.

Phrenology absorbed much of young Sage's time after business hours. He wrote for the Ithaca *Journal* a lengthy and aggressive defense of the system in answer to an attack published by the *Herald*. The attacker promised to continue the debate, and his neglect to do so disappointed Sage extremely. He was probably as eager to display his talents publicly as to propagate the new faith. Sage cherished no mean estimate of his own talents. He prepared a talk for the local discussion club "On the Possibility of Reducing the Practical Conduct of Life to a Science," a talk which he confidently expected not to be "appreciated or even understood at all by more than one or two of our society. But the fault is not mine." At the same time he worked at acquiring an education.

No one needs a thorough course of reading more than I do. My early education was slight, and improperly conducted—and my habits of

[44] George Combe, *The Constitution of Man Considered in Relation to External Objects* (Boston, 1829), p. 17.

life for the past 10 years have been very unfavorable for mental improvement or the acquisition of useful knowledge. . . . My money-making must be brought to a close as soon as possible.

The stress was placed upon "useful" education, not frills. Sage commented in disgust after reading *Laws of Etiquette,* "For any man—seriously—to attempt to dictate about the manner of sipping tea, or placing knives and forks, etc., etc., is supremely ridiculous." In 1836 he earnestly resolved to devote his leisure to study rather than to spend it "in society" in Ithaca.[45] His was a pedestrian approach, but in the search for "useful knowledge" there was also idealism and enthusiasm.

Phrenology was to the self-educated middle class what transcendentalism was to the intellectual elite. Even more than transcendentalism it was a European import. Its roots lay not with the German idealists but with the manipulators, the scientists within the tradition of Bacon. "Gall and Spurzheim's Phrenology laid a rough hand on the mysteries of animal and spiritual nature," wrote Emerson, "dragging down every sacred secret to a street show." Yet even this finely wrought transcendentalist found in it, "a leading to a truth which had not yet been announced." [46] In later years it degenerated into a fad but in the thirties it was pregnant with excitement and appealed, as Sage put it, to "common sense." Its language, though cumbersome to the modern ear and eye, was on the other hand free of the tenuous verbiage characteristic of much transcendental literature.

Through Anne Charlotte Lynch, Henry Sage had gained a slight acquaintance with at least the more sentimental and high-flown elements of transcendentalism. Sage knew Anne Lynch when she was a student and teacher at the Albany Female Academy and he was working for his uncles. For a time they roomed in the same boarding house. This incredible young woman, who was to become the wife of Professor Vincenzo Botta, the hostess of New York's literati and the world's celebrities, wrote in 1835 on the

45 Diary, Oct. 7, 1837; Oct. 10 and 9, Nov. 28, 1836.
46 Ralph W. Emerson, "Historic Notes of Life and Letters in New England," in *The Transcendentalists,* ed. Perry Miller (Cambridge, Mass., 1950), p. 499.

occasion of her twentieth birthday, "Who that knows me would not rather say sixty? I believe I have had every variety of feeling humanity is capable of, and there remains nothing for me now, not even a disappointment." [47] One of her students later wrote of her, "She lived in the high serene region of the Ideal, far above the follies and foibles of this world." [48] The diary which she kept in 1838 exhibits an extraordinary fascination with a kind of disembodied melancholy.

The combination of ingrown transcendentalism, romantic imagination, and haughty isolation evidently captured young Sage for a while. Indeed a sequence of dates suggests that the mournful effusion on her twentieth birthday was prompted in part by the breakup of a romantic attachment between Anne Lynch and Sage. Just a year before to the day each had written the other a letter to be kept sealed for two years. Evidently these contained explanations of the estrangement. Sage had looked forward for weeks to the day on which his letter from Anne Lynch might be opened. But anxiety had raised his expectations too high. "It contained nothing remarkable—at least—nothing but what she had told me fifty times before." [49]

It is not difficult to arrive upon an explanation of their separation. The very elements of dedication and intense scholarship which must have impressed Sage in this period when he was concerned with the unworthiness of business pursuits, must also inevitably have proved intolerable when coupled with Anne Lynch's conviction of her superiority in experience and insight. Miss L., Sage noted,

is a mixture of idealism and selfishness. . . . She creates an ideal being . . . and then imagines herself that being—and expects all others to acknowledge it—this has destroyed my intercourse with her. . . . Although in many respects the most perfect female character I have ever met—she is too selfish to live in the same sphere with me. . . . To use her own language her favors are granted as alms to beggars.

[47] Anne C. Lynch to Miss Anna Platt, Nov. 11, 1835, in *Memoirs of Anne C. L. Botta* . . . , ed. Vincenzo Botta (New York, 1894), p. 237.

[48] *Ibid.*, pp. 24–25.   [49] Diary, Nov. 13, 1836.

On the other hand Anne Lynch would have had to consider that Sage's education was limited, his prospects uncertain. Moreover for all his concern with higher sentiments Sage's tendency was to link moral and intellectual progress to common-sense concepts and the manipulation of natural phenomena. "I am heartily sick of hearing her *notions*—'philosophy—the true philosophy' as she calls them—but they are far from being philosophied—or even tolerably sensible." [50] It is doubtful if Anne Lynch would have entertained for long a would-be phrenologist. If Emerson found phrenology crude, Anne Lynch must have considered it crass.

From phrenology as from religion Sage abstracted what was useful to him, the optimism, the assurance of success if one followed the rules. By the late thirties success meant primarily financial success. The flirtation with the higher life was never given direction. But it did leave a lasting impression on Sage's thought. It sketched in a background of a rational and ultimately sympathetic universe.

With the help of his uncles Sage entered upon an independent business career in 1837, driven by his own need for success and the responsibility of his family, and conscious that

my organization is one which can never be satisfied with a small degree of progress in *anything*—and should my *acquiring* faculties once gain the ascendency—that moment, every higher standard I have ever reared will be struck down—and soul and body—all—everything— sacrificed to the God of Lucre.[51]

He entered business, then, without an idealistic rationale. Yet such gloomy thoughts could not for any length of time absorb one as active and as naturally hopeful as Sage. On his birthday, January 31, 1837, he noted eagerly in his diary:

A New Year! And to me the dawn of a new life—Tomorrow I am to take a stand among businessmen—for *myself* and on my own account. . . . Five years hence—should I live and be tolerably fortunate in my operations my relative position in society will be far different from what it is. . . . Every change has been for the better.

[50] *Ibid.*, June 30, 1837; Nov. 22, 1836.   [51] *Ibid.*, Oct. 17, 1836.

Chapter II
Merchant, 1836-1854

"AT the age of 27 then I propose starting anew—ceasing to toil for money— and entering my proper sphere—in search of knowledge and wisdom." [1] With this compromise resolution duly noted Sage prepared to claim his place as an independent businessman in the speculative trade of the thirties. The compromise was not to be concluded, for the collapse of the boom made retirement impossible and the prospect of success in the late forties made retirement less and less desirable. Years of intensive struggle began for Sage in 1836 and 1837; they were the basis of his title to the self-made-man status. In these years, too, the business practices and prejudices which guided him for the rest of a long life were established.

By 1836 Sage was clearly dissatisfied with an employee's status. The modest but rapidly achieved fortune he desired could not be accumulated on a clerk's salary. In February of that year he invested in a line of canalboats on the Ithaca–New York route. Sage, Thomas Kimball, and David Ogden & Co. purchased the Williams' interest in the line.[2] The source of Sage's funds is uncertain. He may have financed this investment, as he did his land speculations in these years, by means of a mortgage loan, paying a portion of the purchase price of a boat or boats and then mortgaging the boats for the remainder, probably to the seller, expecting to pay the full sum from the profits of operation. The times seemed to promise profit. In communities all along the canal route property values were rising, population was growing, local markets

[1] Diary, June 18, 1837, HWS.   [2] Ithaca *Journal,* Aug. 10, 1836.

were becoming, or supplying, regional ones. Henry Sage was well aware that he was living in the midst of a transporation revolution. His problem was to acquire sufficient capital to realize on the opportunities available.

Restless, anxious about his prospects, Sage had considered moving west. But when J. B. Williams suggested that Sage buy the Williams Brothers stock and take over their Ithaca trade, Sage was enthusiastic. Immediately he wrote a friend, Joseph E. Shaw, asking the latter to join him in the venture. Sage assumed that his uncles would allow the two young men to purchase on long term credit and would also extend their influence on behalf of the younger men so that they might obtain credit in the New York City commercial houses.[3]

Credit was essential, for neither Sage nor Shaw had available capital. Sage, like almost everyone else about him who could command cash or credit, was speculating in real estate in 1835 and 1836. Small as these investments were they must have absorbed all of his ready cash. He made at least three purchases of land, two secured by mortgage loans. His friends evidently shared his high hopes: "Sage is now here & speculating in Ithaca property at a great rate. . . . The young Fellows of Ithaca must all get rich out of the excitement & not leave to the old cocks all the picking." [4] The panic ended both this dream of quick profits and until 1845 further real estate ventures on Sage's part. Sage had evidently been able to raise approximately $1,500 for these speculations.

By February of 1837 he hoped to accumulate "a cash capital of my own—of $2000," [5] exclusive of real estate sales, presumably from his canal-line investment and salary savings. Most of these funds were "unavailable," however, in the fall of 1836 when Sage began to plan for the coming year's operations.

Negotiations with the Williamses continued for some months. While his letters assumed an impatient and independent attitude

[3] Sage to Shaw, Sept. 24, 1836, WF.
[4] L. S. Eddy to Shaw, June, 1836, JBW.
[5] Sage to Shaw, June 12, 1836, WF.

—"I have awaited the motions of others long enough" [6]—entries in his diary for this period reveal Sage's anxiety about the Williamses' decision. In October, Sage asked his uncles for a loan of five thousand dollars for five years on the security of his "business abilities and moral principles," and in his diary he wrote: "This will test their confidence in them. If they refuse, on their insufficiency I shall live to make them ashamed of it. If they grant my request, they shall never suffer." [7] In November, Sage seems to have received definite assurance of help from Timothy Williams. [8]

In January 1837 the firm of Sage and Shaw was organized to transact a general merchandise business at Cayuga Inlet in Ithaca at the old stand of Williams Brothers. Sage and Shaw advertised themselves as the purchasers of "the entire stock in trade of Williams & Brothers." They offered to "sell for Cash, Barter or approved credit as low as any establishment west of Albany." [9] A third partner, Frederick Barnard, joined Sage and Shaw when they organized a "Storage, Forwarding and Salt business" in February 1837. The stock and equipment, including canalboats scheduled to run to and from New York City, Albany, and Buffalo, were bought from the Williamses; there is some evidence that Timothy Williams retained a share of the ownership as a silent partner, in addition to being the creditor of the firm. Sage may also have borrowed from his uncle, Manwell. [10]

The new organization pleased his family as well as Sage, and from Middletown came a congratulatory message: "I am glad to hear that HWS has got into a permanent business and hope he will do well both for your interest and his own." [11] This was of course only a beginning; success was far from assured, and the fears that beset young Sage remained with him. Perhaps they were even

[6] *Ibid.,* June 11.   [7] Oct. 7, 1836.   [8] *Ibid.,* Nov. 26.
[9] *Journal,* Feb. 15, 1837.
[10] J. B. Williams to Williams Brothers, Oct. 23, 1837, WF; Will of M. R. Williams, May 16, 1840, JBW.
[11] C. P. Williams to M. R. Williams, Jan. 14, 1837, WF.

intensified in the uncertain first years of his career. In March he was still

> determined to silence the slanders of my enemies—and to prove to them all that they can neither injure nor assist me—that I am independent—and above them. . . . Many are using every effort to injure my reputation as a social—moral—and business man. I can attribute this . . . to nothing but envy.[12]

Undoubtedly reputation was a crucial factor for a young businessman whose career depended upon credit. Nevertheless this notion of persecution indicates a deep-seated personal insecurity. Success, the ability to "show" the others, seemed to Sage to be the solution.

The pattern of success he found in his uncles' business. This was substantially the pattern of the merchant capitalist, a pattern which describes Sage's career for approximately twenty years. Most characteristic were the short-term "arrangements," partnerships and joint-account ventures organized usually on a seasonal basis. Such arrangements served to pool capital and provide managers but were not oriented toward the development of a permanent business organization. In Sage's case these short-term ventures had real application to the goal of his business activity. Initially he considered business corrupting; his aim was leisure to study. He would then place no emphasis on the development of a business organization as a permanent unit. Since his uncles' business served as the school for Sage's business behavior, it is interesting to note that these men, too, occasionally protested their desire to retire to cultivate higher sensibilities. Whether or not they ever abandoned the idea of cultivated leisure as a practical goal, it was perhaps significant to the organization of their operations in the thirties and forties that the Williamses and Sage had in mind then the real estate and retirement plan characteristic of the merchant capitalist.

Sage and Shaw started out with a store or stand which was the center of a general retail trade. The store also served as a collecting

---

[12] Diary, March 5, 1837.

depot for country produce, grains, salt, and especially lumber. The produce was brought to the store by local farmers and loggers who sought goods or cash in exchange, or by the partners themselves and their agents who contracted for produce in the surrounding area. From the Inlet store and warehouses the produce was shipped to Albany or New York City for sale. Operating on a small margin of cash and desperately anxious to expand their trade, Sage and his partners relied heavily on advances of credit initially from Albany, where their produce was handled through the yard established by Williams Brothers.

The panic of 1837 ushered in five years of depression during which Sage was able to maintain himself as an independent businessman largely through the credit made available to him by the Williamses. The successive reorganizations which Sage and Shaw underwent from 1837 to 1842 are not evidence of the peculiar strain of the depression, since such reorganizations continued into the more prosperous period which followed. They do indicate, however, that the small margin on which the firms operated could not, without danger, be reduced by the loss of a partner, and perhaps that any expansion of interests required the resources of an additional partner. Thus in 1837 Charles Robinson, who had previously been engaged as a purchaser of logs for the joint account of himself and Williams Brothers, joined Sage and Shaw in their mercantile organization, and in the next year replaced Barnard in the shipping and storage aspects of the business. When Robinson joined the firm (SS & R), the new advertisement announced a change in policy. The "ready pay system" was substituted for credit to customers, indicating perhaps the tight situation.[13] Shaw remained with the firm until 1840. It is worth noting in connection with the capital resources of the firm that withdrawing partners, like Shaw and later Horace Mack and Timothy Williams, seem to have allowed some of the funds they were entitled to draw from the firm to remain with the organization.

Reorganizations affected the canal lines as well as the mercantile

[13] *Journal,* June 27, 1838.

establishment throughout the thirties and forties. Generally these lines were made up of boats independently owned and consolidated on a seasonal basis to provide efficient service and to reduce somewhat the fierce competition in this area.

In 1839 Sage took an interest in the Albany lumber yard which his uncles, Timothy, Manwell, and Josiah had organized and which was now managed by their brother Chauncey. Chauncey had been reluctant to undertake the responsibilities of the yard alone. He complained of melancholy and hypochondria, and urged upon his brothers his wish to have their nephew join him. A possibility exists then that Sage was given an interest in this business in return for his services.

When Shaw withdrew from the Ithaca concern, Chauncey joined it. The Ithaca firm, now called Sage, Robinson and Co., seems to have dealt largely if not exclusively through C. P. Williams and Co. in Albany, and in 1841 Chauncey complained that "Sage Robinson & Co. have a good portion of the resources of our business, and they must be putting themselves in condition to help" meet the financial drain on the Albany firm.[14] In 1842 Robinson left the organization, and for one year Sage and Chauncey were the sole active parties in both firms, H. W. Sage and Co. in Ithaca and C. P. Williams and Co. in Albany.

All the concerns in which Sage was interested seem to have had an optimistic policy of continuing to purchase and perhaps of expanding purchases despite the depression period and in the teeth of the seasonal tightening of the money market. In the late summer and fall of almost every year, the manager of the Albany yard was forced to argue against a policy of continuing to buy lumber and continuing to draw upon him for advances. On November 1, 1838, Josiah reported to his brothers that despite promises that they would not draw on Albany further, SS & R had already sent for acceptance drafts of more than $2,000. And in late August of 1839 Chauncey reported that "our folks have drawn

[14] To J. B. Williams, Dec. 31, 1841, WF.

for Sept much beyond what I had anticipated on. . . . I am afraid that our folks [SS & R] have been going most too fast for my bene-fit." In September he advised that SS & R concentrate as far as possible on operating their canal boats for others' shipping, while they themselves ought not to purchase lumber: "Our folks there *must stop buying property there. It will not do.*" Chauncey had come to the end of his patience· "To look at things cooly without being excited by them it looks as though we were going to ruin." [15]

Chauncey was inclined to undue pessimism, however. By No-vember the worst effects of the panic in the money market seem to have been ended and lumber was again selling well. In summing up his financial status Chauncey wrote, "I think all accounts I have standing out and all notes I hold will be paid—perhaps not all at maturity—but I see no prospect of losing a dollar by any bad debts." [16]

For the next two years the new firm held its own, but in the spring of 1842 panic conditions were again apparent. Produce piled up in Albany with no possibility of sale. Chauncey explained that it was *"utterly unprofitable* to raise money enough out of it to pay one tenth of the chgs."

I have received within a week 2341 Bu (nches) shingles and have more on the way. All I have sold is some 200 Bu. . . . I have crowded in upon me 840,000 ft Lumber in addition to last years stock and have not sold a *stick* in the last two weeks.

I have . . . been warning our country customers of the danger, and they . . . have thought I wanted to scare them and have kept on— The only way of making them believe it is to refuse to accept their drafts.[17]

The country producer was anxious to get his products into the hands of the merchant so that he might draw upon the merchant for money. Yet the merchant could not sell in this depression year. Chauncey contemplated postponing his marriage, for if they were

[15] To Williams Brothers, Aug. 21, Oct. 16 and 24, 1839, JBW.
[16] *Ibid.*, Nov. 22.   [17] *Ibid.*, May 7, 1842. JBW.

"to be overwhelmed by ruin and Bankruptcy, I must yield to dire necessity." [18]

The partners had bought far more than they could sell. At the close of navigation they had to retain for the following year, "1,500,000 feet Lumber and 4 to 5,000 Bu. shingles." Moreover they had lost some "$20,000 in bad debts and losses on property." [19] Many years later Sage recalled this crisis period. His young son had been dangerously ill, and yet he had to leave "to save a debt in which more than all CPW & I were worth was involved—No telegraph then. . . . near a week when no letter could reach me." [20] What saved the partners was their affiliation with Williams Brothers.

It is significant that Chauncey's earlier complaints of SS & R's activities and his later descriptions of business conditions should have been addressed to his brothers in Ithaca. Williams Brothers dealt through C. P. Williams and Co. in Albany in much the same way as did SS & R and its successor firms, but Williams Brothers was as well the creditor of C. P. Williams and of the Ithaca firms. Through loans to the principals and credit extension to the organizations, Williams Brothers maintained a real stake in their fortunes.

Credit extension by the Williamses was perhaps the most continuous type of aid extended to the younger firms, particularly after the establishment of the Merchants and Farmers Bank by the brothers in 1838. In 1842 Chauncey had over $19,000 in drafts coming due within the next two months, about $16,000 of which were drafts of H. W. Sage and Co. He was forced to ask for aid. He wrote his brothers apologetically:

Doubtless we are much blamed for being in a situation where we cannot pay all promptly at maturity. Perhaps we deserve blame, but it is for getting into debt rather than not getting out of it.

It pains me exceedingly to ask any help, but what else can we do? We must either do this or let things take their own course to Ruin.[21]

[18] *Ibid.*, July 25, WF. [19] *Ibid.*, Nov. 12, WF.
[20] To W. H. Sage, Aug. 15, 1893, HWS.
[21] C. P. Williams to Williams Brothers, Oct. 7, 1842, JBW.

It was the expansion or perhaps only the maintenance of the volume of business despite the depression that Chauncey singled out as the reason for the firm's difficulties. Yet continued expansion of business interests was to be characteristic of Sage's and Chauncey Williams' behavior. Perhaps confidence in the Williamses' backing kept them from contracting their interests to any significant degree.

The Williamses evidently agreed to aid Chauncey and Sage, for the latter rode out the depression years, and in February of 1843 the inventory of H. W. Sage and Co, disclosed a net worth of $6,791.78. Assets of $26,239.27 included no cash but book accounts, notes, judgments, lumber, shingles, salt, fixtures, eight boats, and horses. The net worth of C. P. Williams and Co. amounted to $2,157.86. Assets included book accounts, notes, fixtures, lumber, shingles and lumber in New York City.[22] Sage had come a long way since 1837. He was now a man of substantial property, which although not "available" promised realization in time.

After the crisis of the 1842 season, the danger of failure was much less apparent. Sage's business behavior followed more or less the pattern established in the previous half-dozen years. There was a series of short-term arrangements accompanied by a rough annual inventory and the characteristic carrying over of balances from one arrangement to the next; this form of credit undoubtedly allowed for expansion.

In 1843 Timothy Williams joined Chauncey and Sage in an arrangement which provided for an establishment in Ithaca to be run by the elder Williams, one in Albany under Chauncey's management, and a third in New York City under Sage. Sage and Chauncey contributed their boats and horses, for which they were to be allowed a proportionate compensation. The partnership extended only to the equal division of profits and losses.[23] The actual functioning of the three organizations was completely separate.

The accounts of one firm appeared on the books of the other two, and each acted as the agent of the others to form a continuous

[22] Memorandum, Feb. 1, 1843, JBW.   [23] Contract, April 8, 1843, JBW.

service following the line of transportation. Yet each was essentially an independent merchant and shipper handling other accounts, charging commissions on transactions for the affiliate firms, and using outside agents. The 1843 arrangement was continued for two seasons and seems to have netted the partners something over $24,000.[24]

Looking back on his career, Sage seemed to regard 1844 as the year which marked the end of his first bitter struggles. So well was business proceeding at the close of 1844 that Chauncey expressed a desire to close out all but his Albany interests: "I have now, and growing to be a *large* business and one that is profitable independent of any connection." [25] Chauncey was anxious to have Sage join him in the active management of the Albany concern, but Sage evidently would not consider moving his home from Ithaca to Albany.

It was in this period that Albany was coming to be more than a convenient half-way point between the New York City markets and the country districts of the western part of the state. Albany's lumber district was developing into a major wholesale market. Dealers from New York City arrived each spring to inspect the lumber shipped to Albany from the southern tier and from northern Pennsylvania. Chauncey reported that the competition of the superior Chemung and Binghamton lumber was making it difficult to sell Ithaca lumber profitably.[26] This factor may very well have influenced Chauncey's wish to sever the connection between the Ithaca and Albany concerns. Probably as a consequence of the petering out of the Ithaca supply of first-quality timber and of the continued growth of the Albany demand, the purchasing agent for Sage and the Williamses, Henry Schuyler, made his headquarters in Corning, accessible to the timber valleys of both the Chemung and Tioga Rivers.

Schuyler and at least one other agent, John Langdon, purchased

[24] Memoranda, "Results of the Business, 1843, 1844," April 13, 1848; "Results Inventory 1844," undated, JBW.
[25] To J. B. Williams, Sept. 4, 1844, JBW.   [26] *Ibid.,* July 20, 1845.

lumber for the Williamses and Sage. Generally these men, who considered themselves independent merchants, operated on a joint-account basis. Contracts seem to have been made for the season; the Sage-Williams interest usually provided the capital for purchases and gave instructions covering the amount and quality to be obtained and the price to be paid.

After two years Timothy Williams withdrew from the arrangement entered into in 1849. More and more absorbed by his banking interests and by politics, Timothy showed a disinclination to pursue mercantile ventures if his personal services were required. His capital was left with the firm and his status seems to have been that of a silent partner. In 1845 Horace Mack entered into a partnership with Sage and Chauncey. Although H. W. Sage and Co. in New York City seems to have been discontinued, the partners advertised their willingness to extend advances on goods consigned to New York and operated a line of boats from Ithaca to New York City. In 1846 Mack dropped out of the partnership, and H. W. Sage and Co. was operating actively in New York City once more.

In 1847 a new contract was drawn up which provided for a partnership to last one year. Timothy, Josiah, and Chauncey Williams were to act as investors and advisers. Timothy and Josiah together contributed $12,500 to the capital of the firm; an equal sum was advanced by Sage, and Chauncey supplied an additional $5,000. A fifth partner, who contributed no capital but who was to manage C. P. Williams and Co. in Albany, was included; he was Charles E. Hardy, the father-in-law of Josiah Williams. Sage was to take over the Ithaca business "with such advice and assistance as T. S. and J. B. Williams can give." The New York branch was discontinued.[27]

The sums contributed to the capital by Chauncey and Sage were drawn from their joint resources, testifying to the progress that their business had made up to this point. The contract was probably drawn in response to Chauncey's anxiety to share responsibility for the Albany concern and to develop it independently of

[27] Contract, Feb. 16, 1847, WF.

the Ithaca interests of Sage and the Williamses. Sage had earlier reported to his uncle, Timothy, that Chauncey "insists upon the right—and avows the intention, to retain that branch of our business, and evidently prefers for a partner Crocker—to us. . . . Our general business will be deprived of the sales (at least $20,000) pr year to the Retail yard." [28]

The relatively small share of the capital provided by Chauncey for the 1847 season underlines the fact that the views of Sage and the elder Williamses prevailed at the annual family conference which was held at the close of navigation to settle the year's business and plan for the following year. One clause did provide that "each of the parties to this contract agrees to use his influence for the benefit of the joint business, and not to be interested in any business out of this partnership which shall conflict with its interests." This may indicate that the Ithaca Williamses and Sage, too, recognized that greater concentration would be more conducive to profits. More probably it was intended to tie Chauncey's hands.

These were not the men to put all their eggs in one basket. In the late forties Sage too began to be involved in many diverse enterprises. With Shaw he took over Timothy Williams' grist mill; he began again to trade in Ithaca real estate; and in 1847 Sage and Chauncey began to invest in timberlands and a sawmill in Tioga County, Pennsylvania.

The lumber trade remained Sage's single most important interest. He early began to operate upon the assumption that in the long run lumber prices must go up, and consequently he was unwilling, while credit was available, to cut prices in order to clear out his stock at the end of the season. Credit became increasingly easy to obtain as his business standing grew. At the close of navigation in 1847 Timothy Williams reported that Sage and Chauncey had on hand an "enormous stock," which Timothy attributed to Sage's unwillingness to sell at the prevailing price level. To Timothy Williams this situation seemed "all wrong," the more so

[28] Copy by T. S. W., Jan. 12, 1847, WF.

34

since he was expected to aid them in carrying through until the next season.[29] Chauncey did not seem disturbed, however: "We have here [Albany] and in N.Y. upwards of two million feet of (Ithaca) lumber—but we shall, I think, work it into cash in the spring." [30] And when Timothy indicated a reluctance to extend a $6,500 note, Chauncey prepared to arrange for a loan through banks other than the Merchants and Farmers Bank of Ithaca. Chauncey's confidence at this juncture in the affairs of the concern contrasts sharply with his earlier pessimism, "for even as bad as it is now to raise money, I feel every confidence that the Banks we do business with would not hesitate at all to give us all the help we should need to pay every cent of our liabilities through the winter." [31] His confidence reflected the established position of himself and Sage. Josiah and Timothy Williams withdrew from their partnership with Sage and Chauncey in 1848 but again probably left their capital in the business to draw interest. Timothy estimated their fair share of the profits of the 1847 season at approximately $5,000,[32] which would represent a handsome return on an investment of $12,500.

The course of business in 1848 was typical of the decade. Lumber opened high and Schuyler, Sage's agent in Corning, was advised to pay $8 per thousand feet of good quality. Five weeks later $7 was made the maximum price; in June $6 to $7 was advised, and Chauncey went so far as to write Schuyler: "It is impossible to name any price it would be cheap at. Dont allow yourself to put a farthing into it." [33] Sage was not anxious to contract operations, however; he advised Schuyler, "I am not afraid to buy in Corning at 6½ for good lots as long as I can raise the money to do it." [34] Meanwhile the partners carried on trade in pork, flour, and coal. Pork and flour were shipped to Schuyler in Corning

[29] To J. B. Williams, Nov. 27, 1847, JBW.
[30] To J. B. Williams, Dec. 7, 1847, JBW.   [31] *Ibid.*, Dec. 16.
[32] To J. B. Williams, April 5, 1848, JBW.
[33] Sage to Schuyler, April 14, May 22, June 8, 1848; Williams to Schuyler, June 3, 1848, DeWitt.
[34] June 6, 1848, DeWitt.

for sale, coal from Corning to Ithaca and Albany. While money was difficult to obtain, Sage advised that Schuyler trade pork for coal.[35] Chauncey was always less sanguine than his partner, but he too was willing to buy cautiously as soon as the "money squeeze" was over. In July and August an active trade was carried on. By mid-August stocks and prices both were low in Albany, and bargains could be purchased by the dealer. Chauncey advised: "I am strong enough in the faith yet to buy all good *real prime* lots Lumber that can be bought in the country at $6. . . . Put in all such lots that are offered and we will ruin our credit to pay for them if necessary." [36]

The year's pattern is clear. The opening of the season meant high prices for dealer and purchaser while stocks were low. When lumber started to come in from the country along the canal, prices began to drop. This situation was aggravated by the seasonal strain on the money market as fall approached.[37] At the end of the season low prices were attractive to dealers who had the resources to buy for the following year. Each year of course the pattern varied. Cholera or canal breaks might impede the lumber crop's coming to market. A tighter-than-usual money market might cut into the line of credit extension that held together banker, dealer, and customer. Dealers had to watch widely and rapidly fluctuating prices in the wholesale markets of Albany and New York City as well as in the producing centers. Rapid communication between the dealer and his agent was difficult. Risks were high; each transaction was something of a speculation. Business policy was consequently geared to highly competitive and individualistic methods. When stocks were not yet purchased it was best to "damp the market as much as you can." [38] When this policy was not successful, its opposite was tried: "It is best not to alarm others—let them

---

[35] *Ibid.*, June 8.   [36] To Schuyler, Aug. 31, 1848, DeWitt.
[37] Margaret Myers, *The New York Money Market* (New York, 1931–1932), pp. 207–208.
[38] Sage to Schuyler, May 26, 1848, DeWitt.

hold up as long as they can—*But dont you* buy." [39] In either case the uncertain future was enough to make Chauncey "blue."

But the continued expansion of Chauncey's and Sage's operations would tend to bear out the analysis of Charles Robinson, Schuyler's partner at this time:

If he [Chauncey] is as Blue as he writes all I have to say is I think him sick   the fact is he & Sage to have Bot to much Real Estate & tied up all their Business Capital But would like to move all about their affairs and make no calculation where it cannot be Relied on.[40]

With capital absorbed in real estate, lumber, and timberlands any stringency in the money market was bound to frighten the partners.

At the end of the 1848 season Schuyler moved his headquarters to Port Hope on the Canadian shore of Lake Ontario. Charles Robinson, his partner, located in Buffalo, across the lake. In March of 1849 Robinson had orders from Sage to provide a stock of some four million feet for sale in Albany, and Sage was also eager for Robinson to expand his shingle trade. Robinson was of course urged to buy on credit: "Get 3 or 4 mo^s if you can." [41] Greater interest in Canadian lumber may have been the reason Sage leased his warehouses in Ithaca in 1849. Although he advertised that he would "continue upon the old stand in the purchase of Lumber, Shingles, and all descriptions of country Produce for Cash," [42] major lumber purchases were made through Robinson and Schuyler and through George Raymond, who was located at Vienna, center of the lumber-producing Otter Creek region of Upper Canada.

Sage's partnership with Chauncey Williams was dissolved at the end of the 1851 season. But he continued to deal in lumber in partnership with Shaw and in a separate partnership with Rob-

---

[39] C. P. Williams to Schuyler, June 3, 1848, DeWitt.
[40] To Schuyler, Nov. 24, 1848, DeWitt.
[41] Sage to Robinson, March 9, 1849, DeWitt.
[42] Ithaca *Journal and General Advertiser*, July 11, 1849.

inson. Their lumber was sold through C. P. Williams and Co. on a commission basis.

With the dissolution of his partnership with Chauncey, Sage was preparing to try his hand at a new kind of business. In 1853 he operated a small steam sawmill which he had purchased in Ithaca, and in the same year he bought from the inventor the right to use in Ithaca a patented "Revel Sawing Machine." [43] Perhaps he sought practical milling experience, for in 1854 he was to begin operations on a large-scale sawmill in Canada. Up to this time, although he had had some contact with milling operations, he had not himself had much experience with the mechanical workings of a mill. The small mill which he and Chauncey owned in Pennsylvania was managed by a millwright.

By the fifties a good number of Sage's associates were drawn into manufacturing. Schuyler, Shaw, C. P. Williams, all became interested in mills in Canada. As merchants, these men had never been completely divorced from the manufacturing process. Often the small mill in the Ithaca area was largely financed by a merchant's advances. In some cases the merchant's contract with a farmer for timber provided that the logs be manufactured at a mill in which the merchant had an interest. Usually the merchant himself did not supervise the mill; if he owned it, he hired a miller who was encouraged to purchase an interest. Within Sage's circle a transition was taking place in the fifties. In some cases the old mercantile pattern of simple investment was retained, but Schuyler, Shaw, and Sage became involved in the operating end of manufacturing. Undoubtedly the consistent upward trend of prices had much to do with the decision of these men to enter a new sphere. From the spring of 1844 to 1854 lumber prices had risen steadily and for the best lots almost spectacularly if we can judge by the scattered reports in the Sage-Williams-Shaw correspondence. Moreover capital equipment did not require a huge outlay of cash; the size of the mills was still small, the machinery crude. Thus the transition to industrial capitalism was gradual.

[43] Contract, April 21, 1853, HWS.

At first these mills were mere adjuncts of the mercantile pursuits of their owners. The short-term partnership and the joint-account venture were carried over into the manufacturing enterprise. Only in time was the merchant to consider himself primarily a manufacturer.

It would be difficult to say just when Sage stepped up from the category of businessman to that of successful businessman. In 1853 he was listed among Ithaca's wealthiest citizens.[44] Yet three years later the economic crisis found him in need of additional credit to stave off failure. The explanation lies in his manner of operating in the forties and fifties—the enthusiastic and continuous expansion of property interests with apparently small attention to liquidity. In the light of Sage's later conservative financial policies and in the light of the pious injunctions of business manuals and the more cautious outlook of his partner, Chauncey, Sage's gambling on the availability of credit to carry him through the periodic financial crises of the period, emphasizes his determination to succeed rather than merely to hold his own. His attitude reflects also his confidence that the Williamses would extend credit, despite some grumbling, on the security of his property and business ability. A significant amount of help was needed to promote the career of a "self-made" man.

Success was still limited. There was no suggestion in these years of the flamboyant profits of the post–Civil War decade. Sage remembered the years from 1837 to 1845 as a period when "there was not stimulus of liberal profit—all went hard & slow—I worked these years *intensely* lived with great economy and had not at the end of 1844 10.000 to show for it. After that to 1860.61 all progress was slow—23 years!" [45]

[44] Henry C. Godwin, *Ithaca as It Was, and Ithaca as It Is* . . . (Ithaca, N.Y., 1853), pp. 59–60.

[45] Sage to Dean Sage, Sept. 15, 1894, HWS.

Chapter III

"The Commercial Men of the Present Day"

IN the years between his thirtieth and fortieth birthdays Sage established himself not only as a businessman but also as a leader in community affairs. His affection for Ithaca was well known. Friends scoffed at the idea that he might ever leave. Here presumably he could measure the distance he had come by walking—or better still, driving his fine team—from the Inlet to the center of town. Here he became a chief patron of the church, a prominent advocate of public improvements, and for a brief time a political contender. He did indeed cut something of a figure in this world.

Somewhere along the line Sage forgot or rejected his earlier resolve that business was to be a temporary expedient. Business became, if not an end in itself, the central force in his philosophy of progress. The change probably came about imperceptibly along with increasing satisfaction, even exhilaration, in business activity. Years later a contemporary, reminiscing about the fifties, recalled particularly Sage's enthusiasm for new projects.

The responsibility of a family must also have discouraged Sage's earlier ambition to retire to a study. Sage's marriage in 1840 to Susan Linn linked him with a family of considerable education and some reputation. Susan's grandfather, the Reverend William Linn, had been a noted minister of the Revolutionary period. Her father, William Linn, was a lawyer who had come to Ithaca about 1812 as agent for his brother-in-law, Simeon DeWitt, the original proprietor of the village. Linn was a colorful figure, well-read, extremely articulate, a vigorous and inexhaustible lyceum speaker, whose subjects ranged from "The Worthies of Virginia" to "Schemes of Happiness." He was as well a lover of fun and mischief, and reputed to be the author of the Roorbach hoax at the time of Polk's presidential campaign.[1] Linn's levity contrasts sharply with the sobriety of Sage's uncles, who were playing so large a role in Sage's life at this time. The contrast may well have provided a welcome relief.

Susan Linn had been a student at the Albany Female Academy. There she undoubtedly absorbed a certain amount of transcendental philosophy and "higher life" sentiments along with the mathematics, French, mental philosophy, physiology and chemistry, ecclesiastical history, and physics of the regular curriculum.[2] It is significant in view of Sage's later sponsorship of coeducation that the women of his family and social circle were at least as well educated and occasionally better educated than the men. His sisters evidently received adequate education despite the family's financial difficulties; the two eldest held teaching positions and the youngest was giving music lessons when she was fifteen. Once, having won on a bet with Chauncey three dollars worth of books —and this in itself is an interesting commentary on the world of the young clerks—Sage chose among others a copy of the *Female Student* to send to his sister Lucy.[3] The ladies seemed as avid for education and self-culture as the men and helped set the tone for a literate, lecture-going society. Such a society in turn helped determine a pattern of philanthropy by the values it sanctioned.

In the first years of their marriage Susan and Henry Sage may

[1] To a description of a slave-driver's camp Linn added the statement that forty-three of the slaves had been purchased from Polk; then he had the description published in *The Ithaca Chronicle* as an excerpt from Roorbach's *Travels through the Western and Southern States*. Roorbach was soon proved a myth but not before the story was widely circulated (H. P. Pierce and D. H. Hurd, *History of Tioga, Chemung, Tompkins and Schuyler Counties . . .* [Philadelphia, 1879], p. 407).

[2] Joel Munsell, *The Annals of Albany* (Albany, 1865–1871), II, 352, quoting George Combe's description of the Academy.

[3] Diary, Oct. 10, 1836, HWS.

have lived in a boarding house, as was customary for young business couples who could not yet afford a house and servants. However, by 1845 at the latest they had their own establishment, and Sage advertised in his characteristic, no-bones-about-it manner for a servant: "A respectable girl to do the work of a private family. One who understands her business (and none other need apply)." [4] In 1853 Sage's name appeared on a list of "owners and occupants of very splendid private houses, and finely ornamented grounds." [5]

The Sages had two sons, Dean born in 1841 and William Henry born in 1844. Perhaps because her family was small, Susan Linn was able to accompany her husband on his trips more often than was customary for wives of this period. In the fifties she went with him to Canada and lived for months in the near wilderness where he was building a sawmill town. It is to her credit that the beauty of forest and lakes compensated this Victorian lady for the lack of comforts she might have enjoyed at home. She was far from enthusiastic about the "lumber piles." These she reported were "not in the least picturesque, but my husband is I am afraid *lost* in admiration of them." [6] Nevertheless she was impressed by her husband's achievement and shared in what was undoubtedly his most creative work.

Unfortunately only a very few of Susan Linn's letters have been preserved. Like most middle-class Victorian wives she remains hidden behind her husband's writings and doings, absorbed in the management of handsome if cumbersome homes. Like her husband Susan Linn seems to have had sincere and unsophisticated religious convictions and a deep interest in philanthropy.

Within a relatively few years of her marriage Susan Linn had to accustom herself to being the wife of a leading citizen and, in keeping with this role, a benefactor of the church, the major social organization of the local community. In 1853, shortly after Henry

[4] *National Archives,* Ithaca, N.Y., March 13, 1845.
[5] Henry C. Godwin, *Ithaca as It Was, and Ithaca as It Is* . . . (Ithaca, N.Y., 1853), pp. 59–60.
[6] To Mary Williams, undated, WF.

Susan Linn Sage (1819–1885)

Sage had offered $1,000 toward the building of a new Presbyterian church, Josiah Williams' wife reported that Sage was discouraged about the amount so far subscribed. "If he will not carry it through, who will?" asked the local banker's wife.[7] Mary Williams may very well have been shocked by Sage's further statement, "He says that if our church is not built, he shall go to the Episcopal." Yet this was characteristic. Because he had even then no strong sectarian bias and because he did have a strong bias toward the successful institution, he might very well transfer his allegiance and patronage. His sons evidently were tutored by the local Episcopal rector.

Sage's earlier participation in the lyceums must have stood him in good stead when he began to come forward as a supporter of public improvements. From campaigning for plank roads and railroads to campaigning for public office seems almost a natural progression. Sage was as intense in this political sphere as he was in business, hoping and expecting to achieve distinction. Years later he complained that this was a dream that had died hard.

Like his uncles Sage entered politics as a Whig. That was to be expected, for the Whig party was traditionally the sponsor of internal improvements and Sage's economic interests as merchant and shipper were directly dependent upon the canal system.

In 1847 Sage was elected representative to the New York Assembly. Seemingly his commitment to internal improvements was recognized by his appointment to the canal committee of the Assembly. Scarcely a week passed after the opening of the legislative session when "Mr. Sage gave notice of a bill to improve the Inlet of Cayuga Lake." [8] This bill, authorizing the canal board to spend up to $1,500 to keep the channel of Cayuga Inlet open to vessels drawing five feet of water, was ultimately passed.[9] Subsequently Sage brought before the house a resolution proposing the enlarge-

[7] Mary Williams to J. B. Williams, April 4, 1853, WF.

[8] Ithaca *Journal and General Advertiser*, Jan. 16, 1847.

[9] *Laws of the State of New York . . . Seventieth Session* (Albany, N.Y., 1847), I, 274–275.

ment of the canals and an amendment of the constitution to permit the state to borrow to accomplish this.[10]

A major incident of Sage's year in the Assembly was a clash between the canal and printing committees over a report on canal frauds. Sage took the leading part in defending the canal committee against the complaints of the printing committee. The latter objected to the canal committee's refusal to release the proof sheets of the report on frauds even for revision to the authors of the document. The implication drawn by the printing committee was that it was left "but one course to pursue, and that is to publish their disclaimer of the responsibility of the correctness of the printed document, and thus seriously impair if not entirely destroy the moral force and influence which it otherwise would and ought to exert." [11] Sage explained that the object of the canal committee was to prevent only injudicious use of the document by restraining individuals from using misleading portions presumably before the whole was ready for publication.[12] Although this seems a reasonable statement of the case, the suspicion was raised that Sage's zeal might have something to do with his desire to protect canal appropriations. It would not have been an illogical assumption. Although the impulse behind canal development had to some extent subsided since the depression of 1842, representatives from areas directly concerned with a canal or the canal system fought steadily for enlargements and improvements.

In the fall of 1847 Sage took part in the political campaign for the next year's officers. In late August he addressed the organizational meeting of a Rough and Ready Taylor Club in Ithaca. Timothy Williams was running this year for state senator, and Sage took part in the electioneering. Williams' campaign was somewhat complicated by his reputation as an implacable temperance man. A letter evidently disavowing his implacability was read to

[10] Albany *Argus,* March 12, 1847.
[11] *New York State Assembly Document No. 84* (Albany, N.Y., 1847), Feb. 25, 1847.
[12] *Argus,* Feb. 26, 1847.

the voters by Sage. A certain amount of money was also necessary to "buy off" a "liquor drinking community." [13] Williams gained the state senatorship, and in the spring Sage was elected trustee of the village, one of the few Whigs to gain office that year.

Now, however, Sage took a singular step. Previously an orthodox Whig, in the fall of 1848 he repudiated the party and its candidate. The issue was free soil. He told one political meeting that it was entirely inconsistent for Northern Whigs to vote for Taylor.[14] Sage's new party, the "Free Democracy," had a conglomerate membership of radical Democrats and conscience Whigs, and a single major plank, the Wilmot Proviso. Sage's convictions on the slavery issue were obviously sincere. His uncles, who held abolitionist sentiments and sponsored abolitionist speakers, evidently felt no need to disassociate themselves from their party on the ground that its presidential candidate was sympathetic to slavery.

As an apostate Whig, Sage was made much of in the Ithaca area, where he spoke repeatedly in behalf of the new party. He was appointed to local and county conventions, but the campaign was a lost one. The free soil faction split the Democrats' long-standing division completely, and the Whigs made a sweeping comeback.[15] In 1849 Sage was defeated at the charter elections in Ithaca. This was, of course, not the end of his political interest. He was chosen delegate to the Tompkins County Democratic Convention and one of the five-member County Central Committee for 1850. The course he must take became clearer with the formation of the Republican party. In this organization were joined the slavery question, on which he felt strongly, and the economic objectives of the old Whig party. Sage became early and remained always a staunch Republican, but never again did he hold public office.

Sage's disillusionment with politics as a career did not mean

[13] Charles Robinson to T. S. Williams, Nov. 1, 1847, JBW.

[14] *Journal and General Advertiser*, Oct. 25, 1848.

[15] DeAlva Alexander, *A Political History of the State of New York* (New York, 1906), II, 143–144.

that he lost interest in political influence or that he was not keenly aware of the aid government might contribute to private enterprise. His enthusiasm for economic development was not peculiar but part of the general boom picture from 1843 to 1857. In the same way the expectation of government aid to economic development was also general. Perhaps at no other time did the interests of the entrepreneur and the community seem so closely identified. "What about our lock at Cayuga?—Cant you get an especial law to enlarge that? . . . If you can get this matter attended to before Spring it will save us here very much.—I have warehouses under way." [16] When Sage asked this of his uncle Josiah, then in the state legislature, he had no thought of compromising himself or of asking undue favors. Special favors were also favors to the community.

Sage's brief political career was to remain his only departure from business. From the fifties on he concentrated his energies exclusively on his business affairs. Hard work and "manliness," the two aspects of virtue, were now very concretely attached to the conduct of business. Perhaps he was rationalizing his own lack of success in politics when he labeled professional politicians as idlers and worse. In any case Sage had come to accept a rationale which identified the success of the businessman with the health of the nation.

In 1849, while presiding at a supper in celebration of the completion of the Cayuga and Susquehanna Railroad, Sage offered a toast to "the commercial men of the present day: The Railroads and Canals which they build while living, will be imperishable monuments to their memory when dead." Sage argued along lines accepted by recent revisionists of the history of American capitalism. He emphasized as a goal what was indeed to be a major contribution of American industrial development, the profound rise in the standard of living of the great majority in the United States. Sage added to this argument his conviction that out of material development would come also a splendid cultural achievement,

[16] March 15, 1853, JBW.

a rich and a Christian society. His own fortunes were rising and so, it appeared, were the fortunes of his community, now having at its command increased transportation facilities.

The commercial spirit of the present day, is no longer that groveling propensity which can be satisfied with mere accumulation, and has no higher aim than to be forever revolving around the circumference of a dollar! But it seeks in the construction of Railroads, Canals, Steam ships and Telegraph lines to facilitate interchange of thought and action—develope mineral and agricultural wealth—encourage labor, and elevate the laborer by so reducing the cost of all necessary articles of human consumption that the lowest as well as the highest may have enough to spare. It is in this way that a true and well directed commercial spirit is the very handmaid of Christianity, and is to-day the most powerful agent in Christianizing—humanizing and civilizing the world.[17]

Sage then proceeded to urge the construction of the Sodus Bay canal, a project sponsored by a group of Ithaca merchants. The necessary note of idealism, of justification, had been acquired.

Sage adopted the rationale of business success in a period when all the world was shouting its merits. Hunt's *Merchant's Magazine* regularly reprinted messages of enthusiasm and encouragement to the businessman in the forties. He was urged to be prouder of his profession, more convinced of its spiritual benefits. "The Moral Influence of Steam," a paper read before the Mercantile Library Association of Charleston, South Carolina, suggested, "To what human means was it most likely for the *Prince of Peace* to refer, for conveying the 'words of truth to all nations,' than to that communication between them, which commerce afforded." [18] Another selection urged the intellectual as well as the religious aspects of trade: "How pleasant and how intellectual a task it is to calculate, at any moment what is most required, and yet what is wanting or hard to find; to prepare for each easily and soon, what

[17] *Journal and General Advertiser*, Dec. 20, 1849.
[18] Charles Fraser, "The Moral Influence of Steam," *Hunt's Merchants Magazine*, XIV (1846), 499–515.

he demands; to lay in your stock prudently beforehand, and then to enjoy the profit of every pulse in that mighty circulation." [19] Who could withstand such praise, particularly when his own fortunes were on the ascendancy? And it was praise, not irony. The pre–Civil War decades were growing years; economic progress at least seemed assured, and the businessman seemed to be the agent of progress. The very words which forty years later might damn the businessman in the forties were meant as glowing tribute. Sage, who was making his way with these phrases in his ear, could not easily dispute them.

[19] "The Intellectual in Trade," *Hunt's,* XII (1845), 587.

Chapter IV

The Canadian Experience,
1854-1869

THE thirty-eight years during which Sage operated as a millman were years of fulfillment. He earned financial success, prestige, and authority. These were sufficient, for in no sense can Sage be considered a man of vision, an entrepreneur on Schumpeterian lines. His gifts were energy, application, ambition. A characteristic picture of Sage was drawn by an admiring member of the Cornell faculty apropos of a discussion of proper study habits.

I have often sat in the outer room of Henry W. Sage's office without announcing myself in order to see the tremendous energy that he put into his work. His attitude at those times seemed to me to be the ideal attitude of a conscientious student. I have seen one or two pictures of Gladstone at work, which reminded me of the attitude of Mr. Sage.[1]

The comparison with Gladstone is perhaps not so far-fetched as it seems on the first reading. Both men were fervent believers in the doctrine of hard work.

Sage had the necessary ability to grasp and weigh all the varied detail of business management. He carried over into manufacturing the technique of working through a conglomerate of partners, agents, employees, and independent businessmen. The result was a highly successful manufacturing enterprise run by a merchant capitalist rather than by a technically competent industrialist.

Sage adopted the role of manufacturer enthusiastically. His

[1] Lucien A. Wait to J. G. Schurman, Oct. 20, 1903, JGS.

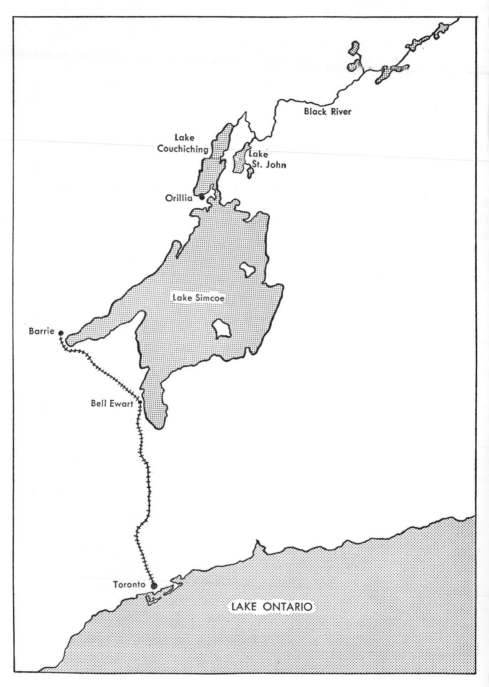

Area of H. W. Sage's lumbering operations in Ontario, Canada, 1854–1869

wife wrote that the noise of his mill was music to her husband's ears; "he is fascinated with this enterprise." [2] The building and operation of the mill were doubly satisfying, for Sage saw in them not only the promise of personal prosperity but also tangible proof that he, as a businessman, was an agent of progress. In 1857 he wrote proudly of his Canadian mill town,

Less than 9 years since this was an impenetrable wilderness—the site of our town having 2 or 3 miserable Indian bark huts. . . . We now have over 400 people here . . . & I venture to say that no town in Canada of its size *produces* so much annual wealth as this I can see & feel that we are doing good—both here & for many miles around us— Setting examples of enterprise & industry.[3]

He, Henry Sage, was bringing the virtues and institutions of his civilization to a frontier: "enterprise & industry," a school, "about 30 scholars," and "twice each month . . . preaching—Methodist." This was exciting and rewarding work, and Sage was far too busy to be smug.

Sage's first milling operation had been limited. Between 1847 and 1849 he and Chauncey Williams bought more than 2,000 acres of pinelands in Tioga County, Pennsylvania, and a millrace on Elkhorn Creek.[4] A mill was either purchased or leased here and operated under the management of A. J. Fisk. The lumber was undoubtedly marketed through the Sage-Williams organization in Albany. By 1852 the operation seems to have been terminated. Sage took title from Chauncey of the remaining acreage, probably as part of the settlement of their partnership.

In 1854 Sage undertook a major manufacturing enterprise in partnership with William Grant.[5] Grant too had been an Ithaca merchant, then had become interested in woolen manufactures. It is probable that Sage was the originator of the project. It was he who was familiar with the lumber trade and the timber-producing

[2] To Mary Williams, undated, WF.
[3] To C. E. Hardy, Jan. 26, 1857, WF.
[4] Deed books, 1847–1852, Tioga County Court House, Wellsboro, Pa.
[5] From 1854 to 1856 the firm was actually Sage, Grant, and Hixon.

region of Upper Canada which in the fifties was being opened ever more generously to lumbermen by railroad construction. In any event Sage claimed full credit for the enterprise a few years later: "In fact it has really been a creation of my own—I have at least wholly originated & developed it—& conducted it." [6] It is true that Sage seems to have done the lion's share of the work, traveling frequently to Bell Ewart, where the mill had been constructed, opening and operating the New York City yard in 1857.

The Northern Railroad had completed a branch from Toronto to Lake Simcoe in 1853 in anticipation of the development of industry along its route. Eager for freight, its directors were willing to strike bargains with prospective customers. Sage & Grant were able to secure rates considerably lower than the published tariff.[7] The partners began at once to build their mill in Bell Ewart at the foot of Lake Simcoe. Bell Ewart was still only a "niche in the woods," containing "three houses, plenty of mosquitoes, and . . . agueish." [8] The Northern had built a wharf and warehouse perhaps as part of its agreement with Sage & Grant. In August of 1854 a reporter from the Toronto *Globe* noted that through the trees that still covered the largest part of the village one could see "a great frame being raised, of massive timber, and several other little frames around it. That is a saw mill being erected by an American firm, who propose to work their way out of the woods." [9]

The Sage & Grant mill was operated by steam power. Its capacity, approximately fifteen to eighteen million feet per year, classed it among the modern mammoths in the fifties.[10] A large part of the lumber product of Upper Canada was still being produced by water-powered mills with a capacity of a few hundred thousand

[6] To Dean Sage, May 13, 1861, HWS.

[7] Sage & Grant to D. Thurston, May 13, 1857; to A. Crook, July 30, 1857, HWS.

[8] *Northern Advance*, Aug. 23, 1854.

[9] *Globe*, copied in *Northern Advance*, Aug. 30, 1854.

[10] A. R. M. Lower, *The North American Assault on the Canadian Forest* (Toronto, 1938), p. 50.

feet per year. As late as 1858 only 154 of the estimated 1,567 mills in the area were steam driven [11] The mill was supervised by A. J. Fisk, whom Sage had brought from Tioga County. The arrangement with Fisk illustrates the merchant capitalist's techniques. Fisk was strictly neither employee nor partner; he owned a part of the mill machinery and was paid for its use as well as for running the mill. Each month the saw bill was reckoned and accounts settled. Although this arrangement operated effectively on the whole, there were inevitably times when a conflict of interest arose. On one occasion, for example, Sage & Grant threatened to charge the loss resulting from damaged lumber to Fisk, who they asserted had used defective saws in order to "economize a few dollars." [12] Nevertheless these relatively independent businessmen were usually able to agree on a common interest. When Fisk succeeded in breaking his own production record and, according to Sage & Grant, that of every other three-gate mill, the firm gratefully presented him with a new suit of clothes and rewarded the laborers, at the same time urging, "If you get out 1300 M in July *something* will happen to you all again." [13]

The mill was equipped with three gates or gangs, each containing twenty to twenty-five saws. There was also a lathe mill. The organization employed about two hundred men who worked twelve-hour shifts; two twelve-hour shifts were necessary during the height of the season. Wages averaged $12 to $16 a month with board, or 90 cents to one dollar per day without board. Initially Sage & Grant had to import both mill hands and logging crews. In 1857 they were still sending workers to Bell Ewart from New York City, the port of debarkation for most immigrants and therefore the best of labor markets.

Although Fisk was supreme in the mill, Sage & Grant also maintained a general manager at Bell Ewart, DeWitt Linn, Sage's brother-in-law. He supervised the stocking, logging, and shipping operations and had general authority over the firm's affairs in

[11] *Canadian Merchants' Magazine,* III (1858), 414.
[12] Sept. 19, 1857, HWS.   [13] *Ibid.,* July 20.

the village. For the project was necessarily more than the construction of a mill. Having imported laborers, the firm had the responsibility of housing and feeding them. A barracklike boarding house was constructed for the bachelors, smaller private houses for those with families. A store for provisions and logging supplies was maintained. Sage & Grant did not consciously assume a monopoly of the economic life of the village. It is clear that the company store was not intended to be a device to return wages to the employers, for in 1857 it was rented to independent businessmen who promised to allow Sage & Grant long-term credit on supplies. The store was a means of supplying the laborers and the manufacturing firm itself. Nevertheless, as the dominant economic unit in the community, the company wielded considerable power.

That power the firm directed toward creating a community of good report. A local newspaper noted, "The employees make a considerable community in themselves, and when controlled by such order and system as is practised at Bell Ewart, cannot fail to make the impress that all good settlers do." [14] Sage & Grant assumed responsibility for the building and maintenance of a schoolhouse and contributed $1,000 to a Methodist church and a lot and one-third of the cost of construction to a Catholic church in the village.

In the fifteen years during which Sage operated the mill at Bell Ewart there was no hint of hostility toward him from the community and no labor troubles. Unlike his later experience at West Bay City he does not seem to have alienated any segment of the village population. Bell Ewart was a much smaller community than West Bay City and more directly dependent on this single firm. During the worst crisis which the community suffered, the panic of 1857, Sage & Grant were anxious to provide sufficient provisions to prevent the starvation situation of many another manufacturing village that year. Moreover, Sage, who bought out Grant in 1861, did not preside over the shutting down of the mill and the consequent stifling of the economic basis of Bell Ewart.

[14] *Northern Advance,* April 25, 1860.

Sage sold the mill in 1869 when scarcity of timber was beginning to tell on profits.

The firm's difficulties arose rather from conflicts of interest with other businessmen, with agents, with its bankers, with the railroad and with the upriver lumberman whose dam prevented the free passage of Sage & Grant's logs.

Sage & Grant did not invest in any great quantity of pinelands in Canada. They had put about $36,000 into the mill property itself,[15] and this may have exhausted available funds. On the other hand timberlands were generally not subject to sale in Canada except to bona fide settlers under conditions much like those imposed by the American homestead law somewhat later. In the ten years between 1857 and 1867 Sage & Grant and H. W. Sage and Co. purchased over 2,000 acres that can be traced in the Crown Land Papers at from $1.00 to $1.60 per acre, a high price compared to Sage's purchases in the Lake States in the sixties. There may have been unrecorded sales, but the high price and the difficulty of acquiring title probably discouraged large purchases. Timber berths were available to lumbermen; payment of ground rents and a tax on the timber cut entitled one to a license. Sage & Grant may have utilized this procedure to some extent. In the fifties, however, the largest part of Sage & Grant's logs were contracted from settlers along Lake Simcoe and the Black River.

Four to five logging crews were kept busy on lots usually contracted for the previous year. The large clear logs were sought, and for these $4 per thousand feet were paid in 1857. Sage & Grant advised their loggers to impress the settler with this price by naming "price pr log for logs 30 to 40 inches—take log book & make calculations—It will perhaps *sound* better than a price pr M—& cost less." [16] Good lots brought $2.50 per thousand feet delivered in the river.[17] Where possible, the loggers would work

[15] Sage to Dean Sage, May 13, 1861, HWS.
[16] To DeWitt Linn, June 26, 1857, HWS.
[17] In this period Sage & Grant generally classified lumber in three grades: Excellent, Good, Common.

out from a tract owned by Sage & Grant, canvassing the small owners in the vicinity. Where money was advanced on the logs, Sage & Grant collected interest until the timber was stripped and in the river. In some cases a farmer was commissioned to buy logs from his neighbors for Sage & Grant, the logs to be cut and delivered in the river. While the timber lasted, it was perhaps cheapest to buy this way, choosing only the very best of the logs and including in the price very often the cost of cutting and delivery in the nearest river. In cutting as well as in buying Sage & Grant advised their crews to ignore the common and lesser grades. They were interested in only the choice.[18] Since in most cases Sage & Grant did not own the land, the practice of a second cutting was not carried through in Canada as it was to be in the Lake States. Wasteful methods of lumbering were encouraged by panic periods when only high-grade lumber, it was thought, could command a profitable price. Sage's career as a "slaughterer" of pine was begun early. But at this stage no protest was heard from the rest of the community. In 1860 the *Northern Advance* commented that the community was "not a little indebted to American enterprise in the development of our resources, and especially along the line of the Northern Railroad." [19] Conservation sentiment did not develop to any significant degree until Sage was an old man, too old perhaps to change his notion that the slaughter of timber represented economic progress.

Beyond the mill and logging staff Sage & Grant built up a sales and shipping organization. Although they continued to sell through C. P. Williams and Co. in Albany, they sent lumber to Buffalo and Toronto for sale on a commission basis; in 1857 they opened their own lumberyard in New York City.

The New York yard had been organized for a wholesale trade. Sage moved his family to Brooklyn and prepared to take over the management. Unfortunately Sage discovered that the rapid turnover of the Albany trade could not be duplicated in New York City. He decided, therefore, to convert the yard to retail as well as

[18] To Hubbard, June 4, Sept. 25, 1857, HWS.   [19] April 25.

wholesale sales. The yard had to be expanded and equipped to store lumber while Sage sought "a shipper-dealer-or consumer, that *wants it*." [20] Sage sold from the New York yard not only the lumber produced by the Sage & Grant mill, but also lots of lumber picked up by his agents and lumber left with him for sale on a commission basis. In June of 1857 he asked a 5 per cent commission if he sold lumber afloat and guaranteed the sale, 10 per cent if he had to unload and pile it in the yard. The larger commission included insurance fees and a guarantee of sale.[21] In true merchant capitalist style Sage & Grant used the yard as a base not only for the sale of lumber but also for ventures in other country produce, largely grains. Purchases were made both on joint-account and commission bases. Sage & Grant's agents and partners were urged always to purchase on credit; at least thirty-day and preferably sixty-day drafts were to be used in payment. The contract was a short informal letter:

If you . . . can buy an occasional cargo of oats or corn so you think it will do—& raise the funds by dft on us at 30 ds from shipment—so the thing will turn itself around, we have no objection to try it for joint a/c & risk—Making no charge either way for services—ie—you buy & ship—& we sell—& no charge—The joint interest to stand the *risks* of sale—interest, & other expenses—If this suits we must keep each other well advised—& act with great caution.[22]

The most important point was to keep from using more funds than absolutely necessary. By the time the thirty-day draft came due, it was hoped that the grain would be sold and its price have paid its cost and a profit besides. Ready money was always short. The customers who paid for lumber paid in notes and long-term drafts just as Sage & Grant did.

Sage & Grant tried to keep in constant touch with all their branches by almost daily letters and a system of weekly and monthly reports. Entry books were sent to the foremen of logging crews so

[20] To Grant, May 28, 1857, HWS.
[21] To L. H. Owen, June 10, HWS.
[22] To Ben Tabor, July 15, 1857, HWS.

they might keep a daily record of the logs cut and skidded. On the selling end agents were also instructed to keep records; entries were made in a duplicate set of books, one set in the hands of the agent, one at Sage & Grant's office in New York. Accurate reports of the amount of lumber shipped on each boat were especially important, since the captains were suspected of selling lumber on the sly, an old canal practice. But while an accounting of lumber was important, an accounting of funds was crucial. Every agent was himself an independent businessman as aware of the main chance as Sage & Grant, as eager to make a killing in oats, to pick up a bargain in lumber or wheat. The man who had the funds would get ahead. No wonder then that Sage & Grant complained continuously that remittances were not promptly forwarded: "What is the matter with your boys at Toronto? Are they using our funds for your business?" And again, "We rec'd from you here in the month of Sept. only *500* cash—out of 3 to *4000*." [23] The temptation existed in temporary partnership or joint-venture arrangements for the partner who received payments to take his share of the profits early,

Our arrangement was that you were to receive nothing till ours [balance] was reduced by *absolute payments* to twice the amt of yours & then we were to receive in the proportion of our interest we two dollars to your one, on such assets as were recd—The fact appears to be that you *took* early in the season a sum which will probably more than pay all you will be entitled to when all is closed up—& leave still due us about $9000—& so far as we can see, nothing to pay it with but the clapboards in London & the Lumber you have in Buffalo.[24]

Competition, the fear of fraud, the physical difficulty of maintaining contact with scattered and independent agents, these were the problems of conducting business as a merchant capitalist in the fifties. Yet all was not suspicion and ill grace; Sage & Grant could write to their shippers with friendly humor: "Allow us

[23] To Latham, Tozer and Perry, Sept. 21, 1857; to D. Thurston, Oct. 1, 1857, HWS.
[24] Sage & Grant to J. Van Vleck, Oct. 5, 1857, HWS.

to call your attention to a few general principles—First to that passage of Holy Writ which says 'Swear not at all.' "[25]

It funds were short in normal seasons, during a panic they dried up completely. The 1857 season opened easily with Sage & Grant predicting a good trade. Cash was as unavailable as usual and the order was given to buy at sixty and ninety days. But by June credit was less easy to obtain, and Linn was urged: "Collect up every dollar of debts owed you—Cut down any possible expense- Use no cash except when you *Must*."[26] By September there were no funds to pay freight charges, by October none for wagon. Typical of the panics of the period but more severe, that of 1857 was related to the pressure placed on the money market when the fall crops came in and by specie drains on other accounts.[27] A chronically weak banking system was unable to withstand the strain.

Sage & Grant's measures to meet the crisis could only be limited. They urged Fisk: "Keep on sawing for if we break we want a large pile of lumber on hand to pay debts with—Drive the mill for the next 45 days as hard as you can."[28] But money for wages was a serious drain and Linn was advised that a reduction in wages was necessary while the labor force must be drastically reduced. Although the firm's principals determined immediately to cut wages, they were anxious "to provide employment as far as possible for those who have families there" and resolved to "try to keep our forces in motion if we can raise the means without sacrifice of Property & credit." At last some of the men were asked "to wait for wages till this storm is over."[29] Most lumbering operations in the Simcoe area had been forced to suspend or to continue at a reduced wage scale, and at that the workers were not to receive wages until spring.

[25] To William Tozer, July 31, 1857, HWS.   [26] June 4, HWS.
[27] Margaret Myers, *The New York Money Market* (New York, 1931–1932), p. 143; Paul Studenski and Herman Krooss, *Financial History of the United States* (New York, 1952), p. 127.
[28] Sept. 19, 1857, HWS.
[29] To Linn, Sept. 25, Oct. 12; to Hubbard, Oct. 1 and 13, HWS.

At the height of the crisis loaded boats were lying at anchor at New York, Albany, and Troy; their masters were without the funds for canal tolls.[30] Despite their inability to get cargoes to New York City, Sage & Grant refused to accept five-day drafts for freight payments while the shippers refused to allow thirty-day drafts. Sales were made even in the worst days of the panic and at good prices, but payment was to be in three, four, and five months, not cash. The risk of accepting five-day drafts which might have to go to protest was too great, and as the panic developed even five-day paper was not acceptable; specie was demanded. Throughout the crisis Sage & Grant's major effort was to keep from "breaking." Bankruptcy now, protest of their notes, and loss of credit would strip them of the organization they had built up and of whose soundness Sage was positive. An angry correspondence began with the firm's ultimate creditor, Josiah Williams, now president of the Merchants and Farmers Bank of Ithaca. Williams resented Sage & Grant's refusal to acknowledge that in his capacity as bank president he had to abide by rules which determined the amount of paper the bank might discount or renew.[31] Sage & Grant countered that it was better to renew a loan when there was reasonable expectation of payment than to call it when the result would be to bankrupt the firm. They held Williams to account for the worst disasters of the crisis:

We could point you to one of our Lumber Shanties on the Black River, in Canada, & 19 men & 2 women, who were for days with no food but bread, (& little of that,) & other scenes of trouble & distress . . . between which, & your letter of 26 Oct° there was a most direct connection as *ever* existed between cause & effect.[32]

Sage was not exaggerating the extreme state of the workers in Canadian mills; in this same period at Port Burwell the employees of a mill that had closed volunteered to operate the mill without wages if only food was supplied.[33] The quarrel with Josiah Williams took on a personal and bitter note. There is a hint of the

[30] Sage & Grant to Latham, Tozer and Perry, Sept. 16, 1857, HWS.
[31] Williams to Sage & Grant, Nov. 17, 1857, WF.   [32] Nov. 21, 1857, WF.
[33] George Raymond to J. E. Shaw, Oct. 23, 1857, JBW.

resurgence of Sage's old resentment of his wealthy uncle and of the old sense of personal persecution. Sage reported to his friend, Shaw, that Josiah had deliberately neglected to call on Sage during a visit to New York: "This man—*our friend*—who arrogates to himself the credit of making us—& you & others—at the time when he could really assist us with no injury to himself—is the only man who *in our case*—withholds his sympathy—& acts oppressively." [34]

Sage's insistence that the banker had nothing to fear in extending loans was based on the conviction of the value of his own property and on an interpretation of the panic which divorced it from the world of actual production. Industry as Sage saw it was healthy; the panic was the result of financial manipulation by speculators and bankers who brought on the catastrophe and then abdicated: "The only way to work out now is for the *men*—the real movers & workers, each in their individual capacity to resolve that the solid affairs of the world shall not be thrown from their bases—& that industry & production *shall* go on as usual—*and it will be done*." The panic had been precipitated as a "senseless" financial squall but had affected business activity in a chain reaction:

There are now a thousand good reasons why the next 6 months will be fraught with still wider & deeper financial evil—To one that existed 60 ds since why there should be any serious disturbance. . . . This stoppage of labor & industry—This forced paralysis of all industrial exertion will be fatal in its effects upon the property already in existence if it continues long—It is like tapping the jugular to save life.[35]

In so far as Sage was placing responsibility for the panic on the banks, he was approaching a modern interpretation. But he was right for the wrong reasons or at least for reasons too unsophisticated to be effective; for Sage it was not the breakdown of the banking system but lack of "manliness" in bankers that ultimately accounted for the failures of 1857. In accounting for business failure Sage had only the vocabulary supplied by Calvinism and

---

[34] Nov. 27, 1857, JBW.   [35] *Ibid.*, Oct. 24.

the self-improvement cults of his youth. Just as earlier he had interpreted his father's failure in terms of character, he now described the panic as a manifestation of cowardice and worse: "Nobody pays (here) or pretends to try to." [36] In explaining his father's situation Sage had only the philosophy of optimism to guide him, a philosophy that made no allowances for failures. In dealing with the panic he had again nothing but the optimism of his trade. Lumber was still in demand, the property was available, only the credit and currency to move supplies were lacking. On the other hand stupidity, fear, and callousness were apparent. The rule of "every man for himself" was in force.[37] Fear and resentment and the inability to see the panic except as a personal and moral phenomenon were reflected in the bitterness of the firm's correspondence:

Banks have credit (if not *souls*) to save, the same as you & I & theres no use in their driving all mankind into a corner—If they wont give you facilities to forward our property—as usual—*keep it there—pile it up*—Let Oswego become a store house—a Lumber yard. . . . Let your banks by refusing to furnish the usual facilities to *move* the trade that centers there—lay up your vessels—drive away Canal Boats—stop commerce—& it will be the shortest way they can find to recover their senses—and regain their lost manhood!

The demand for specie to move freight was considered peculiarly cruel:

In the *abstract they are right*—ie, they have the legal right to demand specie—but in these hard times it is extremely hard if a man wont take a frt bill in funds which are redeemed here at ¼ of pr ¢ disct.[38]

Sage & Grant survived the panic.[39] Indeed in January 1858 Sage was able to assure Josiah Williams that "our Bank liabilities

[36] *Ibid.*   [37] Sage & Grant to N. T. Williams, Oct. 8, 1857, HWS.
[38] To Latham, Tozer and Perry, Sept. 14, 1857, HWS.
[39] Sage may have obtained some of the funds necessary to carry him through the panic from the Tompkins County Bank, a rival of his uncles' bank. See April 29, 1895, entry in Mulks Notebook, Collection of Regional History, Cornell University.

are but little over ⅓ what they were a year ago today—& we have
much larger property assetts to pay with—& have provided already
for full half as much stock on Lake Simcoe, as we had last year." [40]
Cash was still unavailable, however, and credit in the form of
discounts on the firm's paper and bills receivable was sought from
Williams. Credit was extended with less grumbling and bickering,
however, as the panic subsided after the fall and winter of 1857.
Sage continued to reassure the firm's bankers that "we are selling
some lumber, and trying hard to pay our debts." [41] Nevertheless,
just as in the forties, Sage's efforts were directed toward expanding
his operations rather than achieving liquidity.

Meanwhile lumber prices had been climbing steadily.[42] In 1847
the highest grade of lumber brought $28 per thousand feet. Ten
years later, despite the panic, it brought $39 and $44.[43] In 1859
Sage calculated that timber ought to cost $4.00 per thousand feet
delivered at the mill, $3.00 per thousand for sawing, and $5.50
to $6.00 for freight to Albany, a total cost of $12.50 to $13.00. His
sales for that year had averaged $20 per thousand feet, leaving a
net profit of $7 per thousand.[44] Sage told J. E. Shaw that for "the
past two years they had made $54,000 & $48,000 and probably
would make as much this year." [45] When Sage's older son, Dean,
was ready to decide on a career, Henry Sage drew up for him an
evaluation of Sage & Grant's achievement in the six years the mill
had been in operation. Sage calculated the firm's net worth at this
time, May 1861, at $307,375. After deducting an amount for
probable bad debts and allowing for the depreciating effect of
"the political difficulties of our country," Sage hoped that $225,000
would represent a fair figure for the *"solid nett earnings*—for

---

40 Jan. 27, JBW. 41 To C. E. Hardy, June 24, 1858, JBW.
42 For the same period general price indices also indicate a steady upward
trend (Bureau of the Census, *Historical Statistics of the United States 1789–
1945* [Washington, D. C., 1949], p. 232).
43 J. E. Williams to Henry Schuyler, May 18, 1847, DeWitt; Sage & Grant
to A. L. Durand, Sept. 9, and to C. P. Williams, Sept. 11, 1857, HWS.
44 To J. E. Shaw, Dec. 29, 1859, JBW.
45 George Raymond to Shaw, Dec. 9, 1859, JBW.

the 6 years business." [46] This was, as Sage admitted, a large return on the original cash investment of $36,000.

In 1861 Dean Sage took a one-fourth interest in the firm of Henry W. Sage and Co., which was organized when the Sages bought Grant's share of the old firm.

It is probable that in the sixties Sage resorted to timber licenses to stock the mill, although he continued to buy lots of privately owned timber. In the mill organization some changes were made. Fisk was replaced as mill superintendent by William Spooner, who was evidently an employee without independent interest in the mill machinery. The capacity of the mill was not appreciably increased, perhaps because it was apparent that timber was increasingly more difficult of access. In 1867 Sage contemplated the building of a canal from the Black River to Lake St. John and attempted to interest another firm operating in the area in joining him. "With the canal built there will be plenty to do—without it I think business will be limited." [47] At the same time, however, Sage also had in mind the possibility of abandoning Bell Ewart for a mill near the falls of the Severn River.[48] Two years later the mill property was sold for $120,000.[49]

The purchasers were two young men; one of them, Harry Beecher, was the nephew of Henry Ward Beecher, Sage's pastor and friend. Harry had worked at the Bell Ewart mill for a few years as an employee of the Sages. The greater part of the purchase price was apparently not paid in cash but in notes of the new firm, which proved weak from the very beginning. Sage's assurance that the young men could make a net profit of $40,000 a year [50] was not borne out. His own endorsements for the young men worried him considerably in the seventies. Ultimately Sage wrote off as a bad debt $70,000 owed him by Beecher and Silliman.[51] Characteristi-

[46] May 13, 1861, HWS.
[47] Sage to Thompson, Smith, July 10, 1867; see also June 21, HWS.
[48] Sage to D. E. Boulton, July 5, and to H. L. St. George, July 6, 1867, HWS.
[49] Sage to Beecher and Silliman, Oct. 16, 1872, HWS.
[50] To Harry Beecher, Nov. 9, 1872, HWS.
[51] Sage to Dean Sage, Feb. 1, 1884, HWS.

64

cally he blamed their failure on the personal extravagance of young Beecher.[52] He apparently took no account in this appraisal of his own increasing difficulties in stocking the mill in the years before he sold.[53]

When Sage began milling in Canada in 1854, he considered himself primarily a merchant. Fifteen years later when he sold the Bell Ewart mill, he was a major manufacturer. His Canadian experience had provided a model for a much larger manufacturing enterprise in West Bay City, Michigan.

[52] *Ibid.*, Dec. 5, 1872.

[53] Lower points out that the mills at Barrie and the southern part of Simcoe County "reached their height about 1870, after which the pine of the neighborhood petered out" (*op. cit.*, p. 172).

Chapter V

The Michigan Experience: The Mill and the Business Community, 1864-1892

THE Saginaw Valley in the Lower Peninsula was the first of the lumber regions in Michigan to experience intensive exploitation. Some slight settlement of the valley was begun in the thirties. The small and crudely equipped mills, which usually appeared soon after the beginnings of settlement on the forested frontier, increased greatly in number along the river. It was not until 1858 or 1860, however, that lumbermen who were also substantial capitalists began to invade the valley, and that Saginaw lumber began to appear regularly on the eastern markets.[1] Henry Sage had known of the possibilities of the valley since 1847, when he had made a trip to Michigan to purchase lumber. Indeed the "first cargo of clear lumber ever sent from the Saginaws, was shipped . . . in 1847 . . . consigned to C. P Williams & Co. of Albany, N.Y.," the firm in which Sage was a partner.[2]

At the end of the Civil War rapid western development and increased industrial capacity made for a phenomenal rise in the price of lumber.[3] Inevitably, lumbermen began to seek out new, rela-

[1] A. R. M. Lower, *The North American Assault on the Canadian Forest* (Toronto, 1938), p. 141; James E. Defebaugh, *History of the Lumber Industry of America* (Chicago, 1907), II, 448.

[2] W. R. Bates, *The History, Commercial Advantages and Future Prospects of the Saginaws* (East Saginaw, Mich., 1874), p. 40.

[3] [Leeson], *History of Saginaw County, Michigan* (Chicago, 1881), pp. 399-

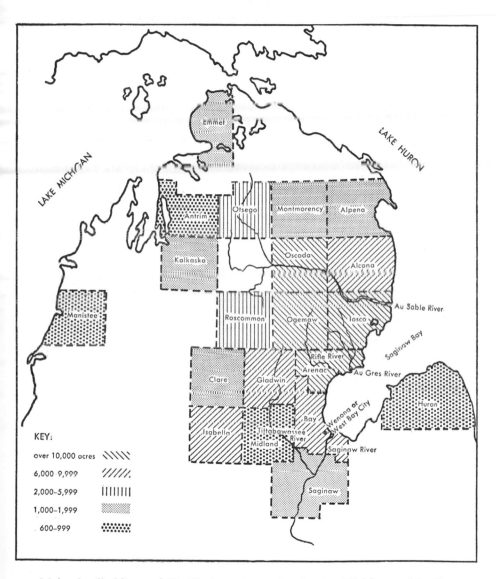

Major landholdings of H. W. Sage, Lower Peninsula, Michigan, 1864–1892

tively cheap and easily exploitable timber resources. Millmen were anxious to expand and more particularly to expand in areas which promised the most abundant resources. Thus, rather than increase the size and capacity of their existing mills, Sage, his partners, ex-partners, and competitors became part of that wave of lumbermen who began to buy up timber stands and mill sites in Michigan. Sage's partner in this new venture, John McGraw, was a lumberman familiar with the New York and Canadian lumber regions. His yard in Albany had been an outlet for Sage's Canadian lumber for a number of years.

The site which Sage and McGraw chose for their Michigan mill was on the west shore of the Saginaw River opposite Bay City. The mill was completed in 1865, one year after Henry Sage and John McGraw had signed a copartnership agreement "for the purpose of manufacturing Lumber and such other business as they think proper to connect with it at Bay City, Michigan." [4] Sage had earlier located the pinelands upon which the mill depended. These were now turned over to the joint interest in which Sage had a three-eighths and McGraw a five-eighths share. Under the terms of the agreement each partner was liable for a sum up to $75,000. The partnership was projected to last only five years, and was actually terminated in July of 1868, when each partner bid on the property of the firms. Sage took the whole for $461,000.[5] McGraw subsequently built a mill in Portsmouth, southwest of Wenona.

Much of the Sage-McGraw mill was built of timber from the trees growing on the site. The floor plan of the original mill was 80 × 140 feet.[6] Contemporaries referred to it as a "mammoth," a "giant," or "the largest saw mill in the world." In the first year of

---

400, quoting the lumber statistics of George F. Lewis and C. B. Headley; Isaac Stephenson, *Recollections of a Long Life* (Chicago, 1915), p. 161; Defebaugh, *op. cit.*, II, 455.

[4] Partnership agreement, Bay City, March 7, 1864, DeWitt.

[5] Statement of property, Sage, McGraw and Co., July 1, 1868, HWS.

[6] George W. Hotchkiss, *History of the Lumber and Forest Industry of the Northwest* (Chicago, 1898), p. 101.

operation, it produced only 9,048,000 feet, but in the next year, 1866, it produced 20,225,000 feet, and its production figures continued to grow higher. A peak year was 1870 with 34,450,972 feet produced.[7]

The mill was run by steam power and equipped with "one mulay for siding down the large logs . . . one rotary saw, two slabbing gangs, and two stock gangs of forty saws each, making a seasons cut of about thirty million feet. [8] A great part of the time and energy of Sage and his mill manager was taken up with repairs and improvements, testifying to the pragmatic method of test by use which was employed and to the stimulus of increased production. Sage relied heavily upon the very detailed understanding of the industry he had acquired. Although he was in no way an innovator of mill techniques and equipment, he kept up with improvements in so far as they were publicized in the trade journals. His characteristic injunction, repeated after instructions on repairs, was to "make some money by *saving*." [9]

Particularly in the first years of the mill's operation, the local newspaper eagerly reported weekly and daily production figures at the mill. In 1866 the Bay City *Journal* challenged: "On Thursday last . . . Sage, McGraw & Co's steam saw mill, in Wenona, cut 218,564 feet of lumber in 12 hours, an average of over 18,000 feet per hour. If there is any mill in Michigan, or out of it, that can beat that, we should like to see the figures." [10] The following year, the Sage mill beat its own record when it cut 370,797 feet in twelve hours.[11] Sage, who was present at this test of the mill's capacity, not only thanked the workers but gave them "a complimentary oyster supper." These sawing records were not typical of the mill's daily output. In 1867 production figures were reported at 125,000 feet per day, in 1872 at 150,000, in 1873 at 150,000 to 170,000, and in

[7] H. R. Page, *History of Bay County, Michigan* (Chicago, 1883), p. 52.

[8] James C. Mills, *History of Saginaw County Michigan* (Saginaw, 1918), I, 397.

[9] To S. A. Plummer, April 21, 1873, HWS.   [10] Dec. 8.

[11] *Ibid.*, Nov. 16, 1867.

1874 at 200,000.[12] Reports of mill production during the rest of the seventies and eighties range between 150,000 and 185,000 feet per day.

Although the Sage mill generally took first or second place among the Saginaw Valley mills in annual production of board feet, it produced less than 5 per cent of the valley's total output. In 1869, for example, when the Sage mill had not yet been rivaled by John McGraw's newer establishment, it produced only twenty-five to thirty millions of the more than 626 million feet cut in the valley that year.[13] The greatest part of the valley's production came from the many small mills producing less than ten million feet a year. Thus Sage held a distinguished but far from commanding role in the valley's lumber market. The structure of the industry in the Saginaw Valley remained substantially the same throughout the period of Sage's milling activities there. In 1882, the peak production year for the valley, Sage's mill contributed 31,500,000 feet to the total cut of 1,012,951,211 feet.[14] The complaints of overproduction and inability to control the market heard throughout the period were undoubtedly a reflection of this type of market structure.

In terms of capacity, however, the Sage mill ranked with the major mills of the Lake States. In the sixties its capacity was unusual. In the seventies it was on a level with the "great mills of the Chippewa Valley" of Wisconsin.[15] Only in the late eighties did its rank slip somewhat, for by the end of that decade in Minnesota "a big mill . . . was cutting not less than 40,000,000 feet in a year." But it is significant that by the late eighties individual proprietorships and partnerships were giving way in the Minnesota lumber industry to corporations in order to provide for higher

[12] *Ibid.,* May 11, 1867; Sage to H. W. Sage and Co., Toledo, Sept. 25, 1872; to Dean Sage, Nov. 2, 1873, and Aug. 18, 1874, HWS.

[13] Hotchkiss, *op. cit.,* p. 102; Page, *op. cit.,* p. 52.

[14] Hotchkiss, *op. cit.,* p. 143; *Lumberman's Gazette,* Bay City, Mich., XXI, 2.

[15] Frederick Merk, *Economic History of Wisconsin during the Civil War Decade* (Madison, 1916), p. 72.

capital costs.[16] Moreover, even earlier the giants of the industry like Knapp-Stout, which could produce between one hundred and one hundred and fifty million feet per year,[17] were corporations whose output represented that of several mills. And it was at this point, when he would have to consider the sale of shares in his business as a means to expand, that Sage's business and personal prejudices would intervene. Sage looked upon corporate status as a threat rather than an opportunity, a threat to his absolute control of the business he had built.

Policy formulation at the mill was almost entirely in Sage's own hands despite the fact that each of his sons took a one-fourth interest in the mill upon McGraw's withdrawal. Sage's impulse toward immediate, personal control was apparent in the administration of the lumber organization. The mill with its manager, mill boss, and engineer was the center of an organization concerned with all phases of lumber production. Logging camps located on Sage's pinelands and purchasing agents provided the timber for the mill. H. W. Sage and Co. lumberyards in New York City, Albany, and Toledo sold the finished lumber of the mill. There was no real bureaucratic hierarchy in this system. Each purchasing agent, logging contractor, camp foreman, member of the mill staff, was in direct contact with Sage and made his arrangements and terms with Sage.

The mill manager was the most heavily relied upon of Sage's employees. He was the general supervisor of affairs at the mill and in the camps and also performed some functions with regard to the location of lands in Michigan for the Sage interest. He was ultimately responsible for keeping the mill adequately stocked with lumber from the camps and for locating the camps and supplying them with food and feed. When he neglected any duty, Sage was not inclined to be lenient. His letters—almost always ending "In

[16] Agnes M. Larson, *History of the White Pine Industry in Minnesota* (Minneapolis, 1949), p. 157.

[17] Paul W. Gates, *The Wisconsin Pine Lands of Cornell University* (Ithaca, N.Y., 1943), p. 126.

71

Haste"—were sharp and exacting without benefit of a personnel-department editing. The point of a self servicing farm-camp-mill system would be defeated if the activities of the three groups were not coordinated. It was the mill manager's job to relieve the owner-manager of responsibility for the details of that coordination. At the same time Sage did not merely define the executive's duties and abdicate. Sage maintained his own lines of communication with all the men in the field, each man's report providing a check on the others, and all the reports providing a comprehensive picture of his business at any given moment. His plea for efficiency and initiative was never a plea for independent action. Although technically an absentee owner, Sage spent a number of months each year in residence in the mill town.

Immediate as well as ultimate authority always rested in Sage, perhaps because Sage was unaccustomed to a system in which able men were expected to make a permanent career in the management of businesses they did not own. In the twenty-eight years of the mill's operation, Sage employed four successive mill managers. Sage helped two of these men to establish themselves as independent businessmen. Only one of his mill managers made a career of his position in the Sage organization. Frank Pierson began as a clerk in the company store, took over the bookkeeping tasks at Wenona, and was at last advanced to manager.

The mill boss was in charge of construction and operation. He hired the mill hands, but wages, hours, and the number of workers were subject to Sage's approval. Sage demanded accurate and detailed information concerning mill costs and production. He ordered "a tabular statement . . . showing each month . . . the cost of sawing—the no. of men employed—the average cost pr day of each man—the average production pr day of each man." [18] With regular weekly and monthly reports, this type of statement enabled Sage to discover immediately any disadvantageous fluctuation and to set standards of production and cost.

In the camps, the stocker was responsible for determining with

[18] To H. W. Sage and Co., Wenona, Sept. 16, 1872, HWS.

the aid of a surveyor the boundaries of the areas purchased by Sage for exploitation by his camps. This was a particularly delicate job, for errors frequently meant long and expensive lawsuits. The stocker was general supervisor of camp operations and of the company farm. Potatoes, turnips, wheat, and oats were raised at East Tawas to supply the loggers through the winter season. The farm was expanded in the early seventies from year to year; the logging crew did the clearing and planting. Horses needed for hauling were kept at the farm and fed with homegrown hay, and cattle were kept to supply the camps with meat.

The camp foremen were expected to see to cutting timber, hauling it to the rivers or booms, constructing booms, and driving the logs to the mill. Camp labor earned between $25 and $30 a month —more nearly the former—plus board.

In selecting his mill staff, Sage was concerned to discover whether they had "industry enough—capacity enough—convictions of moral character enough" to be trusted with responsibility. When he discovered that the mill office was not open and prepared for work at 6 A.M., he labeled the tardiness of his mill manager a "lazy —poor house habit." [19] Plummer, the mill boss, was taken to task for his interest in horse racing. Sage wrote indignantly: "It should be your duty to *prevent and forbid* any notice of Horse racing or similar entertainment being posted upon our premises—No matter whose the horse—He cant run Race course & Mill too—Must choose which." Plummer was asked to choose also between his position in the mill and his position as Mayor of Wenona. Perhaps the fact that Plummer was a Democrat may have influenced Sage. Plummer resigned his position as Mayor. However, he left Sage's employ shortly thereafter, not without Sage's acknowledgment of his "real staunch nobility of character." [20] Sage also asked that Hiram Emery, his stock jobber, be warned "that using fast horses

[19] To James Langdon, April 23, 1867; to Sage, McGraw and Co., June 21, 1867, HWS.
[20] To H. W. Sage and Co., Wenona, June 23, 1873; to E. T. Carrington, Dec. 12, 1873, HWS.

on a race course will *hurt him*—The time & thought it costs, the expense, the associations & habits—are not in line with principles which control success in business or elevation of character." [21]

The camps and the mill did not constitute the whole of the lumber organization. Sage's own logging operations did not suffice to supply the mill or his yards. His logging was confined to pine while the yards had also to be supplied with hardwoods. There were seasons when he did not cut sufficient quantities of pine or was not able to get timber to the mill in sufficient quantities. Consequently he employed purchasing agents.

George Raymond in Peru, Indiana, was Sage's agent for hardwoods for many years. Raymond worked for a salary like the men in Wenona, but in line with the sanctions of the period he was anxious to go into business for himself. He was concerned with buying logs and land. When the opportunity arose he proceeded to buy on his own account with some partners as well as for Sage. Sage was angry but helpless: "There is no basis of reasoning that can justify you in building up an interest hostile to ours while at work for us, handling an important part of our business." [22] To prevent the development of a competing—hence "hostile"—enterprise Sage could only suggest that Raymond arrange to transfer his partners' shares to Sage while Raymond himself would retain his interest if he chose and thereby become Sage's partner in this part of the business.

Sage's other purchasing agent, Brewer, was even more independent than Raymond. He owned in his own right considerable timber lands in East Saginaw; in 1872 he was to build a sawmill in partnership with John C. Owen, whom he was to buy out in 1875.[23] Brewer bought logs for and with Sage, usually taking a one-third interest. The lots of lumber for Brewer's account and for Sage's were separately measured and inspected before shipment from Wenona, and the result charged to each owner's account. Sage's instructions to

[21] To H. W. Sage and Co., West Bay City, June 28, 1878, HWS.
[22] Sept. 22, 1871, HWS.
[23] Gates, *Wisconsin Pine Lands,* p. 109; Mills, *op. cit.,* II, 77.

the Wenona office suggest the general tone of this business relationship: "In shipping the Brewer lot measure & inspect *every* foot."
A few years later Sage seemed even more suspicious:

I want you to send George Russel to the Tittabawassee Boom & have
him stay there a week or so when the Logs are sorted out & see if all
is done right. . . . Now it would be very easy (if any of the sorters
try to do it in B's interest) to select the largest and best logs for
Brewer & give us the poor—It is this that I want R to watch for one
week.[24]

The joint account type of venture which Sage used extensively was
familiar to him from his early years in the trade, when capital was
scarce and numerous partnerships and joint accounts answered
that need. Now there was sufficient capital, but these arrangements,
although hardly as characteristic of the period as of the years before
1860, were still utilized to gain the services of an experienced man
like Brewer.

The problems of junior partnerships and rival interests arose
in connection with the lumberyards too. Whitney, the manager
of the Toledo yard, sought a share of the business rather than a
salary. In order to maintain that branch of the organization efficiently "with very little of our personal service," Sage agreed to
an arrangement whereby Whitney received 20 per cent of the net
profit on sales. The sales were, of course, to be of lumber sold to
the yard by the Sage mill. This made for difficulties when Whitney
felt that he could buy lumber more cheaply than Sage was willing
to sell and indeed made a purchase of lumber outside the Sage organization. Sage demanded that future purchases be left to the discretion of H. W. Sage and Co. which "has logs & mill but not
enough cash." [25] This tug of war between rival interests within
the same organization, although not a continuous phenomenon,
represented the fundamental problem of administration in the

[24] April 26, 1872; June 10, 1875, HWS.
[25] To H. W. Sage and Co., Toledo, June 18, 1873; see also Sage to Dean
Sage, June 8, 1874, HWS.

Sage business. It was perhaps unfortunate for Whitney that he obtained the partnership arrangement just at the beginning of the depression of the seventies. In the few years that followed it was Sage who maintained a philosophic calm in reply to Whitney's fears and complaints: "Don't get blue if we lose money—We *must* carry our part of the burden whether we like it or not—and let us do it cheerfully—The whole year may be better than the outlook is now." [26] Undoubtedly the senior partner could better afford to be cheerful. He had other interests to sustain him should the Toledo yard's business fall off, while he had discouraged Whitney's participation in outside interests both on the grounds that the planing mill in which Whitney proposed to invest was not a safe investment and because: "I should be wholly unwilling to have you as clerk or partner of ours—have an interest in any other business—The scriptures have a rule on that subject which is doubtless familiar to you." [27] Despite the lean years of the seventies, Whitney was able to accumulate enough to purchase the yard from Sage in 1883 in partnership with Frank Tracy.[28]

In 1867, H. W. Sage and Co. set up its own lumberyard in Albany with Dean as manager. Until that time it had marketed its lumber through the McGraw yard. While the lumberyard in Albany was under Dean's management, there were few administrative problems, but in 1875 the yard was transferred to the management of D. L. White, whose own firm had collapsed just before the '73 panic. The change probably came about as a result of Dean's persistent efforts to get out from under the lumber business. White undertook the job on a 10 per cent commission basis, a basis which led to a real conflict of interest with Sage during the depression years. White wanted to sell to collect his commission. Sage was anxious to hold his lumber for a rise in price. From 1875 to 1878 the conflict with White continued, and Sage felt it necessary to remind White that "our right to give you instructions as to prices

26 May 17, 1876, HWS. 27 April 25, 1873, HWS.
28 *Lumberman's Gazette,* XXII, 2.

& terms of credit is complete." [29] In 1878 Dean took over the yard again. The New York yard was under the direct management of the elder Sage, aided by Will, a clerk, and an "outside" man, until it was sold in 1878.

Undoubtedly the effectiveness of Sage's administration rested in his own detailed knowledge of his business and his willingness to expend energy freely in its behalf. Only these enabled him to overcome the contradictions apparent in the business objectives and business practices of his day. The ideal of independent proprietorship was not compatible with the development of a permanent management group divorced from ownership. The fact that Sage's early training came in the thirties and forties, when businesses were relatively small affairs and the owner was his own administrative staff, surely must have influenced Sage's techniques of management. Because the best of his staff were striving to achieve or had already achieved an independent status in which they were capable of acting as competitors, not only was Sage oriented toward acting as his own chief administrator, he was also compelled to keep detailed supervision and control if he expected to maintain a successful business.

By his own test, the test of profit, Sage was a successful administrator. The "eleven fat years from 1862 on" which Sage contended that lumber producers had enjoyed [30] had been relatively undisturbed by price declines. A short depression in the fall of 1869 had driven prices down temporarily, but by fall of the following year they were back to the $6–$12–$35 level, which represented the good prices of the fat years in the Saginaw Valley market. The Chicago fire and a short crop of logs in 1871 drove prices up still higher, and in 1872 the great stike and a short crop again maintained the rise. The drop that came after the panic seems the more dramatic because of the unusually high prices that obtained in the two previous years. Perhaps this explains why Sage

[29] To H. W. Sage and Co., Albany, Nov. 26, 1877, HWS.
[30] Sage to H. W. Sage and Co., Toledo, July 17, 1874, HWS.

included 1873 in the fat years, and why as late as July 1874 he regarded the situation with relative complacency, "Two or three sober years, if they don't utterly destroy, wont hurt them [the lumber producers]." [31] In the fall of 1873 prices dropped to $4–$8–$28 and $30. From 1874 to 1878 they fluctuated between this low figure and one that approached the 1868 price level. In September of 1878 prices dropped again and did not recover until June of 1879, when they were quoted at $6.50–$13–$28 and soon rose to $7–$14–$30, a figure close to that of the exceptionally good prices of 1871. Average prices remained at a high level until the crash of 1884.[32]

In 1880, after seven years of depression prices, Sage estimated "the profit on lumber production will *average $150 M* or more# for past 10 years—(# much more, as you know, only two years of the past 10 *less*)." [33] That is, in only two years from 1870 to 1880 did the firm's profits average less than $150,000. This represents a 37½ per cent or a 30 per cent return on the entire mill property investment, which was estimated at different times as $400,000 and $500,000. Moreover it does not take into account the profits on salt and lath production and the proceeds of rents which Sage estimated as amounting to $33,276 or more than 6 per cent on $500,000. This profit had been made despite a depressed price level.

Sage felt the pressure of fluctuating and declining prices. Yet complaints seem to be directed at relative rather than absolute losses. Thus in 1874 Sage wrote his son: "We can make a little on Lumber this year if we take from it (in sorting up) all there is in

[31] *Ibid.*

[32] All price quotations are taken from Saginaw Board of Trade, *Third Annual Review* (East Saginaw, Mich., 1884), pp. 26–28; Leeson, *op. cit.*, pp. 399–400.

[33] To Dean Sage, Dec. 14, 1880, HWS. Profit seems to have been calculated on "lumber production" after subtracting all costs of production, transportation, and material, including stumpage. With the possible exception of stumpage from the lands purchased in the sixties and considered part of the mill property, appreciation of stumpage values was charged against the profits of production rather than included in them.

it—But it wont be much at best—*Not* 7 pr ¢ in our capital." [34]
In 1878 he repeated that profits were possible but would be small.
"It will be a close business to make *anything* & sell at present rates
but we can by close management make small profits—say 1 to 1.50
pr M at best—We have reached a time when accumulations must
inevitably be slow." [35] A similar comment was made in 1885. Sage
wrote W. J. Young: "I think the worst of our depression in trade
is over & that we are to have increased production in all things,
and a period of reasonable prosperity in business that is *well
managed*—but without very large profits—We must learn to be
content with moderate gains—There is nothing better or safer
than the Lumber trade." [36]

In the last ten years of the mill's life an actual loss was recorded
in only one year, 1890. After the crisis of 1884–1885, however,
the profit level never fully recovered at the mill or the Albany
yard. (See Table 1.)

The unusually high profits of the sixties and early seventies
were based not only on the demands of an expanding economy but
also on the cheap price of stumpage. In the sixties stumpage had
cost Sage ten to twenty cents per thousand feet. But in the eighties
the supply of cheap timber easily accessible to the mill which
Sage had provided in the sixties was being exhausted. By 1885
Sage was evidently beginning to cut the poorer quality timber remaining on his lands.[37] In 1889 Sage predicted, accurately: "Our
lumber manufacturing business is very nearly at end in Michigan—
Three years will use up all the Timber we have." To continue
manufacturing by purchasing pine stumpage now with the price
of stumpage at $6 and $10 per thousand feet did not seem "worth
doing." [38] The rise in stumpage prices and the forseeable exhaustion of their own supply in the eighties lent force to the
Sage sons' desire to sell the mill. In 1882 the mill was actually
advertised for sale, and again in 1885 Sage offered to sell the mill

[34] *Ibid.*, June 2.   [35] *Ibid.*, May 23.   [36] Oct. 3, HWS.
[37] Sage to W. J. Young, Jan. 8, 1886, HWS.
[38] To E. F. Branch, Feb. 27, HWS.

property and three hundred million feet of timber, but he was not willing to sell at a price which did not compensate for the high value he placed upon it even then. The mill property and the returns it represented must not be "wasted or frittered away." [39] In 1890 the valuation of the mill on the books of the firm was reduced to $200,000.[40]

Table 1. Annual profit or loss *

Year	Mill		Albany yard	
	Profit	Loss	Profit	Loss
1882	$148,662		$114,181	
1883	138,032		121,554	
1884	83,740		68,656	
1885	36,330		18,784	
1886	40,937		37,553	
1887	121,211		59,194	
1888	129,154		65,137	
1889	134,829		90,505	
1890		$62,898	68,101	
1891	83,157			$133,133 †
1892	22,966		115,565	

* The figures are taken from H. W. Sage and Co. Day Book, *passim,* HWS.
† This loss reflects a major embezzlement by an employee in the Albany office.

To offset any decline in the profit level Sage relied on "close management," which invariably meant pressure upon the wage level. Sage agreed with the reflection published in the *Lumberman's Gazette* "that the compensations of labor must be regulated by the conditions of trade, and the ratios of profit." [41] The worker's services were factors in production, whose cost was adjusted in

39 Sage to Dean Sage, Oct. 28, 1885, HWS.
40 W. H. Sage to H. W. Sage and Co., West Bay City, April 18, 1890, HWS. This represents a loss in the book value of $200,000 to $300,000, which is reflected in the 1890 figure for "Addition to Stock A/c"; see H. W. Sage and Co., Day Book, March 31, 1890.
41 VII, 20.

terms of the maintenance of production and profit. The adjustment process, Sage believed, was to be controlled by the employer, for "employers know what they can afford to pay for the products of Labor and *will* pay all they can afford to." [42] Worried by the wave of strikes in New York City and by the possibility of a strike at the mill in 1872, Sage wrote, "We cant afford yet, to submit to the charge of an ignorant rubble—the conduct of enterprises upon which the nation's wealth and prosperity depends." [43] Sage justified the unilateral control of the wage level by the employer on the grounds that he produced the goods and provided the capital upon which the community's prosperity was based. His obligation to his workers was defined by supplying them with work.

Over the whole period of lumber production in the Saginaw Valley the money wage of labor did apparently increase. About 1850, when a mill employed seven men for each twelve hour shift, the average wage for all workers amounted to one dollar a day.[44] By 1860 the average wage paid in the valley for common labor had risen to $1.12½. The post–Civil War period brought even higher wages. A Lumberman's Proclamation published during the 1872 strike listed the average daily wage paid from 1865 to 1872 to demonstrate the rise in money wages. The last figure—$2.30—compared favorably with the first—$1.52.[45] The average wage at Sage's mill in July of 1872 was as high as $2.33.[46] However, higher money wages in this period ran parallel with high prices.

In 1873 began a downward swing of both money and real wages.[47] Sage's mill had reduced its average wage to $2.14 by July of 1873, before the panic struck. Sage contended that manufacturers could not long continue "to be deaf and blind to the fact that we must reduce cost, and restrict production—*both*—if we make lumber

[42] Sage to H. W. Sage and Co., Wenona, July 11, 1872, HWS.
[43] *Ibid.,* June 2.   [44] Leeson, *op. cit.,* p. 384.
[45] Bay City *Daily Journal,* July 3, 1872. The *Journal* like the *Tribune* added "Daily" to its title in some years.
[46] Sage to S. A. Plummer, July 15, 1872, HWS.
[47] Chester W. Wright, *Economic History of the United States* (New York, 1941), p. 752.

trade produce anything save *loss and disaster.*" [48] Sage proposed a "concert of action" among the millowners of the valley to postpone sending men to the woods until they were prepared to accept $20.00 a month as wages. The postponement would serve not only to gain lower wages but also to limit production. It is true that Sage did not cut much timber in 1873, but due to the strike of 1872 and unusually dry weather that year, which kept the stock in the woods, he had a plentiful supply in 1873. His own production figure went from the unusually low 12,940,519 feet in 1872 to 20,370,670 in 1873 and 25,111,595 feet in 1874.[49]

In September of 1873 a 12½ per cent wage reduction was agreed on by manufacturers.[50] In April of 1874 Sage considered $1.50 enough for common labor.[51] The *Lumberman's Gazette* quoted $1.75 as the average daily price of common labor in the valley in 1874; by 1877 this had dropped to $1.25.[52] Evidently the price level was not sufficiently low to compensate for wage reductions. Thus, the editor of the Saginaw *Daily Courier* sought in vain to discover "what is to become of the laborers who get only $1.00 a day and are obliged to pay $13.00 a barrel for flour and $1.50 a bushel for potatoes." [53]

There was no significant improvement in the wage level until 1880. Wages then began to advance only to drop again in 1884.[54] By 1885 the wage level of the industry was seriously affected. Of the 4,232 men employed by 77 mills in the valley, 54 per cent earned $1.62½ or less.[55]

Thus the substantial rise in money wages from 1860 through 1872 was sharply curtailed in 1873. Though wages tended to rise again in the early eighties, they did not do so in the same proportion as they had in the first period, and again the rise was

[48] To H. W. Sage and Co., Wenona, Sept. 11, 1873, HWS.

[49] Page, *op. cit.*, p. 52.

[50] *Lumberman's Gazette*, III, 66; Bay City *Tribune*, Sept. 29, 1873.

[51] To H. W. Sage and Co., Wenona, April 22, HWS.   [52] XI, 100.

[53] April 29, 1877.   [54] *Tribune*, July 8, 1885.

[55] Bureau of Labor and Industrial Statistics, *Third Annual Report* (Lansing, Mich., 1886), p. 16.

curtailed by depression. The wage level, then, was highly responsive to a decline in the price of lumber, less responsive to a rise in price.

Strikes occurred in the Saginaw Valley with some regularity. For the most part they were limited in scope, involving only a fraction of the working crew. One lasted only fifteen minutes. Organization of the workers was usually attempted after, not before the outbreak of a strike, and none of the strikes could be said to be successful. In 1867 talk of a strike for higher wages reached Sage, who warned:

Lumber is declining in value and slow of sale at *any price*—and wages *should be,* and *will be*—permanently lower before they are permanently higher. . . . We are willing to pay for labor all our business will warrant—but we can't at the same time increase wages of labor—and sell its products *below cost.*—and lumber could not be sold *freely* today in any market I know—East or West—to *pay* a reasonable business profit over the cost of production.[56]

This stock argument was to be heard even more often after 1873.

If a strike was not justified in a poor year it was considered equally unjustified in 1872 after two comparatively prosperous years. Sage wrote:

Never was there so little good reason for discontent—Never was labor so well paid [this was the year when his average wage at the mill was $2.33]—so fully occupied—If we can keep it well occupied and well paid as now our nations wealth will rapidly increase and every interest will prosper—but destroy the foundation or decrease its flow—and we shall very soon go back to poverty—We cant stand the drain of extravagant expenses and partial idleness.[57]

He referred by this last statement to the demand for a ten-hour day in the mills and/or an increase in wages to meet higher prices.

About the fifteenth of June, 1872, the "murmurings" for a ten-hour strike throughout the Saginaw Valley were brought to the

[56] To J. G. Emery, July 12, HWS.
[57] To H. W. Sage and Co., Wenona, June 17, HWS.

attention of the millowners. Strikes on varying scales began to break out in the first days of July. There was perhaps a deliberate slowing down of production in the mills. Thus Sage complained that his mill, which should have been cutting 100,000 to 120,000 feet a day had averaged only between 60,000 and 70,000. Nevertheless Sage was anxious to keep his mill going as long as possible "on regular time." [58] On July 3 he joined with the millmen of fifty-seven other firms in Bay City, Saginaw City, and East Saginaw in issuing a proclamation to the effect that they would "not submit to any reduction of the hours of labor nor any increase of wages." [59] By July 5 most of the mills had been shut down.

The millowners agreed on a uniform show of resistance toward the strikers' demands. The resolve of the Lumberman's Proclamation was adhered to fairly consistently. A shutdown at this time did not seem disastrous, since the lack of heavy rains that season had resulted in a shortage of logs. Nevertheless, millmen were anxious to cut what they had in expectation of the large returns a scarcity on the market would realize. Sage directed his mill manager as early as July 8 not to "wait to know the real purposes of your men—Get them together and learn how many and *who* want to work on our terms—Then prepare to protect them and our property." [60]

There was real fear of mob violence and destruction of mill property. No effective organization existed among the workers. It was a restless, milling body of men with no apparent leadership which the millmen faced. Sage was prepared to arm his mill staff with six-shooters and Spencer rifles, and gave orders to notify the mob that Company officials were armed and would protect the mill property should the town government prove unwilling or unable to do so.[61] Threats to burn down the mills were received,[62] but never carried out. The mills after all represented the only source of income to the workers.

On July 9, four days after the strike had "officially" begun,

[58] *Ibid.,* July 3.   [59] *Daily Journal,* July 3, 1872.
[60] To H. W. Sage and Co., Wenona, July 8, 1872, HWS.
[61] *Ibid.,* July 5 and 6.   [62] *Ibid.,* July 8.

the laborers organized a union based on a one-dollar initiation fee and a twenty-five-cent monthly assessment.[63] The Striker's Union contributed little toward the organization of the strike movement. Its main function seems to have been to keep the workers' families provisioned. The establishment of the union did not imply success in treating with the mill operators as a group or in organizing the workers of any one mill to treat as a unit with their employer. The concept of collective bargaining was perhaps as alien to the workers in this period as it most certainly was to employers.

The Sage mill was prepared to start up again several times during the strike period with a partial crew who agreed to Sage's terms. However, the resumption and immediate shutdown of his mill led Sage to feel:

The only remedy for this case is to let the whole laboring community feel the burden of the strike till there grows up in their own midst a sense of their folly. . . . Collect your rents promptly—especially from strikers—They must not live on us while their conduct destroys us.

And finally, exasperated, he ordered that the workers remaining at the mill be fired if the hands refused to come back at the old wages and hours. This group, he contended, were probably in secret sympathy with the strikers but holding on to their jobs so that they would not lose anything whether the movement succeeded or failed.[64]

By July 17 the Bay City *Daily Journal* claimed that the strike was about broken. Sage's mill had started up with thirty-five men, and he expected to hire seventy or eighty more that day. By July 19 all the mill except the circular saw was running the full twelve-hour day.[65] The greater ability of the millowners to wait out the strike, particularly in the face of a scarcity of logs, was probably the most overwhelming factor in their success.

Sage contended that the strikers "have against them not alone

[63] *Daily Journal*, July 9, 1872.
[64] To H. W. Sage and Co., Wenona, July 9, 13, 1872, HWS.
[65] *Daily Journal*, July 17, 19, 1872.

the employers—but the whole interests of society—*and quite as much their own!"* His attempt to discover any within his organization who were "doubtful" with regard to the labor movement, to "learn where they are—who they are—and exactly how to count them—they are either for or against and we should know which—" was in line with the position taken by the *Journal,* which declared that "the entire blame" for the strike "can be laid at the doors of a few discontented demagogues."

These men are marked, and will have considerable difficulty in procuring situations in the Valley, and it is perfectly right that all such discontented uncongenial spirits should be debarred from work where an insinuating word does as much harm as it has within the last four weeks in this section.[66]

The vocal element, the "respectable" element in the community did not concede the right of workers to disrupt the processes of production.

The twelve-hour work day was resumed. Perhaps most significant of the results of the strike was the notice: "Before the strike lumber was selling freely at $7.00, $14.00, and $35.00. . . . Since the strike has ended $7.50, $15.00 and $36.00 are the figures at which holders stand firm." [67]

After the panic of 1873 the chances for an effective labor protest were weakened still more. Riots were reported in May of 1876.[68] A few months later Sage directed his manager to "hire your men *low* and pay them from the store—We *cannot raise* cash and there must be no reliance on it." [69]

In the late fall of 1879, when the depression began to ease, a fifteen-minute strike for higher wages among Sage's workers occurred.[70] In May of 1882 fourteen men at work at the salt block of H. W. Sage and Co. struck for a 12½ cents advance which

[66] To H. W. Sage and Co., Wenona, July 11, 10, 1872, HWS; *Daily Journal,* July 19, 1872.

[67] *Lumberman's Gazette,* I, 4.   [68] *Ibid.,* VII, 20.

[69] Nov. 28, 1876, HWS.

[70] Bay City *Chronicle and Tribune,* Oct. 8, 1879.

would bring their pay to $1.75 a day. Their places were soon filled by others "quite willing to accept the company's terms, which are the same as all other blocks along the river are paying." [71] Again there were more than enough workers for the places available, and no opportunity for a better-paid job in the mills of the valley.

During the spring of this year the coopers of Sage's mill commenced a series of strikes for a raise in wages. The most interesting notice connected with these strikes was of the existence of a union organization.[72] In 1874 during a workingman's meeting a Mr. Allen, who may have been a local merchant, had risen to express his thought that "the workingmen had all the privileges they wanted already and that we should be careful in organizing to consider the rights of capitalists as well as that of the workingman." [73] Subsequently the meeting carried the motion to convert this "society for the benefit of workingmen" into "a benevolent protective literary society." From this time almost no notice seems to have been given in the newspapers and trade journals to labor organization in the valley.

Nevertheless, the Knights of Labor had been active. Out of an estimated 4,232 men employed by the Saginaw mills in 1885 the Knights claimed to represent 3,000.[74] This did not make it the focal point of militant labor protest, however. The Knights' membership roll was a heterogeneous sort; it included on its lists tradesmen and city officials. Indeed during the Great Strike of 1885 "the official aid rendered by the Knights complicated matters, because nearly all of the city officials in Saginaw, East Saginaw, and Bay City were members of the order." [75] Perhaps because of its motley membership, the Knights tended to be a conservative agency, cautioning the strikers to moderate their demands. While

[71] *Daily Tribune*, May 9, 1882.   [72] *Ibid.,* June 13.

[73] Bay City *Morning Chronicle,* Feb. 11, 1874.

[74] Bureau of Labor and Industrial Statistics, *op. cit.,* p. 119; *Tribune,* July 14, 1885.

[75] Sidney Glazer, "Labor and Agrarian Movements in Michigan, 1876–1896" (dissertation, University of Michigan, 1932), p. 96.

the Great Strike of 1885 was neither organized nor led by the Knights of Labor, individual Knights played a prominent role.

This strike seems to have originated in a misconception of when the ten-hour law, whose passage had been promoted by Thomas Barry—a laborer, Knight, and Democratic-Greenback member of the Michigan legislature—was to take effect.[76] The workers of the valley were convinced that the law was to go into operation on July 1, although it is clear that the law was not to be effective until September 15. About the fifth and sixth of July the Rust mills in Bay City were shut down by the strikers. Soon the whole valley was affected by the agitation.

The years 1884 and 1885 were severe depression years. Sage contended in 1885 that "this year and last year the wages we have paid have been more than our profits." He wished that "all the mills in the Valley would close for 60 days—that would do great good"; that limitation of production which the millmen could not achieve among themselves, the labor force was carrying out for them. "We should welcome with joy an absolute shut down of the mills for the whole of this season—it would enable consumption to overtake production and in that way restore values of property already produced." [77]

With this the prevailing attitude among employers, the workers could hope to achieve little for themselves by striking. Nevertheless, the strike continued. On July 11 the mill hands of Bay City and West Bay City made their dramatic trip to the Saginaws by foot and barge to rout out their fellows with the slogan "Ten hours or no sawdust." Some of the millowners, although by no means all, had no objection to a ten-hour day. The crucial issue was the workers' demand that the reduction in hours be accompanied by no reduction in pay. This the millmen were universally unwilling to concede.

Although the mill operators were indifferent to or even welcomed the closing of the mills, they resented bitterly the "mob

[76] Bureau of Labor and Industrial Statistics, *op. cit.*, p. 110.
[77] To H. W. Sage and Co., West Bay City, July 9, 10, 1885, HWS.

action" which precipitated the shutdown. Sage was convinced that his own employees were willing to work but "forced to quit by mobs,"

We clearly recognize the right of men to fix for themselves the price of their labor, and the hours they will work—and also the right of employers to agree or disagree with their terms—the rights of mobs, or illegal combinations of men to enforce their views upon men willing to work, and satisfied with their wages we wholly deny.[78]

Sage himself was sure that "the strike did not originate with the laboring men," that it was the "influence of Labor Knights and Politicians" which had kept it going so long.[79] Nevertheless, a meeting of the employees of the Sage mill resulted in a refusal by the workers to return at the old terms.[80]

The lack of a comprehensive organization among the men was illustrated again and again during the course of the strike by just such meetings of the crews of an individual mill. While indecision and successive proposals marked the stand of the strikers, Sage maintained a fixed policy: The old terms or a ten-hour day and a one-eleventh reduction in pay. By August 23, fifty of his workers were willing to accept the latter proposal. But when the mill started up again on September 1, it was upon the old terms, eleven hours and no increase in wages.[81]

During the course of the strike, Sage noted that valley officials appeared too sympathetic to the laborers' cause. Sage wrote angrily, "Bay City authorities' concessions to mob rule *wrong*—this to be avoided at *all cost*." And again, "If the Bay City authorities had not been so weak-kneed the strike would never have assumed its present proportions." [82] Undoubtedly the unwillingness of officials to clamp down harshly upon the strikers was due to the fact that many of them were themselves Labor Knights. Also, despite the protests of mob rule made by the employers, there was surprisingly

[78] *Ibid.*   [79] *Ibid.,* Aug. 6; to Dean Sage, Aug. 3, 1885, HWS.
[80] *Tribune,* July 16, 1885.   [81] *Ibid.,* Aug. 23, Sept. 1, 1885.
[82] To H. W. Sage and Co., West Bay City, July 11; to Thomas Cranage, Aug. 21, 1885, HWS.

little evidence of violence over this long period. Governor Alger addressed the strikers as freely as did Blinn and Barry, strike advocates, although he spoke as a lumber manufacturer and warned that "to hinder others from working is illegal." On one occasion when a strikers' meeting, complete with band, was ordered to disperse, a Negro jumped to the platform to shout: "In this free country a white man can't speak but a wooly headed nigger can. I advise you to join your hands like an eagle's claw and a lion's paw and hang together and stay away from the mills till they send for you!" [83] And with such colorful advice he bade the strikers goodnight as they "gradually dispersed." The lack of violence and the affiliation with the Knights may have influenced many in "respectable" places to sympathize with the strikers. Rumor had it that even Sage's chief engineer, Roundsville, who had been with Sage about twenty-five years and was a personage in West Bay City, many times an alderman in fact, sympathized with the strikers and was perhaps himself "a member of the 'skilled laborers association.'" [84]

There may have been yet another reason for sympathy for the workers among the middle class of the valley, and that was the knowledge that the mills could not continue to operate many years longer in the valley because the lumber supply of their hinterland was nearing exhaustion. The closing down of the mills would necessarily affect adversely the basis of the entire community's economy. Such knowledge could not but influence the attitude of the community toward the mill operators, particularly toward the absentee millowners. Though certainly not actively expressed, some feeling of hostility may well have existed. Sage thought it wise to have "the authorities . . . and the People" informed that if nothing were done to curb "rule of mobs" "we propose to close our mill and all business there and not resume it." [85]

[83] *Tribune,* July 15, 16, 1885. Daniel C. Blinn was editor of the *Labor Vindicator.*

[84] W. H. Sage to H. W. Sage and Co., West Bay City, Aug. 21, 1885, HWS.

[85] To H. W. Sage and Co., West Bay City, Aug. 15, 1885, HWS.

By the last days of August the strike had been broken. In general the mill operators' terms were accepted in full: either the old eleven-hour day or a ten-hour day with a one-eleventh or 10 per cent decrease in wages. Sage disagreed with the millowners who insisted upon holding out categorically for the old system. He pointed out that to do so would mean a renewal of the contest when the ten-hour day went into effect by law. He noted that the laborers "certainly have gained nothing except the questionable privilege of an extra hour's rest per day, which they ought to be welcome to enjoy so long as they are willing to pay for it themselves."[86] Nevertheless, a millowners' association was formed in the Bay City area and Sage was influenced by his neighbors to insist on the eleven-hour day. Perhaps the personal tragedy he had experienced in these weeks as a result of his wife's death made him less able and less inclined to press his own point of view. He expressed objections to the methods by which others were attempting to break up the "Labor Organization combination," although he held no brief for the combination itself. Earlier he had advised his mill manager that "we had better avoid saying anything to irritate—such as that we will discharge all 'Knights' etc."[87] The sixty-day shutdown he had welcomed had done its work, and Sage was eager to get back into production. The labor struggle had resulted in substantial gain and outright victory for the employer; future problems could be met as they arose and with less show of aggression on the part of the employer.

On September 3, Sage reported to his son that the mill was running "full crew—old hours and price—cut first day 153 M with considerable not piled."[88] But as he predicted, September 15 meant renewed difficulties. Brief, sporadic strikes occurred in the valley during the next few weeks until a formula was accepted at each mill. Sage acceded to the ten-hour demand and settled for a 5 per cent rather than a 10 per cent reduction.[89] Ten hours

---

[86] To L. L. Hotchkiss, Aug. 24, 1885, HWS.

[87] *Ibid.;* to H. W. Sage and Co., West Bay City, Aug. 19, 1885, HWS.

[88] To Dean Sage, Sept. 3, 1885, HWS.   [89] *Tribune,* Oct. 13, 1885.

were accepted as the general work day in the valley. Wage reductions from 10 per cent down were general, although an occasional mill did not enforce a reduction at all.

The slightly higher wage was won only by a minority of workers in the valley. It was the employer who gained most directly in money terms because of the higher price his limited output could and did obtain on the market. Far more important in long-range terms was the fact that this last significant protest on labor's part came when the industry had reached peak production. H. W. Sage and Co. closed its mill in 1892. Many had done so earlier; many others were to follow shortly. The industry died and with it died the possibility for growth in many Saginaw communities.

The great strikes of 1872 and 1885, one undertaken during a period of relative prosperity, one in the midst of a depression, were both met by the superior resources of the mill operators to wait out the strike and the determination of the operators that labor be reduced once more to its position as a factor in production. By the time the community expressed even a passive sympathy for the workers, it was too late for that sympathy to change the established pattern. The millowners were already investing in new lumber frontiers in expectation of the exhaustion of the valley's timber. Without effective labor organization, the final arbiter of the reasonableness of profit remained the employer with the sanction of a community which depended upon him for industrial and civic development. And the employer was most absorbed by the effort to reduce costs.

In dealing with the mill staff and the mill crew Sage found it desirable and necessary never to relinquish authority or responsibility, nor would he tolerate the attempt to share in the determination of wage and hour policies. He was prompted by an assurance that he best understood his own interest and by a genuine belief that his success provided the basis of the community's prosperity. A comment to a fellow lumberman, "An organization like yours which can produce nearly 10 millions pr month and sell 70 pr ¢ of it, is one to be proud of—both for the efficiency of its work and the Generalship which directs it," [90] provides a clue to the way in which Sage regarded his own role. The mill was his creation, his "life work" to which he had given, as he suggested his sons give, heart, zeal, and earnest purpose. He was repaid not only in profits but also by a sense of real achievement.

In dealing with his fellow lumbermen Sage's authoritarian temper had to be curbed somewhat. The lumbermen of the valley organized several successful boom companies and joined in an equally successful pool to market the salt produced by their mills. They cooperated on occasion to force down freight rates or to reduce taxation. Their efforts to organize and curtail lumber production, however, failed. Cooperation in the first instances led to the formation of what were essentially service agencies for the individual mills, the boom companies providing adequate facilities for getting the logs to the mills from the timber country, the salt association making possible economies in transportation and marketing and eliminating the competition of independent sellers. The profits and long duration of these companies testify to their success.

Cooperation was achieved despite the strong individualism and the profound jealousy of the millmen. The internal history of these associations reveals constant conflict and persistent attempts of individual members and of groups within the organizations to gain and maintain control. The millman sought from these organizations not only the benefits all producers might derive and the dividends all stockholders might claim but also whatever special privileges, contracts, or agencies the general organization had to bestow upon individual lumber firms. Moreover, he felt that he had to guard his own interests against the special privilege seeking of his neighbors. The boom company or salt association was regarded as the instrument of the men who controlled it, not necesssarily of those who owned it. Since these men were competitors, it was most important to keep within the controlling group.

[90] To W. J. Young, Oct. 3, 1885, HWS.

The Michigan Salt Association was perhaps the most successful of the combinations of millowners in the Saginaw Valley. Salt was produced by the lumber mills of the valley almost as a by-product. Production was largely confined to pumping up and refining brine rather than to mining rock salt. Therefore costs were low after the initial investment in pumps, wells, and refining plant, for fuel, the major cost item, was supplied by waste lumber and sawdust. Consequently manufacturers were tempted, when competition prevailed in the relatively inelastic market, to cut price to the minimum which would cover operating expenses.[91] The Association emerged after several false starts as the result of a high degree of competition in the salt markets of the Middle West, particularly Chicago. Competition was two-fold, within the group of Saginaw producers and between that group and the older established producers of central New York who were organized in the Onondaga Salt Association. A continuous decline in price spurred on the drive toward combination.

In 1866 the first combination of manufacturers in the Saginaw Valley was achieved by the Saginaw Salt Company.[92] In 1868 that company was superseded by the Saginaw and Bay Salt Comany, which controlled four-fifths of the valley's salt production in that year. This organization lasted until the spring of 1872 when Duncan Stewart, one of the largest salt producers in the valley, withdrew from the association. His withdrawal and the higher prices which independents obtained negated the immediate advantage of selling through the company. As highly as he regarded the long-run function of the association, Sage was willing to sell independently in December of 1871.[93] By March of 1872 Sage reported that he was receiving from the association $1.35 per barrel, "less by 25¢ than current rates in the Valley," [94] and he was disposed to

[91] H. R. Seager and C. A. Gulick, *Trust and Corporation Problems* (New York, 1929), p. 87.

[92] J. W. Jenks, "The Michigan Salt Association," *Political Science Quarterly*, III, 81.

[93] Sage to H. W. Sage and Co., Dec. 11, HWS.

[94] To John McGraw, March 9, HWS.

drop out of the organization entirely. By May the Saginaw and Bay Salt Company had been dissolved.

Sage did not believe that much could be accomplished in the way of effective organization until the valley producers had increased their output. In 1872 Sage expected to produce 20,000 barrels, and he thought McGraw might produce 50,000.[95] The output of the entire valley amounted to 724,481 barrels.[96] An increase in output would enable the Saginaw Valley to compete on more equal terms with New York producers and would perhaps force the valley producers to combine. The years from 1872 to 1876 did see an important increase in production. In 1874 the valley's output went over the one million mark and in 1876 reached 1,462,729 barrels.[97] In 1873 Sage produced on an average of 150 barrels a day; in 1874 his salt works were manufacturing 250 to 275 barrels a day.[98]

From 1872 through 1875 Sage sold his salt independently at the mill, through the Toledo yard, or through a commission agent in Chicago. Freight rates represented the most serious problem in marketing the salt. In 1873 Sage estimated that the total cost of production, including the barrels and a sinking fund to cover interest and depreciation was 78 cents. With sales at the mill reported at $1.73 in June, this left a net profit of 75 cents on a barrel or almost a 100 per cent profit.[99]

In the Toledo area railroad difficulties were persistent. On one occasion the Flint & Pere Marquette evidently charged Whitney higher rates than Sage had contracted for. Sage's indignant outburst reflected his most persistent attitude toward all business "corporations."

All corporations that I have dealt with are without soul, or common honor—will rob—cheat or lie whenever it suits their interest or caprice,

95 To A. J. Latham, April 4, HWS.   96 Jenks, *op. cit.,* p. 80.
97 *Ibid.*
98 Sage to Dean Sage, April 25, 1873, May 22, Aug. 6, 1874; to H. W. Sage and Co., Wenona, Nov. 20, 1873, HWS.
99 To Dean Sage, June 27, HWS. Prices were not constant, however.

& the only way to deal with them is to make them do right (if you have the power) as you go along—Not trust them.[100]

Strict accounting, immediate and continuous reckonings, and the maintenance of control were the necessary techniques to ensure success in working with or within a corporation. A major grievance of Sage against the railroad was the matter of rebates. In 1875 he learned that the F. & P.M. was charging Duncan Stewart only 15 cents per barrel to carry salt to Toledo. Sage's efforts to gain the same advantage from the road were apparently ineffective, for a year later he was still confident that Stewart was receiving a preferential rate. In those years before the Interstate Commerce Commission and effective government regulation the shipper could only "ask them . . . squarely" [101] to extend to him the same low rate received by his competitor. An association undoubtedly would give the salt shippers as a group a better bargaining position in relation to the railroads and perhaps would prevent discrimination among those within the association.

The lack of effective association, aggravated by the depression, resulted in lower prices at both Wenona and Toledo. In March of 1874 Sage was willing to sell at Wenona at $1.30 to $1.35, while by July of 1875, he advised sale at $1.10 if no higher price was possible, and was willing to accept $1.35 at Toledo if that low price would enable Whitney to "get in ahead of others & close out any considerable portion." [102] Sage was willing to adopt sharp competitive techniques; in 1874 he suggested making "a raid" upon the customers of one of his low-selling competitors to "force him to *desire* fair profits." [103]

In an effort to gain higher prices two organizations were formed in the valley during this period, the Saginaw Salt Company and the Michigan Salt Company, neither of which proved effective. In

[100] To H. W. Sage and Co., Wenona, Jan. 3, 1874, HWS.

[101] *Ibid.,* Dec. 22, 1875.

[102] *Ibid.,* March 23, 1874; July 6, 1875; W. H. Sage to H. W. Sage and Co., Toledo, Jan. 3, 1874, HWS.

[103] To H. W. Sage and Co., Toledo, Oct. 2, HWS.

the summer of 1875 plans for combining the two associations were proposed. Sage rejected an early offer of the presidency of the new association and was unwilling to commit himself to membership. From the outset, Sage's primary concern was the answer to the question, "Who was to control the new organization?": "If we can feel sure that an arrangement based *on equity* & in the hands of men who will *do equity*—can be established we will cooperate with it heartily." [104]

A trip to Wenona confirmed Sage's apprehensions about control of the new organization. The backers of the Saginaw Salt Company, millmen of the Saginaw City area, were anxious to have their already established agencies in Chicago, Milwaukee, and Toledo adopted by the new salt association. [105] Among these men was the largest producer of salt in Saginaw County. If they succeeded, Sage's interest in marketing through his Toledo yard would be eliminated. On the other hand should Sage gain the Toledo agency for his own yard, he would profit from commissions on sales for the association as well as from the higher prices a combination of producers could command.

From 1876 to 1878 Sage was the leading salt manufacturer in Bay County, while the output of the McGraw mill was second largest in that county. Sage hoped to persuade his former partner to join the association so that together they might maintain the control "at our end of the Valley." [106]

When Burt, his Saginaw rival, gained the presidency of the new association, Sage feared for his own interests. In January of 1876 at a meeting of the Michigan Salt Association, Sage voiced his objections to the assumption of the contracts and obligations of the old organization, i.e., of the Burt organization. He accepted a directorship but moved that the association make no attempt to operate until enough members had been acquired actively to control the price of salt. Evidently, Sage *did* expect the organization to become effective in short order, for two weeks before he

[104] To H. W. Sage and Co., Wenona, July 19, HWS.
[105] Sage to John McGraw, Aug. 2, 1875, HWS.   [106] *Ibid.*

had urged Whitney to hold his salt while others sold low.[107] His disparaging comments at the meeting "Mr H. W. Sage said that the association was never half born, its mid-wife having previous engagements to occupy her time [a comment on the Burt group's obligations]. The present prospects of the organization were not favorable" [108]—seem to have been in the nature of a maneuver to gain support for his own interests.

Dean Sage advised the mill manager at Wenona to offer a rebate to the association in return for the agency at Toledo.[109] Undoubtedly the agency was a highly regarded plum. A compromise was finally struck between the Burt and Sage interests, by which Sage's agent in Toledo was to receive half the salt sent by the association for sale in Toledo. Immediately, however, the agents of the old Saginaw Salt Company in Toledo began to sell in competition with Whitney. An attempt at a pooling arrangement urged by Sage does not seem to have been successful. By July of 1876 Sage estimated that competition had reduced the commissions of the Toledo agency from 8 cents to 4 cents per barrel. Early the following year Burt wrote that H. W. Sage and Co. in Toledo "will probably be made sole agents" at a commission of 6 cents per barrel. Sage was not enthusiastic about the low commission, nor was he confident of gaining the exclusive agency for the association's sales. Consequently Sage refused to handle the salt agency in 1877.[110] In effect, the Burt group had successfully maneuvered Sage into surrendering the agency by the very methods the association was created to eliminate.

The price of salt continued to decline in both the Saginaw Valley and Chicago markets after 1876. However, the rate of decrease was less rapid after 1876,[111] while the decrease in the cost of production was startling. From an estimated cost of 78 cents

[107] To H. W. Sage and Co., Toledo, Jan. 3, 1876, HWS.

[108] Saginaw City Daily Courier, Jan. 21, 1876.

[109] March 16, 1876, HWS.

[110] Sage to H. W. Sage and Co., Toledo, April 27, July 26, 1876; Feb. 8, 9, March 16, 1877; to Thomas Cranage, April 27, 1876, HWS.

[111] Jenks, op. cit., p. 93.

per barrel in 1873, Sage's costs went down to 44 cents in 1878.[112] The association accepted the entire output of its members, paying an advance upon delivery. If the market was subject to an over-supply, the association could and did stop paying advances in order to curtail production. Sage was convinced of the worth of the association. Although independents were sometimes able to make a few cents more per barrel than the association, Sage contended that, "if there had been no association this year [1878] 50¢ or less would have been the price—The follies of competition and the weaknesses of holders would have put it to the very lowest cost of production."[113] The average price in 1878 was quoted at 85 cents.[114] The association maintained a profitable price for salt and achieved for the manufacturers the economies possible in handling large quantities, particularly in the area of transportation. Sage estimated his average annual profits on salt production alone during and immediately after the depression seventies at figures ranging from $25,000 to $30,000.[115] Thus, when independents threatened the prices that the association maintained, Sage advocated ruthless and ruinous competition to force them to terms. "Put the knife to the jugular and *bleed all concerned* till they are anxious for equitable arrangements."[116]

Boom associations were another form of highly successful combination. The Tittabawassee Boom Company was formed in 1864 and remained the largest of the booms servicing the valley mills until the pinelands were exhausted. The company apportioned boomage costs by the thousand feet. Its rates were set at the beginning of the season, but rebates to the log owners were frequently distributed at the end of the season. That the company was a success financially is evident from the high dividend rate that prevailed during its years of operation. The first dividend, issued in 1866, was 50 per cent on the capital stock. The records indicate

112 Sage to Dean Sage, Sept. 19, HWS.

113 To H. W. Sage and Co., West Bay City, Oct. 2, HWS.

114 *Lumberman's Gazette*, XIX, 3.

115 To Dean Sage, June 8, 1874, Sept. 19, 1878, Dec. 14, 1880, HWS.

116 To H. W. Sage and Co., West Bay City, May 10, 1880, HWS.

that all during the depression the Tittabawassee Boom Company provided a generous return on investment: [117]

Year	Dividend
1867	40%
1868	45%
1869	30%
1870	25%
1871	15%
1872	Dividend passed
1873–1878	20% each year
1879–1880	15% each year

The passing of the dividend in 1872 probably reflects the results of the drought of that year, which prevented the logs from being floated down to the booms. The 5 per cent decrease in dividends in 1879 resulted from the movement to limit by state law the dividends on all boom companies' stock.

Sage's original investment in the Tittabawassee Boom Company was made in the name of Sage, McGraw and Co. and in partnership with A. P. Brewer. The company held a two-thirds and Brewer a one-third interest in seven shares of stock. In 1869 Sage held in his own name only twenty shares of the 1,000 issued by the boom company.[118] Although he was one of the largest owners of the logs rafted by the company, he did not, therefore, hold a major position among the directors of the company. W. R. Burt and Amasa Rust were prominent among the directors and log owners in this group. Here also when conflicts arose between the boom company and Sage, Sage tried to ally McGraw with himself to strengthen his position as against the "Boom ring."

In 1874, for example, when the company granted a contract to Brewer to tow logs from its boom to those of the individual mill-owners, Sage was convinced that the contract had resulted from the machinations of a "Boom ring" whose object was to force the

[117] Minutes of the Tittabawassee Boom Co., Michigan Historical Collections (Ann Arbor, Mich.), pp. 50–406, *passim*.

[118] Sage to Sage, McGraw and Co., June 22, 1867, HWS; Minutes of the Tittabawassee Boom Co., p. 165.

log owners to accept Brewer's high rates. Sage suggested that the ring included Brewer and Burt "or some other Boom man" who had an interest in Brewer's business. Sage protested to both Brewer and the company that he had received offers to do the job for substantially less than Brewer asked. Sage and McGraw were willing to accept the company's services at its terms "except as to the towing from your Boom to ours—and as to that . . . we will do it ourselves—or allow you a reasonable price." For some reason the company agreed to McGraw's conditions and not to Sage's. Sage suggested: "Possibly they prefer fighting me alone to both of us—and if so I dont object—I shall fight them alone (at my own convenience) if need be." His convenience dictated that Sage allow the company to carry out the job of towing. However, he refused to pay the rates it demanded, upon which the company reimbursed itself from dividends owing to Sage. Two years later Sage reminded his mill manager, "Remember to keep in debt to the Boom Co enough to cover all they have appropriated of stock dividends to pay that old disputed balance." [119]

Sage's awareness of a boom ring does not seem to have been based on this single incident. It is possible that the underlying basis for hostility was a division between a group of the largest stockholders and the group of log owners who, like Sage, held only a small share of stock. One question which such groups may have found a persistent reason for conflict may have been that of rebates as against dividends. Before 1885 there was no legal limitation on the rate of dividends the boom company might issue. Yet the rebates distributed were extremely large. In 1876 at 4 cents per thousand they amounted to $12,392.34, while dividends amounted to $20,000. In 1877 the rebate was 26 cents per thousand or $109,767.01, in 1878, 30 cents per thousand or $98,466.75, while the dividends remained at $20,000.[120] Undoubtedly the pressure for rebates came from the log owners, and it is

[119] Sage to John McGraw, Feb. 14, March 24, 1874; to A. P. Brewer, March 2, 1874; to the Tittabawassee Boom Co., April 27, 1874; to H. W. Sage and Co., Wenona, July 24, 1876, HWS.

[120] *Lumberman's Gazette*, VII, 40; XIV, 520.

probable from log owners who held only a small amount of stock or none at all. Sage held only twenty shares while he was one of the principal customers of the company. Therefore, he may have sought rebates to the possible disadvantage of larger stockholders and helped to create a "ring" of interests hostile to himself.

In contrast to his position in the Tittabawassee organization, Sage played a leading role in the Au Gres and Rifle River Boom Companies. Sage and McGraw seem to have organized the Au Gres Boom Company in 1867, although they were not the only stockholders. From the outset Sage took a position with regard to Au Gres affairs that was distinctly a stockholder's as opposed to a log owner's. He wrote:

I regret the low prices fixed for Boomage & am sure that *half* the price chd by other Companies which are well organized & equipped is not enough—It will result—either in poor attention to the business—or a *loss,* which the stockholders must pay for the benefit of the public— or of individual stockholders who have more interest outside the Boom than in.[121]

In terms of logs rafted the Rifle and Au Gres booms seem to have been about equal; their combined capacity was considerably below that of the Tittabawassee, however. In the seventies and eighties Sage was a director of both the Rifle and the Au Gres. Over the latter organization Sage seems to have had special influence. Until he decided that the management of the Au Gres accounts was less profitable than annoying, H. W. Sage and Co. had the contract for that task, and a portion at least of the company's supplies were purchased at H. W. Sage and Co.'s store.[122] Among the directors and the officers of the company, not only Sage but also his mill managers always figured, although the latter never held more than a token number of shares.

In order to keep control of the company in his own hands Sage was forced to a certain amount of maneuvering. In 1872 he was anxious to buy enough stock to control a majority and secure him-

[121] To John McGraw, March 2, 1867, HWS.
[122] Sage to H. W. Sage and Co., Wenona, June 22, 1872, June 29, 1874, HWS.

self against Ferdinand Johnson, a fellow stockholder in the Rifle Boom also. Sage gave no specific reason for fearing Johnson but merely commented, "Johnson is *after the control,* and it will be just as well that he dont get it." Yet in 1875 Sage was anxious to cooperate with Johnson within the Rifle River company as against a "machine" being formed by Bay City and East Saginaw interests to gain control.[123] Ten years later Sage, as president, was again striving to maintain control of the Au Gres, now the Loggers Boom Company, in opposition to Johnson, at this time the company's treasurer. Sage tried to acquire the proxies of a number of Philadelphia investors who owned shares of the boom company. This group was apparently interested in the boom company solely as investors, which may explain why Sage could be troubled by Johnson, who in 1883 held only 61 shares of stock as contrasted with the 234 controlled by Sage.[124] Working through the Philadelphia group, either Sage or Johnson could attain control. The reasons for the struggle for control in 1885 are suggested by Sage's letters. He charged Johnson with mismanagement and with making private gains at the company's expense. Moreover, by 1885 the possibility of the company's continuing many more years in successful operation was limited. Dividends had been reduced by law to 12 per cent on capital stock. Sage noted, however, that at the dissolution, "there will be some thousands of dollars in land to divide—But much depends on the *man* behind it." [125] Sage's concern was to be the man behind the division.

In 1867 the officers of the Rifle River Boom Company were H. W. Sage, secretary, Ferdinand Johnson, treasurer, and Luther Westover, president.[126] The composition of the stockholders was similar to that of the Au Gres in so far as it included Sage, Johnson, and at least two large Philadelphia investors. A larger number of Bay City and Saginaw City millmen, including D. W. Rust,

---

[123] *Ibid.,* Feb. 9, 1872; to Ferdinand Johnson, Dec. 24, 1875; to D. K. Hontz, Dec. 13, 1875, HWS.

[124] *Lumberman's Gazette,* XXII, 5.

[125] To Richard C. Dele, Sept. 16, HWS.   [126] *Journal,* May 25, 1867.

seem to have been investors in the Rifle than in the Au Gres. Sage was therefore in a less advantageous position in this company than in the Au Gres, though he held 227 out of a total of 1,000 shares.[127] In Rifle River matters Sage sought the aid of Johnson, whom he had opposed on the Au Gres board. He adopted a conspiratorial tone, advising Johnson to *"be careful"* in determining which interests were behind the "machine." He advised also, "It had better not be understood that you have any communication with me." And in 1876 Sage suggested that either he or Johnson assume the position of treasurer should Westover resign. Westover was a fellow stockholder with Sage in the Second National Bank of Bay City, yet Sage reminded Johnson that "there are several reasons why the change would *not be undesirable."* [128] Sage did not seem to find that acting together in several business ventures inevitably led to mutual confidence. As a stockholder in both the boom company and the bank, however, Sage was anxious for these organizations to complement each other. He suggested that the question of whom to vote for as boom treasurer "be handled somewhat with reference to where the Bk a/c is kept." [129]

Evidently the rivalry and competition within the groups of stockholders did not impair the worth of boom stock. Until 1884, when state law limited dividends to 12 per cent, the Au Gres record was impressive: [130]

Year	Dividend
1877	25%
1878	18%
1879	21%
1880	30%
1881	30%
1882	10%
1883	25%

[127] *Lumberman's Gazette,* IX, 77.
[128] Dec. 24, 1875; Feb. 5, 1876, HWS.
[129] To W. L. Plum, Dec. 9, 1876, HWS.
[130] Sage to R. A. Alger, Feb. 12, 1885, HWS.

In 1883, probably as a direct result of the impending legal limitation on dividends, the Au Gres was sold to a new company organized for that purpose, the Loggers Boom Company, whose capitalization was $100,000 as compared to the $75,000 capitalization of the Au Gres. Presumably the higher capitalization helped to make up for the lower dividend rate. The Rifle Boom Company paid similar dividends. In 1878 it paid a 20 per cent dividend and in 1883, 35 per cent on a capitalization of $100,000.[131]

The profitability of boom companies expressed by high dividends led to a movement to limit the dividend rate by law and force the distribution of profits above the fixed rate among log owners in the form of rebates. The services of the boom company were looked upon as public in character. Each mill and log owner was dependent upon them and jealous of the profits that accrued to their stockholders. In 1879 Sage learned that the movement against high dividend rates had gained such strength that the boom companies of the valley preferred to enforce upon themselves a 15 per cent maximum dividend rate rather than risk legislation. The treasurer of the Rifle Boom Company suggested that the funds in the treasury be distributed among the log owners rather than the stockholders. Sage was vehemently opposed and protested that the company could operate profitably only a few years longer, during which time its primary obligation was to *"its owners."* Evidently some years before a group of boom companies had agreed, "under pressure" Sage maintained, to limit their dividend rates. The Rifle Company had participated in these discussions, but whether or not it had agreed then to adopt the uniform rate, Sage now recognized "no moral obligation" nor "legal binding force" to comply. If a legal obligation did exist, Sage was inclined to demand proof "that all other Co's adhered to it before I accept it as binding." [132]

Sage was anxious to see that the bill was killed and killed

[131] *Lumberman's Gazette,* XII, 27; XXII, 2.
[132] Sage to Dean Sage, March 28; to A. Cheesborough, March 1; to E. T. Carrington, March 1, 1879, HWS.

"without special inquisition into the profits—which are *nobody's business*." [100] He was incredulous that the Tittabawassee Company might favor the bill, but as the largest of the boom companies of the valley, the Tittabawassee must have been most subject to criticism. Moreover, Sage himself admitted that should the bill be passed "it can perhaps be provided that Boom Co[s] *can live*." He noted that if a law were passed which "all must abide by," business, presumably successful business, could be carried on, "with reference to it." Sage seemed willing to accept an arrangement which appeared, superficially at least, to be disadvantageous if others did not achieve a privileged position. Yet he believed it was better to "spend time & money fighting against interference" than in making preparations to ease the burden of the law on the stockholders.[134]

Sage was urged to become a member of the lobby of boom men at Lansing, but he was occupied elsewhere, nor did he feel that the defeat of the bill would be difficult. He approved of one, Hauptman, as "a wise manager" for boom affairs at Lansing. "He wont talk too much—nor put on airs—He is right as to the probable source of difficulty—There has been too much talk." [135] Evidently Hauptman's direct action and unassuming manner obtained results. The matter was dropped temporarily. It was not until 1885, when the lumber resources of the valley were seriously depleted, so that the booms in any event could be operated only for a few years longer, that the log owners succeeded in getting an even more stringent limitation on dividends enforced. This law set the maximum dividend rate at 12 per cent. All profits above that were to be distributed as rebates. It may have been the depletion of the timber areas and the anxiety to keep mills and camps in operation which persuaded the legislature at this later date to ignore the pressures of boom stockholders.

Sage's contention that the profits of the stockholders were not

133 To E. T. Carrington, March 10, 1879, HWS.
134 To H. W. Sage and Co., West Bay City, March 5, 28, 29, 1879, HWS.
135 *Ibid.*, March 17.

a matter of public concern reflects his attitude toward the boom companies. These were profit making, private enterprises. A business "affected with the public interest," and hence subject to public review and government regulation of its rates, was an alien concept. When Sage declared that "as well may the Legislature fix & define the profits of any corporation—as Banks—Rail Roads —factories—" as the boom companies' profits,[136] he was expressing a genuine indignation and a genuine sense of injustice. Government "interference" was a relatively new as well as an unwelcome experience to the businessman. In this conflict between log owners and stockholders, then, it was natural that the battle he viewed and fought as one between pressure groups and lobbies, as the expenditure of "time and money" by two opposing groups of businessmen, while government action or nonaction was the expression of the success or failure of the tactics of one or another of these groups.

Combinations, leagues, associations, and counterassociations were constant factors of the business scene. Yet an effective association of lumbermen per se was not achieved in the seventies or eighties. In the depression years mill operators consistently blamed the poor state of the market on oversupply and as consistently maintained a high level of production. The *Lumberman's Gazette* urged millmen to avoid overstocking the markets, and Sage commented in 1874, "It will be a blessed thing if the mills have to rest for want of Logs." [137] Since the decline in itself seemed to produce little in the way of natural contraction, efforts were made from time to time to gain an organization of lumbermen which could, among other things, effect limitation of production. In 1873 The *Lumberman's Gazette* urged the formation of a national lumber association to establish uniform qualities and gain reductions in insurance and transportation rates for the millowners.[138] This appeal went unanswered. A lumberman's conven-

136 To E. T. Carrington, March 10, 1879, HWS.
137 To A. P. Brewer, July 22, HWS; *Lumberman's Gazette*, III, 67.
138 II, 141.

tion in March of 1874, at which both McGraw and Sage were present, resulted in the organization of the Michigan Society for the Protection of Timber, whose primary purpose was to achieve a combination for the fight against high taxation of pinelands. This new association caused a violent outburst from the editor of *The Saginawian,* who castigated the millmen for their irresponsibility to the needs of the Michigan communities in which they operated. He declared:

[The millmen,] in their recent gathering, upon mature deliberation for ever so many hours, bring out this one puny proposition, that the only bond of sympathy between owners of timber in Michigan is the necessity for "protection" against "barbarous" taxation. It is nothing that by aiding and developing collateral interests, this, the sponsor for the leading manufacturing interests, may do the State much good, . . . it is nothing that it is the part of prudence to obtain correct statistics that wise calculations thereon may be made for the future . . . nothing that it [the timber resource] is part and parcel of the resources of the Commonwealth of Michigan, and ought, in justice, to be managed when it can be done so without detriment to the owner's interests, to promote the interests of the whole people; nothing to nobody but a big fifty million dollar baby that will have some sort of soothing syrup of fight. *Something should be done to preserve and develop* as well as merely *to protect timber.*[139]

The *Lumberman's Gazette,* on the other hand, upheld the lumbermen and, indeed, commented disparagingly upon those "few who had not the courage to utter their just causes of complaint." [140]

Sage recognized that the problem of high constant production in the face of a weak market could not easily be solved by curtailment. There was the fact that despite declining prices profits were still possible so that strong organizations were not willing to curtail and weaker lumber firms did not feel themselves able to curtail. Sage wrote McGraw: "You and I may close our mills

[139] *The Saginawian,* March 14, 1874, quoted by M. E. Hetherington, "A Study of the Development of Journalism during the Lumbering Days of the Saginaws, 1853–1882" (M.S. thesis, Northwestern University, 1933), p. 74.
[140] IV, 67.

and our neighbors will produce more as a consequence—Let our neighbors close theirs and we run ours *nights* to fill the gap." [141] Nevertheless, Sage felt that something might be gained by attending the National Association of Lumbermen's meeting at Chicago in 1875. He urged McGraw to attend also, and gave lip service at least to the idea that overproduction might possibly be avoided. [142] At the convention Sage's speech was devoted to demonstrating the limited amount of the timber resources of Michigan and Wisconsin, perhaps in an effort to gain support for curtailment. [143] Sage had another and perhaps primary interest in the National Association of Lumbermen. He urged upon G. E. Stockbridge, its secretary, the need to cooperate with other manufacturing interests to "stave off reciprocity" with Canada. [144]

As the 1876 meeting of the association approached, lumbermen interviewed by the *Gazette* were skeptical about its ability to affect the lumber market. Philetus Sawyer, a great lumber baron of Wisconsin, declared that the most important task was curtailing the production of 1877, but he had "very little confidence" in the ability of the association to achieve this. [145] Both Sage and McGraw were reported as uncertain on the question of attending the meeting. Nevertheless they did attend, and Sage was made a director. Among the purposes of the association, along with the customary maintenance of uniform standards and achievement of more economical methods, were listed three of peculiar interest: "To discuss ways and means of regulating supply and demand. . . . To stand in readiness to avert the recurrence of adverse legislation. . . . To demand that State and National aid be given to guard our timber lands from spoliation of fire." [146] The association then clearly defined itself as a pressure group anxious to obtain special privileges from government and to prevent legislation it considered inimical. It had no authority and presumably

141 Oct. 28, 1874, HWS.   142 To J. G. Thorpe, Sept. 3, 1875, HWS.
143 *Iosco County Gazette,* Tawas City, Mich., Oct. 14, 1875.
144 Nov. 22, 1875, HWS.   145 *Lumberman's Gazette,* VIII, 144.
146 *Ibid.,* p. 259.

little real influence in the definition and maintenance of standards. The lumbermen employed their own inspectors in purchasing timber and their own graders in sorting lumber. The reputation of the firm was the consumer's major safeguard in the purchase of lumber. The association claimed some responsibility for regulating market conditions, although its statement on that point was vague. In the convention Sage and McGraw gave their support to a movement in favor of publication of a report of the amount of standing timber in the Michigan, Wisconsin, Minnesota area. This action led to an attack upon them by a critic who contended that their anxiety to prove the necessity of curtailment was a hypocritical move intended to make their own large production more valuable by influencing others to reduce production: "They talk buncombe! advising retrenchment, curtailment, forest protection for others, but put themselves outside their own logic." [147] Sage, it is true, did not make any effort to curtail his own production, yet curtailment of production by any one firm would hardly have affected the market. Sage was probably sincere in advocating the principle of curtailment and equally sincere in believing that curtailment could not be achieved so long as the lumber business proved profitable to any degree.

In 1877 the National Association was pronounced dead. "Peace to its ashes. An indebtedness of $72 and a corps of unhonored officials are its only heirlooms" [148] was the epitaph contributed by the *Gazette*. Sage wrote the secretary of the association: "I regret that the general interest in our association is so small— But all the questions which need discussion and cooperation are being worked out by natural processes, and possibly, in the broad way, as wisely as conventions would do it." [149]

Undoubtedly the physical problem of coordinating and regulating lumber output or, if a marketing pool like that of the Michigan Salt Association were attempted, of holding and selling the combined output was beyond the capacity of the organizations

[147] *Ibid.*, VIII, 355–356; IX, 35. [148] XI, 132.
[149] To G. E. Stockbridge, Aug. 15, 1877, HWS.

of that period. Even in the field of salt an attempt at a national pool failed miserably. There was perhaps a more formidable obstacle than administrative capacity. How could a highly individualistic, ambitious, and acquisitive group of mill operators be forced to submit to production restrictions even if it were possible to achieve a successful organization on a less than national scale? The surrender of his ability to determine his own output was never contemplated by the millman. Most important, while a profit margin existed, curtailment and organization to achieve curtailment could not succeed. Sage and his competitors were willing to leave the market to its "natural" course the more readily because they did not seem to suffer absolute losses on lumber production. The efforts at combination for curtailment purposes failed because they were not half believed in by the producers. The National Association of Lumbermen was more immediately concerned with its function as a pressure group than with its ostensible trade-regulating purposes.

Combination among the businessmen of the valley was achieved in forms ranging from this loose national association to the well-organized and profitable salt pool. The individualism which the millmen manifested in their drive toward personal profit was thus mitigated to some degree by the possibility of greater profit and security in cooperation. Nevertheless that individualism remained strong; it was apparent in the internal conflicts of even the most successful association; it was responsible for the millman's thinking in terms of "rings" and the necessity for achieving control. Despite combination and cooperation, Sage viewed his society as essentially individualistic, competitive, its primary drive that toward personal privilege and profit.

Chapter VI

The Michigan Experience:
West Bay City, 1864-1892

THE influx of industrial capital speeded up and shaped the processes of settlement and growth in the Saginaw Valley. The mill village was created and anxiously looked forward to its development into a mill town. Lumbering was in that era a mining operation; the lumberman invested, realized his profits, and pulled out to invest again in a new area. In the process, however, "lumbering made towns, banks, harbors, farms, railroads and fortunes. It ended the fur trade and opened the way for the farmer." [1]

By 1865 the Sage-McGraw mill was completed and producing; it served as chief inducement to settlement of the village. In 1867 it was proudly announced that Wenona had seven hundred inhabitants.[2] By 1868 the population was expected to reach one thousand, while "the total number of houses cannot be less than 150," and "on the main streets lots 50 x 100 feet are valued at from $1500 to $2000." [3] Physical growth was Wenona's most marked characteristic for two decades. Self-conscious reports of population increase, of new construction, and of the rise of property values filled local newspaper columns.

The new mill had been set down in a frontier area. In the year it was built, the local paper still carried an advertisement

[1] Ormonds Danford, "The Social and Economic Effects of Lumbering in Michigan, 1835–1890," *Michigan Historical Magazine*, XXVI, 357.

[2] Bay City *Journal*, Aug. 10, 1867.

[3] H. R. Page, *History of Bay County Michigan* (Chicago, 1883), p. 177.

of a fur trader.[4] With the coming of the lumberman invasions
by the "red-sash brigade," revival-temperance meetings led by such
colorful figures as the Reverend Henry Chance, otherwise known
as Buck-Eye Broad-Axe, the decade-long battle on the question of
impounding stray cattle, continued to give evidence of frontier
conditions. Superficial as they may have been, incidents of frontier
rawness, violence, and vice in the community he had helped establish disturbed Sage. Early in the community's history he wrote
his mill manager:

I hope your Town Government may be speedily reformed. . . . Clean
out the Liquor Shops—Shut up Swine—and all stray cattle—So that
cleanliness and sobriety may walk together—Above all—when you
pass a just and proper ordinance *see that it is executed to the letter*.[5]

For Sage the building of the mill and participation in the building of a community to service that mill were primarily business
ventures. Yet, even if he had wished to, Sage could not withdraw
into an exclusive sphere of mill management. The mill was central
to the life of the village. Moreover, Sage's economic interests in
Wenona were not limited to the mill. The company's housing
facilities and its store, Sage's underwriting of many of the enterprises of the village merchants, his financing of the purchase of
lots by the new residents tied him intimately to economic, and
thereby to social and political, activities in Wenona. Particularly
in the first decade of the village's history, when the executive
staff at the mill became, by virtue of their being Sage's representatives, leading citizens and active formulators of the village's political and social scheme, mill and village were closely tied.

Sage appreciated the significant relationship between the accumulation of wealth and the development of a community. His was
that stake-in-society philosophy which declared it to be the right
and the necessity of the property holder to determine community
development. To this philosophy was added the moral imperative
of a puritan background which converted "right" into "duty."

[4] Bay City *Press and Times,* March 12, 1864.
[5] To J. G. Emery, April 20, 1867, HWS.

His primary objective was to create a community which would protect property and advance its interests. Such a community would ideally be industrious, sober, godly—and probably Republican. Superficially frontier Wenona was neither sober nor godly. Although it may have been industrious and was most certainly profit-seeking, it was not consistently Republican.

The means by which Sage helped to shape Wenona's economic and social structure are clear. The mill, of course, dominated Wenona's economic life, particularly in the first decade before other large enterprises were established there. The laboring class depended upon the mill for its livelihood; the middle class depended on the custom of the laborers.

Certain of the aspects of a company town were immediately imposed upon Wenona. Company tenements, a company boarding-house, and a company store were at once necessities and profitable ventures. The 116-acre initial purchase was bare of buildings except for the shack of a ferryman. Sage and McGraw had to build a boardinghouse for their men; it was a comparatively small structure, 30 by 80 feet, and two stories high.[6] The company was not anxious to manage the boardinghouse, and in 1867 leased it. However, the company maintained substantial, if indirect, controls over the prices boardinghouse keepers might charge and the prices which they had to pay for supplies. This was true not only in the case of the boardinghouse the company had leased but also of those built by men independent of the company within a few years of the village's establishment. The regular boarders were the mill hands; so Sage's order to his mill manager, "Don't pay Rouch 6½ pr week for his board—let him quit there and go where he can board for $5"[7] undoubtedly had much to do with the price scale as well as with the quality of food and service provided for the worker. Evidently direction of the workers from one to another of the boardinghouses by the mill manager or by the manager of the company store did take place. The basis of that

[6] Page, *op. cit.*, p. 176.
[7] To H. W. Sage and Co., Wenona, Nov. 20, 1873, HWS.

direction was in some cases the amount of trade the boarding-house keeper brought to the company's store.

Workers with families required more elaborate housing facili-ties than the boardinghouses. The tenement house built by Sage and McGraw was "400 feet long and twenty-four feet wide, two stories high, divided into twenty-five suits of apartments, each having a brick yard and woodshed." [8] These accommodations came to be called the "Barracks" and acquired a reputation to equal that disparaging title. As "the headquarters for rats, mice, cockroaches, bedbugs, and lice" [9] the mill row meant for its in-habitants physical discomfort as well as a social stigma. A resident of the community recalls that his mother, the wife of a local mer-chant "instructed the teacher to seat my sister with some girl who did not live in the barracks." [10] Sage's constant complaints of depredations upon his houses and the tenements may have helped determine his unwillingness to invest in improving them beyond an occasional whitewashing. The money he spent on the houses was devoted to protecting them from "depredators" and "incendiaries."

In 1875 the mill row was burned down.[11] Sage himself admitted that the loss of the Barracks was one "that we and the village of Wenona can well endure." But the relief of the villagers to see the Barracks gone was expressed by a complacency toward the seeking out of "the villains" who fired it, which distressed Sage. He urged that the minister "preach a sermon on the subject and

[8] Page, *op. cit.*, p. 176.

[9] G. X. Allen, speech to the Exchange Club of Bay City, 1950, Bay City Historical Society, Bay City, Mich.

[10] *Ibid.*

[11] The year was one of the severe ones that followed the panic of 1873, and there is some evidence to indicate that Sage had ordered tenants who had not kept up with their rent payments evicted. "We are sorry tenants go from mill row—but can't help it. See that all the houses are well fastened up—offer the reward for discovery of the incendiary (evidently an attempt at arson was made before the mill row was successfully burned down) — . . . if you ever rent any of them again rent to good parties *or none*" (Sage to H. W. Sage and Co., Wenona, Dec. 1, 1875, HWS).

try to arouse the moral sentiment of the community to a sense of their danger." [12]

In addition to the Barracks and the boardinghouse, Sage built cottages to house workers with families. In a good many cases during the hard years of the seventies, rents tended to fall in arrears. In these times much depended on the good will of the millowner and the discretion of the mill manager. Instructions to "collect sharp" were given often in the seventies, indicating the severity of the times and the impracticability of such a policy for the manager who lived in the community. At times Sage advised a more lenient policy with regard to those tenants the manager felt to be "worthy" and "who are certainly to work for us." But that policy was not a uniform one, and just a year later he ordered his manager to "eject tenants that don't pay—*uniformly*—relaxing only in cases where there is moral purpose and disability through sickness." [13] Control of housing facilities and the ability to demand rents during strike periods, when the income of the working population had been cut off, was perhaps the most obvious weapon the employer could command in labor conflicts. Certainly it was a weapon which was *used*. The company town—even when modified by the entrance of new enterprises of a similar nature—tended to give the employer substantial and direct controls over his working force. Because in this case the pattern of the company town ran parallel with the boisterous, sometimes violent, usually drunken, and unsanitary picture of the lumberman's frontier, and because in this period the wage level did not permit of a substantial rise in the standard of living, which might have transformed this picture, the employer gained from the cycle substantial indirect controls. What sociologists have termed the "utterly unhypocritical combination of high profits, great philanthropy, and a low wage scale" [14] seemed justified at least to the vocal portion of the community.

[12] *Ibid.,* Dec. 9, 10. [13] *Ibid.,* March 22, 1873; March 30, 1874.
[14] Robert S. and Helen M. Lynd, *Middletown in Transition* (New York, 1937), p. 76.

The company's store in Wenona was not the sole store of its kind in the village, but it had peculiar advantages due to its connection with the mill and Sage's logging interests. The store was established by Sage and McGraw, like the company's housing facilities, largely because they were initially the only ones in the new community with the resources to invest in this kind of enterprise.

J. H. Plum was employed as manager at a salary of $1,000 a year.[15] As in many other instances, Sage discovered that capable employees would not long continue in salaried posts. In 1866 Plum was made a partner. There were some difficulties in administering a business under these conditions. Thus in 1867 Plum attempted to prevent Sage, McGraw and Co. from buying from the store at 10 per cent discount materials it wished to use or resell to its men. Obviously such an arrangement would cut down on the store's profit, consequently on Plum's share of the profit. But obviously also such an arrangement was to the advantage of the senior partners, one of the reasons for their establishing the store. Sage, somewhat disgruntled, wrote McGraw that Plum "exhibits a width of track too narrow to stand much running on." [16]

The men who came to Wenona in its first years were all of them anxious to make or increase their fortunes. The motive was legitimate and earned the approval of their society. The means to that end, when not scandalous, were accepted without comment. Thus when Plum bought for himself some lots he knew Sage was interested in, he was operating in an approved business manner. Sage himself did not believe Plum "intended wrong in this," but nevertheless he failed "to see how he could reconcile it with his sense of duty to us." [17]

The store sold provisions to the laborers at the mill, to lumbermen and to logging contractors. Oil, smoked and pickled hams, oats, corn, flour were its main line of merchandise. With the growth

15 Page, *op. cit.,* p. 178.
16 Sage to Sage, McGraw and Co., Oct. 4; to McGraw, Oct. 7, 1867, HWS.
17 To John McGraw, Oct. 7, 1867, HWS.

of the community it did branch out into the sale of luxury goods, coffee and millinery, printed materials and fancy edgings. But it remained heavily committed to the sale of lumbermen's supplies. Thus, while Sage approved the advance the store had made in attracting customers for "fancy goods," he urged that Plum keep a firm grasp on the trade of lumbermen who had to outfit themselves for the logging season. The store operated to a large extent on a credit basis. Individual lumbermen when "perfectly sound" were advanced credit for their outfits as were the logging contractors on their supplies.

The store's connection with Sage's other interests earned it considerable advantages. In the agreements Sage made with logging contractors a clause was sometimes included binding the contractor to purchase his supplies at H. W. Sage and Co.[18] Through Sage's contact with other men in the lumber trade, he sought to direct business to the store. And the town's boardinghouses were also directed to buy at the store. The store seems to have been a highly successful venture, even during the depression years after 1873. So profitable was trade in 1876 that Sage warned Plum, "Don't mention to the public what you are doing—but bear your good fortune modestly—*meekly* even and work and pray for *more*." [19] On one occasion at least during the severe years of the seventies, the store enabled Sage to reduce his cash needs temporarily. In 1876 Sage directed the mill manager to "hire your men *low* and pay them from the store—We *cannot raise* cash." [20]

The store was primarily, like all of Sage's Wenona interests, a sound business. As far as the community was concerned, the H. W. Sage and Co. store provided credit and helped increase property values. Moreover, Plum was committed to Wenona as Sage was not. He was resident there, and all of his interests were centered there. It was through Plum as well as through his successive mill

[18] E.g., Sage to J. B. Ostrander, March 19, 1875, HWS.
[19] To H. W. Sage and Co., Wenona (store), Nov. 6, HWS.
[20] Nov. 28, HWS.

managers that Sage attempted to influence Wenona policy. Plum acted for the joint interest in distributing relief after the great fires of 1871, under the characteristic injunction that he see "to it that every dollar is wisely distributed to those who need it most." [21] Again it was "Sage's store which opened the boom for a free road to Auburn yesterday, with a subscription of $500." [22] Most important, perhaps, it was through Plum that Sage transmitted his objections to any given act of "your people."

Sage was for many years Wenona's only great capitalist. His mill managers, his chief engineer, and Plum acted as his representatives in the village. In so far as his values were the dominant values of the village council, however, it was not because of the two or three votes commanded by his partner and employees, but because the middle class, which was predominant in village politics, shared his outlook. It too was concerned with the accumulation and advancement, hence with the protection of property. In so far as Sage came into conflict with the community, it was because of his peculiar position as absentee owner and because of temporary clashes with the property interests of groups of residents.

Despite its frontier qualities, despite evidence of immaturity, Wenona had from the beginning a well-defined social structure. There were roughly two classes, the mill hands and a middle class of mill executives, merchants, and professional people. The mill hands were largely Germans and, increasingly in the seventies, Poles, with a substantial number of "Frenchmen . . . from Canada, and Irishmen . . . from everywhere." [23]

The middle class provided the social and political leadership of the village. It was very largely their excursions, church socials, glee club meetings, and political debates which the newspapers recorded. They came in the years after the mill was built—some even while the mill was being constructed—to what was still largely

[21] Sage to J. H. Plum, Oct. 19, HWS.

[22] Bay City *Evening Press*, Feb. 24, 1880.

[23] Henry S. Dow, *The History Commercial Advantages and Future Prospects of Bay City, Michigan* (Bay City, 1875), p. 50.

a paper town to set up as grocers and tavern keepers. Their resources, usually limited at first, grew with the community, until they became fellow investors with Sage in the property and prosperity of Wenona. By 1875, the Babo block, the Allard, Aplin, Campbell, and Moots blocks were held up as objects of pride along with the Sage block.[24] It was this group which welcomed Sage's promotional activities, and which to a considerable extent drew upon his capital resources in the form of loans and mortgages.

Of the owners of the five blocks completed in 1875, three, Charles Babo, Henry Aplin, and Henry Allard, had borrowed on mortgages from Sage, $6,000, $2,400 and $100 respectively, between 1867 and 1874. Newcomb Clark, Wenona's first village president, borrowed $1,000 at 10 per cent annual interest from Sage in 1870. David G. Arnold, first treasurer then president of the village, borrowed $6,034.95 in 1865 and $2,400 in 1873. George A. Allen, the first grocer in Wenona, somewhat later the village's insurance broker, borrowed $1,950 from Sage in 1867. Sage generally accepted mortgages from those to whom he sold lots and financed home as well as commercial building. Moreover, this lending function did not end with the first years of settlement but continued throughout the period of Sage's association with Wenona.

Sage loaned upon the collateral of land and lots. Interest ran from 6 per cent to 10 per cent, most generally the latter. At times Sage sought borrowers for funds he had idle; he directed the surplus funds of his relatives and friends to investment in Wenona mortgages. Investment in mortgages was as legitimate an aspect of his business as investment in the mill. On those rare occasions when he loaned on the basis of a personal note, though he was anxious to help the friends who were borrowing, he insisted upon a reasonable profit. Thus when Carrington and Plummer, former employees who had gone into business on their own, with Sage's approval and Sage's financial support, found themselves in difficulty when their note was due, Sage wrote them, "We *do need* all

[24] *Ibid.*, p. 86.

120

the cash due us—but if your necessities are greater than ours, we will renew half of your note due July 1st at four months,"[25] However, Sage requested his mill manager to discount that renewal at 10 per cent.[26] He was anxious to contribute to the community's development and to his friends' prosperity but the maxim upon which he acted directed him to help where he could help himself. If a venture was worthy of support, it must be sound. The test of its soundness was its profitability. The investment in real estate in Wenona was profitable. In the first year of settlement lots were offered by Sage and McGraw for $200. Subsequently the price was raised to $300 and $950. Choice locations on the main street sold within a few years for over $1,000.

Sage was proud of the leading role he had taken in supplying Wenona with a railroad connection. In this area personal interest and community welfare were linked as closely as they ever could be in promotional schemes. Sage, McGraw, and Daniel Fitzhugh, one of the original proprietors of the land on which Wenona had been built, contracted to build an extension to Wenona of the Jackson, Lansing and Saginaw Railroad in return for "$80,000 in paid stock of the road."[27] The contract for the building of the road proved profitable. The three men sold their stock in 1871 for $56,000, a sum which according to Sage "gives us back all we put in—with interest and a respectable profit—after we have secured all the objects and benefits which first prompted us to engage in the enterprise."[28] These "objects and benefits," efficient transportation facilities, were of equal importance to the village. While the proposal was being discussed, it was reported that Wenona had succumbed to a bad case of "Railroad on the brain."[29] The enthusiasm of the community evidently resulted in the voting of town bonds to aid in the construction.[30] But Sage was interested in gaining more than a railroad outlet for Wenona. He urged

[25] June 22, 1875, HWS.   [26] June 29, 1875, HWS.
[27] George N. Fuller, *Historic Michigan* (Chicago, 1939), III, 61.
[28] To D. Fitzhugh, June 28, HWS.   [29] *Journal*, March 2, 1867.
[30] Sage to H. A. Hayden, May 14, 1867, HWS.

upon officials of the road that they invest in the construction of slips and docks along the river front. He repeated optimistic estimates of the business that the railroad would do should it build extensively in Wenona. More significant perhaps, he offered to lend the money for the railroad improvements. Sage was in 1867 already thinking in terms of the extension of the railroad north into the pine country. He wanted to make Wenona the collecting center for the timber of that area. Thus he encouraged the railroad people to expand their facilities in Wenona not only by promising to lend capital for that purpose but also by hinting that he would aid in the extension of the road. The railroad people accepted Sage's offer, and Sage and McGraw advanced the money for the Wenona improvements in return for a $47,000 mortgage on the lands of the road. All of this represented good business investment for Sage and McGraw. Ample railroad facilities would promote their lumber interests. They would also benefit by a rise in property values, especially along the river front.

That Wenona did not remain a single company town was perhaps due to its excellent location and to the fact that Sage and McGraw evidenced no desire to keep Wenona exclusively within their own control. They had originally purchased only 116 acres. When the village grew beyond that area, they bought and platted the Sage-McGraw addition. But others also platted additions to the village, including E. C. Litchfield, an easterner like Sage and a fellow investor with him in projects like the Brooklyn Transit System; Litchfield too built a mill in Wenona, though not of the size or capacity of the Sage mill. In 1875 two shipyards and a plaster mill were in operation in Wenona. By 1885 there were at least half a dozen sawmills.

Early in the community's history Sage had rejected the possibility of making Wenona his exclusive province. When J. H. Plum wrote that a new project for a bank in Wenona might preclude the possibility of a bank which the Sage group might control, Sage replied: "There will be no harm if Mr. Roberts and his friend establish Bank at Wenona—Nor will it interfere in the least should we want one hereafter—Encourage every man to come that desires to." And when Plum, obviously prompted by the desire to corner another type of enterprise in Wenona, suggested that Sage enter the warehousing business, Sage wrote: "Don't see how it will pay much—we can't prevent others from having them if they need—nor *ought we.*" [31]

In 1874 the Second National Bank was organized with W. L. Plum as cashier. Sage took $10,000 of its stock despite typical reservations and suspicions:

I want to belong to the ring that becomes stockholders by giving their notes—& dont desire to advance cash to disct notes to pay for other peoples stock—I believe in equal rights for all—& no inside bargains to which all may not be parties—I will pay all cash—or all note—or part cash & part note as my associates do.[32]

Sage also helped the new organization to gain depositors. The bank proved a profitable concern for more than twenty years. Eventually the Sages became its major stockholders.

The mill, the railroad project, the company's store, tenement houses and boardinghouses in Wenona were sound business ventures. The underwriting of the merchants of Wenona was also a profitable undertaking. Perhaps because he was an absentee owner, perhaps because his resources and energies were widely scattered, invested in Ithaca, Toledo, Albany, New York City, the Chippewa Valley of Wisconsin, the Upper Peninsula of Michigan, as well as in Wenona and the pinelands of Michigan's Lower Peninsula, Sage did not take the exclusive view with relation to Wenona's possibilities that Plum, who lived and worked in the community, did.

Nevertheless Sage did not resign that modicum of power which his strategic position in the economic life of the community afforded. As it was exhibited in Wenona's political affairs, it was by no means an all-pervasive power. It was called into play almost

[31] Nov. 14, Dec. 27, 1872, HWS.
[32] To W. L. Plum, May 25, 1874, HWS.

exclusively over the issue of taxation, or what Sage considered an attitude of "hostility whose *only basis is greed to tax* for . . . enriching political cliques." [33] Sage had almost always in his executives in residence at Wenona a nucleus within the village Council upon whom he could count in any conflict. John Emery, E. T. Carrington, W. I. Tozer, and Frank Pierson held successively the chief position at the mill. Each of these men took an active part in the community's life. Lafayette Roundsville, chief engineer for more than two decades, and Plum completed the small group through whom Sage worked directly. At the village's first election, both Emery and Roundsville were chosen trustees, and they were maintained in that office the following year.[34]

With the growth of the community the more or less typical split between Democratic and Republican parties became evident. Needless to say, those men mentioned above—at least while they remained in Sage's employ—remained also within Republican ranks. It may have been the growth of the Democratic party in Wenona which led to Carrington's defeat for re-election in 1871.[35] Soon after the new village government took office Sage found himself in opposition to its plans for a sewer development. As he viewed it, the Council had "plotted" to let a contract to a group of its friends and then to arrange the assessment so that Sage would be taxed $7,000 of the total cost, $9,723.50. Evidently his lawyers were able to find legal grounds for preventing the "plot," or else pressure was exerted through Carrington and others in the community to prevent its completion. It was through Carrington that Sage expressed his congratulations to "the Town Council and the People of Wenona that the Sewer project—in its present shape is dead." [36]

Within a short time Sage was in conflict once more with Wenona's Council, this time with regard to a platform which the com-

[33] To J. H. Plum, July 8, 1871, HWS.
[34] *Journal*, May 31, 1866; April 6, 1867.
[35] Sage to H. W. Sage and Co., Wenona, March 16, 1871, HWS.
[36] *Ibid.*, June 13, 1871.

124

pany had built and which was judged to be a public nuisance. His advice to Plum was in singular contrast with his earlier expressed desire that Wenona's ordinances be enforced with vigor:

Obey the law when you *must*. . . . Offer to build . . . a good plank walk outside—and in all ways you can avoid resistance—open—Nevertheless—*don't remove the platform* till you see it will certainly be down by force. . . . You are called to obey an arbitrary and unkind exercise of authority and we are only bound to do so from compulsion —not cheerfully—nor with Christian zeal."

The matter was adjusted without "conflict." In commenting upon it Sage defined his position with relation to the community:

What seems strange to me is that any one can think it wise for the authorities to be in constant conflict with the largest taxpayers and property owners. . . . We ought to work together there—as a unit. . . . If we are to have improvements involving outlay of capital there *must be* a reasonable acceptance that there will be no unjust official action with reference to it. . . . Without a reasonable assurance on the point I would never invest another dollar there for Rail Road or improvements of any kind—Nor will McGraw or Litchfield. . . . How much of the prosperity of Wenona thus far has been dependent on what we have done?

Business enterprise made for material advance, the acknowledged goal of business and government, hence the link that bound them. The profits of enterprise gave the businessman power:

It has been my intention to build there a Public Library—and to so endow it that all the citizens of Wenona would have forever the means of education and culture—but I can have no thought to do even a good or a necessary work when all my interests and purposes are met with hostility.[37]

Democratic control of the village Council was "generally conceded" before the 1872 election.[38] Nevertheless, the Republican candidate for village president, Roundsville, was successful, and

[37] July 1 and 8, 1871, HWS.
[38] Bay City *Daily Journal*, March 6, 1872.

a Republican recorder and assessor were elected over their Democratic rivals, although the trustees were uniformly Democratic.
Sage was pleased by this evidence "that when good men try they
can establish their supremacy" and offered to "share expenses." [39]
The conflict with the village authorities had given additional stimulus to his desire to have his interests represented in the government of Wenona.

The fall campaign for congressional office must have been of
special interest to Sage. Coming shortly after the strike of that
year, the labor issue was paramount. Republican strategy turned
on identifying the Democratic candidate with "the leaders of the
Workingmen's Union [who had stirred] . . . up a feeling of bitterness toward the mill-owners of the Valley," while at the same
time defending their candidate, N. B. Bradley, a millowner who
had not acceded to the ten-hour demand, against charges of undue
bitterness toward labor.[40] At Wenona's Republican party meeting
E. T. Carrington presided while Bradley defended "the financial
policy of the Republican party" and "showed why it has been
for the advancement of business and the general prosperity of
the country." [41] Evidently his arguments convinced the voters for
he retained his post. If he had not known him before, Sage grew
to know Bradley quite well during the latter's term in Congress.
In 1874 Sage loaned him $7,000 on mortgage, and in 1876 he con-
ferred with Bradley on Republican politics in Wenona. There
the Republican party, the party of business and prosperity as Bradley had defined it, was out of power and could not prove an efficient guardian of Sage's property interests. In 1873 the Common
Council had redefined the fire limits to exclude Sage's property
from communal protection.[42] The ever-disputed question of taxation was reviewed once more in 1874. As Sage saw it, the local
demagogues sought power to tax the large property holders for
improvements which would be "acquiesced in by many" who stood
to "be relieved from their just share of payment for public im-

[39] To H. W. Sage and Co., Wenona, April 4, 1872, HWS.
[40] *Daily Journal*, Oct. 30, Sept. 17, 1872.   [41] *Ibid.*
[42] Sage to J. H. Plum, Aug. 21, HWS.

provements." At the same time men "in the Council and in the ring which helps run it" would gain substantial plums in the form of paving and planking contracts. Exasperated, Sage wrote to the village's state senator in Lansing: "The Wenona Common Council are legitimate results of the New York Tweed dynasty, and have unbounded faith in the power of Taxation." [43] He sought the senator's aid in preventing legislation which would have permitted unequal taxation.

This attempt was blocked, but the following year the omnipresent sewer project was brought forward again accompanied by similar proposals of "unjust" taxation. The Wenona Council submitted charter amendments to the legislature which would have permitted the building of a sewer "from the Bayou to the River taxing the village for the street crossings— and the property through which the sewer passes ¾ of the remainder." Three-quarters or more of that property was owned by Sage. Sage was particularly distressed because Carrington, now an independent businessman, was a Council member and had presumably participated in these proposals. He wrote directly to Carrington to urge that the admendments be revised so that the tax would be laid upon the village as a whole.[44] With the town Council in hostile hands, Sage had to marshal other resources to protect his interests. He called upon the agent for the Litchfield estate and upon John McGraw, his old partner, to aid him in blocking the measure. These three men represented the largest property interests in the community, and all of them were absentees. Special pressure was exerted upon Carrington:

We shall need to play sharp to defeat their purposes—By the way—I wish you would dun Carrington for something on his land article. . . . It is over five years since he paid anything and it will soon outlaw— which we must not permit—I shall dun him when there and wish you would independently.[45]

The project was once more temporarily defeated.

[43] To W. L. Webber, April 10, 1874, HWS.   [44] March 31, 1875, HWS.
[45] Sage to John McGraw, April 9, 1875, HWS.

Other issues, however, continued to disturb the relationship between the community and its largest property holder. Sage decided to adopt a more positive tactic:

Perhaps we had better take hold of politics a little and learn some of our present masters that they can't have all their own way. . . . If we can control 50 votes we can *elect* or *defeat* such candidates as we please under ordinary circumstances. . . . We can find an easy way (when we try) to protect our rights.[46]

With the growth of the village certain trends became apparent. Interest in the advancement of property did not always serve to bind the absentee millman and the middle class of the village together. Improvements seem to have been sought at the expense of the absentee. The success of the Democratic party and of the Greenback party tended to reinforce the gap between the community and the absentee owner and employer. Carrington's apparent "desertion" of his former employer's interests is indicative of the trend. Plummer, Carrington's partner, Sage's former employee, and a prominent Democrat, was accused by Sage of seeking to injure Sage's interests "by an appeal to popular prejudice." [47] Sage's interest in strengthening a Republican party in Wenona was essentially an interest in strengthening that group within the party which would respect his conception of property rights. He was anxious to sort the sheep from the goats and "see to it that positions of most influence and responsibility be given . . . to really sound, respectable men." [48] Thus, his relationship with Van Liew, a leading Democrat and later a Greenbacker, was consistent despite his expressed fear of Democratic control. When Sage wrote Van Liew, "We have no need now for expensive sewers," [49] he seemed confident that the latter agreed with him. It was from Van Liew that Sage sought information about the interests behind the perennial sewer project: "Tell him to write so I can understand *all*—

[46] To H. W. Sage and Co., Wenona, Dec. 8, 1875, HWS.
[47] *Ibid.*, June 19, 1876.   [48] To N. B. Bradley, Dec. 21, 1876, HWS.
[49] Feb. 19, 1876, HWS.

He will know how." [50] It was the sewer project again which made Sage urge upon Tozer that "Emery and Roundsville and others of our force should take some interest in Politics and see that the town don't run wild." [51]

The problem of evaluation and taxation of his Wenona properties meant a second continual battle. Sage contended that his quarrel was not with taxation but taxation based on an unfair assessment: "Tozer can show you how much more our property has been assessed than other property of similar productive capacity." [52] In absolute terms Sage argued that his mill property ought not to be evaluated at more than $25,000. Two years before, in 1874, and shortly after the panic, he had placed a resale value on the mill and salt works of $400,000.[53] In 1878 the valuation of Sage's total property in Wenona was reported to be $301,500, which again is low when compared to his own estimate of the mill property's worth in the depths of the depression. And this figure was the result of a general increase of that year in the valuations. The year before, the tax on a lower evaluation had been 3.3 per cent. In 1878 *because* of the increased valuation the tax was lowered to .7 per cent.[54] The reason for lowering the tax is expressive of the pressures against high taxation.

In his battle with the Wenona Council in 1876 Sage obtained a "considerable" tax reduction, but nevertheless he considered the evaluation of the mill property too high and was confirmed in his view that it was important to protect himself by keeping "scallawags out of power in Town and Corporation." [55] His methods were direct. In the fall of 1876 he entrusted T. F. Shepard with $100 for use in election expenses in Wenona. His object was "to keep the Democrats from control." [56] The Democrats continued

[50] To H. W. Sage and Co., Wenona, June 23, 1876, HWS.
[51] *Ibid.*, Feb. 26, 1876.   [52] To T. F. Shepard, May 15, 1876, HWS.
[53] To H. W. Sage and Co., Wenona, May 4, 1876; to Dean Sage, June 8, 1874, HWS.
[54] *Ogemaw County Journal*, West Branch, Mich., Aug. 8, 1878.
[55] Sage to H. W. Sage and Co., Wenona, May 20, 1876, HWS.
[56] To T. F. Shepard, Oct. 30; to H. H. Aplin, Nov. 1, 1876, HWS.

to report victories at the polls in Wenona (West Bay City, after 1877), but in almost every year after 1876 one or more of Sage's mill staff competed successfully for office. Indeed the boast of West Bay City in 1878 was "the fact that the Common Council is composed of men who have a direct interest in keeping the taxes as low as they can consistently be kept, as they are . . . men who . . . represent $\frac{5}{13}$ of all the taxable property." Prominent among these men was "Mr. W. I. Tozer who represents the interests of H. W. Sage and Co." [57] Sage was able to write his mill manager, "Glad you watch the Treasury of the corporation and *sit down* on all unlawful attempts to capture it!" [58]

After 1876, except for an occasional caution addressed to Tozer on the town board—"Aren't you *increasing* expenses rapidly? Is it necessary to vote *everything* the People ask for?" [59]—Sage seems to have had little difficulty with the town government. The sewer project was never again advanced, despite the fact that Democrats, Greenbackers, and Republican-Greenbackers—it is interesting to note that Roundsville was one of the latter—gained office. Sage's exertions in 1876 directed to clearing out a group hostile to his interests seems to have succeeded. In 1881 Tozer either failed of election or did not run, yet Sage did not seem to be much concerned. He was sure that he could get "fair treatment as to Taxes etc from the present administration." [60] Indeed he seems to have struck a balance in acting with the community. On the one hand, he agreed: "As to *paving streets, we will go with the People*. We fear they will be overtaxed—but we will try to bear our share." Immediately he went on: "Will you discuss with Love the matter of petition to the Council to open and grade the S[age] and Mc-G[raw] lots. . . . We have paid taxes to improve everybody else's lots and should have some benefit for our own." [61] The relationship between Sage and the community was for the most part a

[57] *Ogemaw County Journal,* Aug. 8, 1878.　　[58] Aug. 20, 1877, HWS.
[59] June 27, 1877, **HWS.**
[60] To H. W. Sage and Co., West Bay City, April 14, 1881, HWS.
[61] *Ibid.,* June 4.

complementary one. In almost every case of conflict with the Council over taxation Sage obtained relief if not all the reduction he sought.

The promoter, of his own interests and those of the community, had to command the support of the vocal and responsible portion of the community. This was the essential condition of success and of profit. Thus Sage had welcomed in 1876 the Wenona *Herald's* "expressed purpose to expose corrupt rings." And Sage promised that "if the editor . . . takes bold ground upon the corruption of Wenona Tweeds he will *grow* in the respect of all good men." Sage identified respect for property and the contribution of the property holder with morality and good order. If the Wenona Tweeds were eliminated, so also would be the "Sunday grog shops —and houses of ill fame on your best streets—Your arsons will be less." [62]

Sage had contributed the economic basis of the community. He and his partner, McGraw, had built the mill upon which the working class was directly dependent and the middle class only a little less directly dependent. He had financed the middle class to a large extent. He had brought a railroad to Wenona. In return he expected and received large profits.

Investment and promotion led directly to a second pattern of investment and control. The mill and the Barracks inevitably reinforced social distinctions. The German or Polish or Irish laborer who lived in the company tenement was an animal apart from the merchant and businessman who bought his house or store lot from Sage. Yet Sage maintained a hold on both; he controlled the wages and rents of the laborer and to a certain extent the prices of his necessities. He held the mortgages and notes of the town's businessmen. There was nothing malicious in this pattern of control. It developed in an era when the goal was material development, in an era which gloried in the transformation of frontiers into industrial communities. The universal urge to accumulate wealth, in a community, in a nation, whose resources

[62] To H. W. Sage and Co., Wenona, April 11, 1876, HWS.

were abundant and easily available, made entirely realistic the possibility of rapid development. Development left to autonomous individuals led also to intense competition. Competition on one level made it necessary for Sage to maintain a close scrutiny and control over the affairs of his business organization. On another level competition made him anxious to maintain a position from which he could exert pressure on government authorities to protect and advance his property interests.

On the occasion of the dedication of the Sage Library in West Bay City, its donor remarked, "I have helped to build your churches, your schools, your railroads, and in all ways, so far as in me lay, to promote your interests, while promoting my own." [63] Sage felt no hesitation in reminding his audience that self-interest was the key to community welfare. This was the maxim of his society, of Wenona, which measured the health of the community by property values and real estate improvements. The library, dedicated in January of 1884, was the culminating gift of Sage to Wenona. The building, lot, books and furniture were estimated to have cost $50,000.[64] The donation had been preceded by several others of lots and money to the churches of the community. It was characteristic of his type of philanthropy that a Sage quintette and a Sage debating club graced the community, that the library had been designed with a special alcove for the minister and that it had been expressly provided that it be kept warm and open in the evenings so that the young people of the community might enjoy its facilities after work. Although Sage was somewhat skeptical of the regenerative capacity of a temperance reading room, he agreed to aid it too, at the same time advising that the users contribute something toward its expenses. Paying for what one used would inculcate respect for the facilities and respect for oneself. Sage was most concerned not with saving the fallen, but with aiding the climbing. Ambition, self-respect, ability, success, profit were all

[63] Speech of Henry W. Sage, Jan. 16, 1884, *Michigan Pioneer and Historical Society, Publications* (Lansing, Mich., 1880), VII, 339.
[64] *Tribune*, Jan. 16, 1884.

linked in his mind, and indeed these were constructive forces.

Combined with the available resources, these had developed the Saginaw Valley. But in the very years when Sage Library was being built, it was becoming apparent that the resources of the valley were being depleted. By 1883 the community was deeply concerned with promoting new industries. Real estate owners who raised prices when new industrialists showed interest in the community were rebuked by the Bay City *Tribune*.[65] Alderman Pierson, Sage's mill manager, urged that "immunity from taxation on personal property be granted any parties or corporations who would build a vessel to cost not less than $25,000," and this was hailed as "merely an expression of the liberal policy which the council would adopt toward other manufacturing concerns could they be induced to locate here." [66] Rebates on taxes were generously voted. Sage's claim for a rebate was met with a tie vote in the Council and resolved by the mayor's vote for the rebate.[67] There was evidently some opposition to a general rebate policy, but the Bay City *Tribune*, which reflected the property interests, ridiculed Alderman Braman's fight against "the injustice to the poor taxpayer contemplated by the rebate of 25 cents excess of taxation to a 'bloated corporation.' " [68]

The loss of the timber reserve was not easily made up, however. The report which Sage received in 1885, that the "Saginaw Valley mills won't cut this year over ⅔ stock and that they will *never* cut more than that from Timber now available," [69] determined the course of the millowners. Within the next few years the mills of the valley were closed down. Their owners moved on to the next lumber frontiers, or like Sage confined their interests to the purchase and sale of pinelands. The centennial edition of the Bay City *Times* noted that the collapse of the lumber industry precipitated a quarter of a century of retrenchment and rehabilitation in the valley.[70]

---

[65] *Ibid.*, Oct. 17, 1883.   [66] *Ibid.*, Oct. 28.   [67] *Ibid.*, Sept. 20.
[68] *Ibid.*, Nov. 14.   [69] Sage to Dean Sage, June 10, HWS.
[70] Feb. 28, 1937.

The promoter and investor had been welcomed in the valley. When the lumberman left, a new type of investor was anxiously sought. There was anxiety to repeat the cycle of investment and promotion, but very little concern to examine the process, to deal with the problems of ultimate control in the village's economic and political structure, of the purposes of taxation, of the exploitation of resources. The promoter and the community had been in substantial agreement upon the goals of rapid growth and accumulation of wealth. That the millman turned to the next lumber frontier, leaving behind a library, the churches, a railroad, and the shell of the great mills—soon to be burned down—was justified by the values of his society.

Chapter VII

Investment in Lands

BY the time the West Bay City mill ceased operations, H. W. Sage and Co. had become a major landholding concern. In 1893 the Sage Land & Improvement Co. was organized. The capitalization of the firm, $40,000, was divided into 400 shares distributed among Henry W., William, Dean, and Henry Manning Sage, Dean's oldest son. To this firm were transferred the lands owned by H. W. Sage and Co. and by Henry W. Sage, approximately 200,000 acres in Michigan, 162,856 acres in Wisconsin and Minnesota,[1] 146,296 acres in Alabama and Mississippi, 1,611 acres in Washington Territory, and 563 acres in Arkansas.[2]

The unusually high profits of lumber manufacturing from 1862 to 1873 were based on cheap stumpage and a large constant demand for lumber; these profits were reduced by the depression of the seventies. In the eighties, while overproduction was the perpetual complaint of lumber manufacturers, Sage observed repeatedly that manufacturers must now be content with smaller profits more laboriously earned. Although manufacturers did not often acknowledge this as a source of their difficulties, the profits of manufacturing were being affected significantly by the rise in stumpage prices as the pinelands of the Great Lakes states were exhausted or privately engrossed.

In Michigan Pine Lands were no higher in 1865 than in 1835—ie, they could be bought at Govt prices all any body wanted. We bought the

---

[1] Of which 106,392 acres were cutovers owned jointly with D. P. Simons.

[2] Report, Olaf Holter to the stockholders of the Sage Land & Improvement Co., 1940, HWS.

most of ours from '63 to '70—From '73 on there was a large advance and stumpage which was on selected land then 6 to 10 M pr acre, sometimes more, ranged from $1 to 2—then 2½ & 3—4. 5. 6.—in '88 to 95.[3]

In 1886 and 1887 Sage sold stumpage in Michigan, which had been purchased to service the Sage mill, to other manufacturers. Evidently $6 per thousand feet for white pine and $3 for Norway were more advantageous prices than could be obtained from manufactured lumber. Small wonder then that an increasing proportion of H. W. Sage and Co.'s funds were invested in lands which were to be held for the expected rise in price rather than in expanded plant capacity.

Speculation in pinelands involved major risks: trespass, fire, the mounting costs of interest and taxation. There were no safeguards against fire, and only the limited recourse of damage suits in cases of trespass. Charges against the lands could be justified in many ways, however. In locating the lands quality and accessibility were of primary importance. Here the experience and ability of the landlooker were the investor's safeguards. Number, size, and quality of trees in any tract had to be accurately noted, for on these facts the ultimate value of the land depended. The location of the lands was of course decisive. The landlooker's reports would show the accessibility of the lands to rivers and railroads capable of transporting the logs to existing or future mills. It was the investor's responsibility to determine which of the lumber-producing areas he would choose, whether the Lake States or the South for example, or if the Lake States were decided upon whether Michigan, Wisconsin, or Minnesota, and further which timber area within the state. Although exploitation in these states overlapped, there were clearly successive waves of exploitation, and the time factor involved in holding lands until peak prices could be demanded had to be considered. Sage's experience as a millman stood him in good stead, for he could determine with some accuracy the probable time of de-

[3] Sage to H. M. Sage, Sept. 21, 1895, HWS.

pletion in one area and predict the field most likely to be next exploited to serve a given market. In the Lake States, for example, he need only ask himself where he would build his next mill when the Saginaw Valley's timber was gone.

Quality and accessibility of the timber and the length of time it was necessary to hold the lands before exploitation were then the crucial points for the success of timberlands investments. Sage bought timberlands in Michigan at their lowest price and at the strategic moment, when large-scale exploitation was begun. As a millman his profits reflected this cheap stumpage, and as an investor his profits reflected the engrossment and exploitation continuing from the sixties on.

In Wisconsin, particularly in the Chippewa Valley, Sage's position as a large holder was safeguarded because there were other major holders in the area, like his former partner John McGraw and McGraw's partner, Timothy Dwight,[4] and most spectacularly Cornell University, whose land investments Sage himself handled. There would be little danger of undercutting by small or weak holders. Moreover, the market was there; the mills of the Chippewa and Mississippi valleys would depend on these lands. Under Weyerhaeuser's leadership the millmen of the Mississippi Valley had chosen to invest heavily in expanded plant and boomage facilities rather than to tie up their capital in pinelands.[5] Their mills were to be hungry customers. This is not to suggest that the investor could set the price exclusively; while the mills needed the lands, the lands also needed the mills, and buying together in a pool, again under Weyerhaeuser's direction, the Mississippi Valley lumbermen eliminated competition to a considerable degree. Thus, although it was often only a matter of time until the millmen would agree

[4] Paul W. Gates, *The Wisconsin Pine Lands of Cornell University* (Ithaca, N.Y., 1943), pp. 109–110.

[5] Paul W. Gates, "Weyerhaeuser and Chippewa Logging Industry," *The John H. Hauberg Historical Essays* (Rock Island, Ill., 1954), pp. 55–56; Agnes M. Larson, *History of the White Pine Industry in Minnesota* (Minneapolis, 1949), pp. 141–142.

to Sage's prices for his own and the University's land, during this time the land's charges would mount against the profits of the investor.

In the South also Sage invested when major holders had already selected and engrossed large tracts so that the mills' dependence on the speculators in the near future was apparent. The southern lands like the Wisconsin lands were held only ten to fifteen years before extensive sales were made.

Sage's investments in timberlands may be roughly divided into three periods. In the sixties and early seventies he concentrated heavily and bought cheaply in the pineries of Michigan and Wisconsin. In the early eighties he made major purchases of hardwood and farming lands in the Upper Peninsula of Michigan and added to his pineland holdings in Michigan and Wisconsin. Beginning in 1888 he began to invest in Alabama and Mississippi.

Between 1863 and 1868, with John McGraw, Sage purchased approximately 75,000 acres in the Lower Peninsula and 24,000 in the Upper Peninsula of Michigan. Except in rare instances the highest price paid for these lands was the minimum government price, $1.25 an acre. Most of these lands were purchased with agricultural college scrip at a cost of 55 cents to 60 cents an acre. Sage reported that much of this land ran to 10,000 feet per acre, but even on the basis of more conservative estimates of 6,000 to 8,000 feet, and including the 20 cents fee that went to the landlooker, stumpage averaged only 10 to 20 cents per thousand feet. These were the halcyon days of the lumberman, and in later years Sage remembered them perhaps nostalgically as a time when "timber didnt average cost 15¢ stumpage." [6]

In 1868, when Sage bought John McGraw's interest in the West Bay City mill, he bought also McGraw's interest in more than 32,957 acres largely on the Rifle, Au Gres, and Tittabawassee rivers.[7] The timber on these lands was the basis of the mill's produc-

[6] To D. P. Simons, May 30, 1891, HWS.

[7] Statement of Property, Sage & McGraw, Preparatory to Sale, June 16, 1868, HWS.

tivity. Lands and mill were sold to Sage, the highest bidder, for $461,000.[8]

About 40,000 acres, entered with agricultural college scrip at 60 cents an acre and located by W. S. Patrick for 20 cents an acre, were left undivided by Sage and McGraw.

Sage & McG sold ¼ intst to Thos [Thomas McGraw, John McGraw's nephew]—for 5½ pr acre—bought back at about $8 pr acre—After that sold & cut a part, and what remained something over 30 M acs I bought McGraw estate half of on basis of about $2 stumpage & 10/ for Land $267,500 in 1882.[9]

Appreciation had been considerable in the intervening years. These lands, near the Au Sable River, included some of the richest timber tracts owned by Sage and McGraw. Sage estimated their original cost at $35,000, their value in 1882 at $817,600.[10] Their relatively great distance from the Sage mill meant that only a portion of the lands were used to service the mill. In 1882 some of the lands were lumbered and manufactured at the mill of one Gramm. Sage took the characteristic precaution of acquiring a mortgage upon this mill, "so as to keep some control." [11] More than a million feet of lumber, which was manufactured for the Sages by Gramm at $2.50 per thousand feet, were sold by Dean Sage at $17.75 per thousand feet. After deducting all costs Sage estimated that the stumpage value amounted to $10.40 per thousand feet.[12] Rising stumpage prices and the costs of transportation resulted in the sale of much of these "Sauble" lands in the eighties. Sage's single most spectacular sale in this area was made in 1887 to Henry Stephens and Co.: 2,818.55 acres at $108 an acre, or $305,000.[13] Sage himself was so impressed by this sale that he expressed regret, perhaps the only time he did so, that he had entered upon manufacturing at all: "If we had been wise enough 25 years ago to buy all the land we could pay for instead of building Mill we should have had more

---

[8] Statement of Property, Sage & McGraw, July 1, 1868, HWS.
[9] Sage to Dean Sage, Dec. 17, 1887, HWS.   [10] *Ibid.*, Feb. 15, 1882.
[11] *Ibid.*, Aug. 3, 1881.   [12] To George Frost, Aug. 3, 1882, HWS.
[13] Memo, Land Sale, Dec. 13, 1887, HWS.

profit & less labor"; however, he immediately qualified his statement, "perhaps less wisdom—as a result of the labor." On the whole of the tract, including what they had lumbered at their own mill, Sage expected the profits to average slightly less than $5 per thousand feet of timber.[14]

Almost 20,000 acres were located by W. S. Patrick for Sage and McGraw in the summer of 1867 near the mouth of the Two Hearted River on Lake Superior.[15] Most of this seems to have been entered with agricultural college scrip; some may have been entered with cash, since the Michigan quota of lands that might be entered with scrip was filled in that summer.[16] This land clearly was too far from the Sage-McGraw mill to provide it with logs. Patrick was anxious to "take an interest" with Sage and McGraw and "build a mill at once." Sage was enthusiastic about the purchase either as an investment or as the basis of a new mill: "I consider it a grand investment and think it should find a ready purchaser at $5 to $7 pr acre—Oh for youth, & vigor, to *reap* the fields before us!" [17] Investment won out. On second sober thought Sage probably rejected a proposal which would involve him once more in partnerships and settlements. In 1882 Sage sold his half of the lands, 9,827.39 acres, at $10 an acre, almost $100,000.[18]

In 1867 also A. P. Brewer located 4,000 acres for Sage and McGraw in the Upper Peninsula near Ontonagon. Brewer's crew collected minutes for an additional 4,000 acres, which were entered by Sage and McGraw in 1871 for cash at $1.25 an acre.[19] The Sage half of the Ontonagon locations was sold for $20,000.[20]

After the dissolution of his partnership with McGraw, Sage con-

---

[14] To Dean Sage, Dec. 17, 1887, HWS.

[15] Sage to John McGraw, July 6, 1867; to Robert D. Perry, Feb. 11, 1882, HWS.

[16] Sage to W. S. Patrick, Aug. 14, 1867, HWS.

[17] To John McGraw, July 6, 1867, HWS.

[18] Sage to George Frost, Feb. 11, 1882, HWS. The sale was negotiated by Frost for a 5 per cent commission.

[19] Sage to Thomas McGraw, Oct. 16, 1871, HWS.

[20] Sage to Dean Sage, Feb. 15, 1882, HWS.

tinued to buy pineland tracts accessible to the mill independently or occasionally as a joint venture. From about 1870 on federal government lands accessible to the Saginaw Valley mills grew more and more rare, and competition for them among the millmen more and more keen. Sage employed landlookers to examine and take minutes of reserved government lands even before official notice of restoration had been announced. As soon as the notice of restoration was received, he instructed his agent: *"Take the minutes we have*—and make our application for them promptly—so we shall be first on record—*Say nothing—for I know there will be great efforts to get those Lands. . . .* Avoid asking questions or exciting curious attention." So anxious was Sage to acquire these lands that he was unwilling to share the advantage he thought he might have even with his old partner: "If MG reaches there before I do say nothing to him—I think he may be after it." This was one of the occasions on which Sage sought "friends" in public office. He counted on getting the lands by having his applications the first to be registered. This might "involve being on hand when the office opens on the day designated—or—having our applications— (by arrangement with the Register) made first in order—Is the Register Robinson? Is he any friend of Driggs?" [21]

John F. Driggs, a New Yorker, had moved to Michigan in 1856, become president of the village of East Saginaw in 1858, and had served as a congressman from Michigan from 1863 to 1865 and from 1867 to 1869.[22] In that post he had won the anathemas of James Birney: "You had not one particle of that moral or personal courage absolutely requisite in the atmosphere of Washington." [23] By 1871 Driggs had fallen on bad times financially, and Sage offered him "enough to *reconstruct* you to some extent," i.e., one-quarter of the profits of the restored lands if Driggs could manage things so as to get "the *whole batch* if not over 20 to 25 M acres" for Sage—"Can you go to Washington & *get it?*" [24]

[21] Sage to H. W. Sage and Co., Wenona, May 5, 6, 9, 1871, HWS.
[22] *Michigan Biographies* (Lansing, Mich., 1924), I, 253–254.
[23] Quoted in the Saginaw *Courier,* Oct. 26, 1864.   [24] May 12, 1871, HWS.

Unfortunately Driggs could not be of help in this instance. "Sages man" indeed "stood at door and when opened at ten o'clock he was first to enter and his application was received first." [25] However fifty-three others also applied, and many of the applications were for the same lands. The receiver of the land office decided that the only recourse was to postpone the sale, hold a public auction, and sell to the highest bidder. In the interval Sage did his best with friends and lawyers in Washington to gain recognition of his claim of priority. Ultimately the commissioner decided that the fact that Sage's man had managed to hand his applications in first despite the crowd at his back did not represent a prior claim.

Sage's reactions to the incident were typical. Despite his own attempts to assure his acquisition of the lands by extralegal means, he insisted that his "legal" rights had been ignored, that he had been deprived of what was "rightfully" his. He charged that the register was intimidated by the powerful interests contending for the lands and chose to place the responsibility for a decision with the Washington office. When it was clear that the decision was to go against him, he seems to have become more and more convinced that "there was undoubtedly a division between the purchasers and the Register." [26]

The 795 acres Sage's agent purchased at the auction were to be held jointly by Sage and McGraw, with whom Sage had decided to join forces after all. The total cost of the lands, $3,064.49, included not only the price paid the government but the landlooker's expenses and "all . . . expenses incurred in the getting & attempts to get the Land." [27]

The scarcity of timber created both by engrossment and by use not only raised stumpage prices but also made for less direct

25 W. B. Bates, Register, to the Commr. General Land Office, June 15, 1871, Letters Received, General Land Office, National Archives.

26 To Horace J. Frost, June 27; to John McGraw, Aug. 29, 1871, HWS.

27 Sage to Thomas McGraw, Oct. 24; to H. W. Sage and Co., Wenona, Aug. 31, 1871, HWS.

142

methods of obtaining lands and keener competition. Forties as well as thousand-acre tracts were now in demand. Sage's land-lookers acquired for him during the seventies state lands in small quantities as well as occasional tracts at federal auctions. Sage began to buy also private holdings of pinelands accessible to his mill at considerably higher than government prices. In 1870, for example, he purchased with A. P. Brewer 2,528 acres at $5.50 per acre.[28]

These pressures perhaps influenced Sage to become less cautious than was his wont about security of title and less scrupulous. In 1871 Sage was lumbering on Indian lands in the Isabella Reservation in Michigan, lands which had not yet been patented: "The Govt plan to collect pay for all Logs taken from Indian Land not patented *looks formidable.*" "We need the best counsel we can get—and if there is any ground for us to stand on let us give the needful security for timber taken and then fight for the rights we have." [29] A special agent sent some years later to investigate frauds perpetrated on the Isabella Reservation reported:

At the time the selections were made, there was a great struggle on the part of various speculators and lumbermen to obtain title to the lands selected. Prior to the making out of the lists, these parties had by competent agents been over the whole reservation and estimated the timber on the tracts. When the lands were selected and before the lists were approved or patents issued deeds to the timber on large quantities of the pine lands were taken by various parties, among them by . . . Henry W. Sage . . . and for a large portion of which but a mere tithe of the actual value was paid. A subsequent decision of the Supreme Court of the State having cast a cloud upon the title acquired by these deeds, they afterwards, on the issuance of patents, for a small additional consideration, secured deeds to the lands, thus perfecting their title. . . .

Mr. J. E. Arnold, of Mount Pleasant, who selected and purchased most of the lands for H. W. Sage, says that he paid a fair price for the lands, or at the rate of five dollars per acre, but this is denied by the Indians.

[28] H. W. Sage and Co. to H. W. Sage and Co., Wenona, Feb. 11, 1871, HWS.
[29] Sage to A. P. Brewer, March 8; to H. W. Sage and Co., Wenona, April 4, 1872, HWS.

As near as I could learn, in the brief time allowed, Mr. Sage bought at least 250 selections.[30]

Apparently then Sage did not give security for the timber he had taken but instead secured deeds to the land. It is very unlikely that Sage paid $5 per acre for the lands at the same time others involved in this operation paid $1.25 or less. Appended to Brooks' report was a tale of wholesale debauchery and intimidation of the Indians, fraud in the listing of Indians entitled to allotments and competent to receive deeds in fee simple. How aware of these proceedings Sage was it is difficult to say. He employed an agent to gain the titles to lumber and land for him, J. E. Arnold, who in collusion with the Indian agent at the reservation continued these practices at least until 1876.[31] Sage did recognize that his title was not safe. At the same time the temptation was too great to resist; 250 selections meant a minimum of 10,000 acres,[32] all of them carefully selected for timber. Ultimately many of these patents were canceled, but not before the timber had been cut. Investigations of the Isabella Reservation frauds continued into the eighties with periodic outbursts of newspaper interest but few prosecutions.

The drying up of cheap investment opportunities in the Lower Peninsula in less than a decade led Sage and McGraw to investigate the "Timber Lands tributary to Lake Superior—That will be in a few years the next resource for Eastern and Lake Markets"— [33] and the Wisconsin pinelands. By 1870 they were negotiating for substantial holdings in the Chippewa Valley of Wisconsin. Cornell University, of which they were both trustees, was experiencing severe financial difficulties. The University's major asset was the pineland located in that area by Ezra Cornell with agricultural

[30] Report of Edwin J. Brooks, Special Agent, Jan. 18, 1878, Records of the Bureau of Indian Affairs, Mackinac, Letters Received, National Archives.
[31] *Ibid.,* Oct. 25, 1879.
[32] The smallest allotments made were 40-acre tracts.
[33] Sage to John McGraw, Oct. 18, 1871, HWS.

144

scrip. Sage and McGraw, combining business and philanthropy, agreed to take together 100,000 acres. McGraw planned to take an additional 50,000 acres with another partner and after hearing the early enthusiastic reports of the land Sage and McGraw contracted for a second purchase of 100,000 acres. The thorough examination of the Cornell lands which Sage and McGraw insisted upon proved the lands less well timbered than they had been reported.[34] Despite the philanthropic aspects of the purchase Sage and McGraw were anxious to obtain only the very richest of the pinelands. In the late fall of 1872 Sage proposed that the original contracts be re-called and that Sage and McGraw be allowed "to select Fifty Thousand acres of such Lands as we please which shall be taken by us in place and in complete satisfaction of the Two hundred thousand acres contracted."[35] Although there was a certain amount of dis-agreement, particularly as to the right of Sage and McGraw to select their 50,000 acres as freely as they wished, Sage's proposal was acted upon substantially. Of the 50,000 acres Sage and McGraw finally took at $4 an acre, Sage retained 25,279.07 acres when the partners divided the property in 1876.[36]

From the outset Sage believed that his purchase from the Uni-versity would prove immensely profitable. He pointed out to Mc-Graw that even if Ezra Cornell did not agree to their terms with regard to the selecting of the lands "we shall make at least *a quarter of a million* by letting things stand as they are."[37] Sage looked upon the land purchase from the University in a strictly business light; the rules of business competition were not to be held in abeyance. Ezra Cornell's "unbusinesslike" attitude fre-quently exasperated Sage; in the final settlement Cornell was anxious to have the partners pay for all fractional 80's and 160's in excess—"for the excess—for those *deficient*—enough as if they were full." Later he offered to take in compromise "pay for half only of the acres deficient." Sage was annoyed and amazed:

[34] *Ibid.,* June 29, 1872.
[36] *Ibid.,* Nov. 27, Dec. 2, 1876.
[35] *Ibid.,* Nov. 27.
[37] Dec. 19, 1872.

I hope the next time he buys a Barrel of Flour his grocer may put him up half a barrel—present bill for a whole one; & finally, to avoid any difficulty with a man who so hates to be imposed on as Ezra does, will finally propose to settle on receiving pay for three quarters of a Barrel.[38]

Sage had promised to return to the University all of the profits of the transaction, a promise which was more than made good. That commitment was not to prevent his handling the transaction as though the profits were to come to him, however. His commitment to the University was personal. His transactions with it were business matters. The same attitude was shared by many critics of the University and of Sage and McGraw who attacked the sale to the trustees. Sage had had some objections initially to purchasing property of which he was the trustee, but had allowed them to be overridden. He was nevertheless seriously disturbed by the charges that he and McGraw had paid much less than the lands were worth. He wanted to make it clear that "our motive in the purchase was more to do the University good than ourselves—and that we paid for the Land more than we could have bought others as good for." [39] Undoubtedly $4 an acre was far less than the price Sage and McGraw eventually obtained for these lands, but in these same years Sage and McGraw were actually entering government lands in the Chippewa Valley at no higher than $1.25 per acre, which gives substance to Sage's statement.

To supplement their purchases from the University, Sage and McGraw sent W. S. Patrick in 1871 and 1872 to locate additional lands for them in the Chippewa Valley. Patrick entered 37,762 acres, one-fourth of which he retained as his fee. In 1873 when Hiram Emery examined the Wisconsin purchases of Sage and McGraw, he entered an additional 3,708.97 acres, in which he retained a one-third interest.[40] Subsequently this land was divided between the partners, Sage retaining 1,846.60 acres. The Patrick and Emery locations were made on government lands and entered

38 To F. M. Finch, March 26, 1874, HWS.
39 To John McGraw, Dec. 9, 1873, HWS.
40 Land Book (Wisconsin Lands), H. W. Sage and Co., pp. 1 and 2, HWS.

with cash at $1.25 an acre and with military land bounty warrants.[41]

Although the Patrick entries were "well mixed in with the University Lands" purchased by the partners, they do not seem to have been on the whole as richly timbered, although individual tracts proved extremely valuable. In 1889 the pine timber on 2,064 acres of the Patrick locations was sold for $87,410, approximately $42 per acre, to Frederick Weyerhaeuser.[42] Between 1880 and 1895 the Sages sold pine from 9,064.29 acres of the Cornell lands for a total of $366,884. Between 1882 and 1895 they sold the pine from 13,939.92 acres of the Patrick locations for $967,076.[43] Undoubtedly the Sage-McGraw selections were among the richest of the Cornell lands and the higher price paid for them justified on purely business grounds. The sale of 16,803.64 acres of the Cornell lands brought $639,524.40.[44] The initial cost of the lands Sage purchased from the University was $101,116; the total receipts from the sales of pine and land amounted to $1,006,468.40. The sales of land and pine from 1,727.50 acres of the Emery locations brought in a total of $41,998.50 between 1881 and 1896.[45] Appreciation of stumpage values within a twenty-year period had operated in Wisconsin as in Michigan to make timberland investment more attractive than lumber manufacturing.

In the ten years from 1863 to 1873, then, Sage alone had acquired more than 155,000 acres of timberlands in Michigan and Wisconsin. Stumpage costs on this land, located largely for pine, ranged from 6 cents to 20 cents per thousand feet except on the Cornell lands. Huge profits seemed inevitable. Sage was, naturally enough, extremely enthusiastic about these investments. Yet he never lost his marked caution, and before the heavy plunge into

[41] See Sage to H. C. Putnam, Sept. 29, 1871, for use of warrants, Henry C. Putnam Papers, Cornell University Archives.

[42] Sage to John McGraw, Oct. 27, 1874; to Dean Sage, Feb. 8, 1889, HWS.

[43] Memorandum of Sales of *Pine* CU Wisc. Lands; Memorandum of Sales of *Pine* from Wisc. Lands—Patrick's Locations, HWS.

[44] Memorandum of Sales of *CU Lands*, HWS.

[45] Memorandum of *Sales* Wisc. *Lands* Emery Locations; Memorandum Sales *Pine* Wisc. Lands Emery's Locations, HWS.

Wisconsin lands he reminded himself and McGraw that "you and I cant own everything—and may be just as well without them." [46] Sage's caution was exemplified in 1873 when he attempted to sell the Patrick locations for $6 an acre. Fortunately for Sage he was underbid by others anxious to sell large tracts in that year.[47] Sage's interest in a sale at this time was undoubtedly influenced by the decline in trade already apparent in the spring before the panic. He was probably afraid of being caught land poor. The panic did end further extensive investments in land for about seven years. Indeed in 1874 when McGraw proposed that Sage buy the former's interest in their Wisconsin lands, Sage was forced to refuse. Sage urged instead that both men "hold all these over the present squall & get all they are worth to somebody else when we sell." [48]

Sage was able to maintain his investments over the depression years of the seventies, and about 1880 he began a second period of investment in the Great Lakes states. In 1879 he began negotiations with David E. Miles, a speculator, for the purchase of 109,876.60 acres of tax-delinquent cutover lands in Chippewa County, Wisconsin, at approximately 24¼ cents per acre, a price which included the $4,660 paid to Miles "for his interest." The exact nature of Miles' interest in the lands was not spelled out in the correspondence. Evidently he had not bought the land from the county—Sage did that—but held an "equity" in it, which Sage recognized. Sage reported that "the Chippewa Co Board have passed a resolution to sell to a party to be named by D. E. Miles." [49] It may be that Miles arranged this sale, so advantageous to any purchaser, with county officials for a price. This was suggested by the Chippewa *Herald*, which reported complaints of a pinelands "ring" that sold to an insider.[50]

[46] June 9, 1871, HWS.
[47] Sage to A. G. Curtin, April 22; to John McGraw, June 3, HWS.
[48] Oct. 27, HWS.
[49] To Dean Sage, April 22, 1880; Nov. 25, 1879, HWS.
[50] Prof. Paul W. Gates called these charges in the Chippewa *Herald*, Oct. 27, Nov. 3, 1882, to my attention.

Conscious of the danger of insecure title, Sage attempted to protect this purchase by providing for a contract enforceable against the county "to hold us in possession of the Lands, and pay all damage incurred by us in the use of such as the county cannot maintain the title to." He insisted also that the county provide him with a contract enforceable against itself guaranteeing that "taxes shall not exceed 1¢ pr acre annually for ten years." [51] Although it is doubtful that Sage was able to secure these guarantees, he went through with the sale. His risk was well rewarded. These cutover acres were found to contain more than 70 million feet of pine.[52] Even at $1 or $2 per thousand feet—and by the late eighties Sage rarely sold for less than $3 per thousand—the remaining stumpage provided a handsome profit over the original cost of $26,635.72. Moreover the land itself was left for sale.

About this same time Sage became interested in lands in Minnesota along the St. Louis River and near the then unpretentious towns of Duluth and Superior. When H. A. Emery reported that any company willing to make the St. Louis River rapids navigable for log transportation could obtain a charter enabling it to exact a 50 cents toll for every thousand feet of logs passing through, Sage was instantly enthusiastic. He thought in terms of the development of "a second Saginaw," projected the building of a boom below the rapids where a 75 cents boomage fee might be charged "by *another Co*, but all in our control," and concluded, "I would as soon undertake it as anything I know." [53] However, his enthusiasm found no echo. Periodically Sage was to suggest with eagerness and vigor a new productive enterprise, but his age, his sons' unwillingness, and the certain profits in simply holding the lands for the rise in stumpage values seem to have discouraged his plans. Sage himself may have grown more cautious when he considered the lack of development in the area. He urged W. H. Dean, an old friend, to invest with him in the river frontage: *"Let it rest*

[51] To D. P. Simons, Nov. 25, 1879, HWS.
[52] Sage to H. Atworth, Nov. 18, 1889, HWS.
[53] To Dean Sage, Sept. 2, 1879, HWS.

Someday—when the rocks are cleared from the River so as to permit a clear run for Logs there will be a large use for it for mills and yards." [54]

Sage was also buying timberlands in the vicinity of Duluth and Superior. James Bardon located for Sage 6,253.11 acres in Wisconsin and 1,280 acres in Minnesota, while D. P. Simons located an additional 1,981 acres in Minnesota. [55]

The end of the depression seventies seems to have stimulated investment despite the fact that stumpage costs were higher. Sage's investments in timberlands in this area were made entirely with cash. Bardon entered $2.50 as well as $1.25 lands and took as his fee 50 cents per acre for lands with more than 5,000 feet to the acre and 37½ cents per acre for lands averaging less than 5,000 feet per acre. [56] This represents a marked reduction from Sage's earlier standards; previously he had rejected land containing less than 6,000 feet to the acre. Simons' entries averaged $1.51 per acre, and Simons took a one-quarter interest. [57]

Sage also bought with Bardon a rather dubious title to lots in Superior. Although they tried in the nineties to sell their titles to the lots at $75 each, they were forced "to come down like Crockett's coon every time any one points a gun at us, i.e., commences a suit." [58] Their titles to some of the lots were sold for as little as $25. Others evidently proved valueless.

From 1881 to 1884 Sage purchased 90,292.37 acres in the Upper Peninsula of Michigan. [59] These were largely hardwood and farming lands, less valuable than those located for white pine, but a "safe" investment. Sage wrote of them, "There is no cost of carrying except annual taxes—no large risks from fire or trespass—and

[54] Jan. 5, 1880, HWS.

[55] Index of "Bardon" Lands, Land Book (Wisconsin Lands), p. 3; W. H. Sage to D. P. Simons, Dec. 26, 1893, HWS.

[56] Sage to Dean Sage, Nov. 1, 1880; to James Bardon, Nov. 12, 1880, HWS.

[57] Memo: Minn Lands Jt a/c, Simons, HWS.

[58] James Bardon to Sage, June 29, 1893, HWS.

[59] Index of Ripley Lands Mich; Index of Lands in Upper Peninsula, Mich., Land Book (Wisconsin Lands), p. 3, HWS.

value improves as the country is settled." [60] These lands, stretching across the peninsula from Sault Ste. Marie to the Gogebic Range, reputed to be rich in minerals, were entered for the Sages at $1.25 an acre, standard government price, by L. V. Ripley, who retained a one-fifth interest in 20,000 acres. Although stumpage costs of 16 cents to 18 cents per thousand feet were absolutely the same as the price paid for some of the white pine investments made in the Lower Peninsula in the sixties, relatively, since hardwoods were thought to have less certain value, this investment illustrates a rise both in the investor's costs and in his confidence in eventual value.

What might be called the investment frontier for timberlands was moving away from the Great Lakes in the eighties, while the Far West and the South came increasingly into prominence as investing areas. Sage's unfavorable attitude toward investment in the South was conditioned in part by a number of unfruitful propositions submitted to him in 1882–1883. For example, W. A. Rust proposed to locate in southern Missouri and Arkansas for Sage, taking in payment one-fourth of the lands. Sage authorized Rust to spend up to $50,000 for state and federal government lands.[61] It may be that Sage's disappointments in securities investments about this time made him the more eager for a large investment in timberlands. He wrote his son, "I am satisfied that we can make no wiser safer use of $250 M than *plant it* there." [62] Rust's report, however, confirmed Sage's suspicion that "the pine lands in Southern Mo are a myth." [63]

Sage's hesitation about investing in the South is particularly interesting in so far as it illustrates some noneconomic factors operative upon his business decisions. In 1883 he wrote with reference to investing in Virginia, "In any southern State . . . you meet restrictions—limitations, possible disasters." This statement

[60] To Erastus Brooks, July 16, 1881, HWS.
[61] To W. A. Rust, Dec. 27; to Dean Sage, Dec. 15, 1882, HWS.
[62] To Dean Sage, Dec. 28, 1882, HWS.
[63] To W. A. Rust, March 5, 1883, HWS.

was clarified in later remarks which explained his hesitation not in terms of legal restrictions but in terms of the moral standard of the people of the area who seemed to figure in Sage's mind still as traitors and proslavery men. "Why don't you stop in Virginia," he asked facetiously of a prominent lumberman who had at one time been a clergyman, "and *convert the State!* The Gospel of New England, the Gospel of the Sauble River even (if that of N.E. is too high) would be an immense uplift for them—and perhaps prepare them for the time when a Michigan lumberman could consent to live there!" [64] Sage's prejudice was undoubtedly a hangover from Civil War enthusiasms. He wrote Rust: "We are content to confine our business and investments to those states where *men* grow—There's room enough yet in the North & Northwest." [65] It was not until 1888 that Sage began to invest in Alabama and Mississippi. His decision to do so was undoubtedly influenced by his disappointment over the investment situation in Washington Territory.

Sage was an essentially conservative investor; he was anxious to have reproduced in a new investing area the conditions which had made for earlier successes in terms particularly of stumpage per acre, stumpage costs, and secure title. Beginning in 1887 a large percentage of his land purchases were no longer made directly from the government. In 1889 cash sales of the public domain were abolished, and Sage dealt almost entirely with private holders. Sage tried when dealing with private holders to keep the price as near as possible the old government price of $1.25 an acre. He was especially concerned when buying from private owners to be sure that he received a perfect title. Many tracts, particularly in the South and particularly those owned by southern railroads were rejected because Sage doubted the validity of the title. In Washington Territory the stumpage situation was foreign to Sage's previous experience, but in the South, where the situation more nearly duplicated that in the Great Lakes area, Sage attempted to acquire only lands which contained more than 6,000 feet to the

[64] To H. Loud, Dec. 20, HWS.   [65] March 5, 1883, HWS.

acre. Merchantable timber was defined to the seller as all sound timber which measured "12 inches & *over* at the top end of the log." However, Sage's landlooker estimated and kept a separate account of trees which measured from 8 to 12 inches. By 1893 Sage had reduced his standards in buying southern pine from 6,000–8,000 to 5,000 feet per acre.

Sage was not in the advance guard of investors in any given area. He made a small investment in 1887 in Washington Territory, and then withdrew to the South, where heavy investment buying had been going on since the beginning of the decade.[66] His investments in the Far West were not developed during his lifetime. It was not until 1902 that the Sage Land & Improvement Co. began buying on the west coast.

When Sage sent Hiram Emery to Washington Territory in 1887, he authorized Emery to invest from $100,000 to $250,000 in timberlands. But difficulties arose almost immediately. Emery and Sage had assumed that they could enter government lands, as had been the practice in the Lake States. However, the only legal method of entering government lands in Washington in 1887 was through the operation of the homestead, preemption, and timber and stone acts, none of which was intended to dispose of timberlands for commercial use. Lumbermen and timber speculators were active nonetheless; they resorted to types of fraud which lax law enforcement and a clearly inappropriate land policy made surprisingly easy. Fraudulent homestead claims were filed by men who intended to exercise the preemption privilege immediately and sell to lumbermen. In many cases the lumbermen initiated the process; in others the ostensible homesteader was himself a speculator on a small scale. In the same way the timber and stone act, by which homesteaders and miners were permitted to acquire 160 acres of timberlands at $2.50 an acre for building purposes, initiated a traffic in timber claims. So prevalent was the custom that Sage was openly approached more than once by speculators who out-

[66] Paul W. Gates, "Federal Land Policy in the South 1866–1888," *Journal of Southern History*, VI, 303–330.

lined the process and suggested that they be commissioned to acquire land for him in this manner. Sage generally refused to do business with these dealers. The proposition, he pointed out, was illegal and dangerous, for "no title so obtained can stand if contested." [67]

Sage's letters to Emery indicated that he was interested only in clear titles purchased from the owner *after* the latter had paid the government: "It seems wholly certain that it is not safe to buy land in any way tainted with the collusion of parties to get the Land in evasion or breach of the Law. Buy nothing to which you cannot get a *clean title*." Sage clearly hankered after the old system. He suggested, "Perhaps you had better make some inquiry about Oregon Lands—I think you can buy of Govt there." [68] Evidently the provision that he work within the law prevented Emery's purchase of any great quantity of land. He bought in small sections only 1,611 acres for the joint account of Sage and the Emery brothers. There was also the factor of price. At $15,806,[69] this land averaged almost $10 per acre. Although the land was expensive, the amount of stumpage per acre—largely fir—was high. One 971-acre tract, Emery reported, averaged 44,000 feet to the acre, at which stumpage amounted to only "24 ¢ & a fraction." [70] This was only four cents higher per thousand feet than the pinelands entered at government price in Michigan and Wisconsin twenty years earlier. Nevertheless the price per acre seems to have dampened Sage's enthusiasm.

Sage took into consideration still another factor that emerged from Emery's survey of the situation. There was in Washington and Oregon a large amount of timberland still in government hands. This land when proved up by homesteaders would be made available to lumbermen cheaply, too cheaply, "perhaps, to permit large profits to outside holders." [71] The continuous opening of new

---

[67] To Jno. Sherburne, March 17, 1890, HWS.　　[68] July 28, 1887, HWS.
[69] Washington Territory Lands—Jt A/c Emery Bros, Land Book (Miss., Ala.), p. 130, HWS.
[70] Sage to Dean Sage, Sept. 1, 1887, HWS.　　[71] *Ibid.*, Aug. 26, 1890.

lands for exploitation in the area would reduce the value of purchases made in the eighties and nineties for investment purposes.

Meanwhile the southern timber states were widely advertised among lumbermen and investors. There the great proportion of the lands had been offered and until the prohibition on cash sales in 1889 could be purchased of the federal government at the standard $1.25 per acre. Moreover these were pine states and as such closer to Sage's own experience than the far western timberlands. Also many large timber holdings had already been acquired; so it seemed that the eventual engrossment of the timberlands by active speculators and investors might occur here sooner than in the West.

Sage had received repeated offers of land in the South, particularly from one firm of commission dealers, Spencer and Berry of Birmingham. Soon after Emery's return from the west coast he went to Alabama to investigate these offers. Emery was impressed by the quality and availability of the timber. From January to August of 1888 he located 123,333 acres in Alabama and Mississippi.[72] Approximately 50,000 acres were bought through Spencer and Berry at $1.75 per acre.[73] A little more than 73,000 acres were government lands entered at $1.25 an acre.[74] On the entire tract Sage estimated that stumpage would cost about 16¼ cents per thousand feet on the basis of 8,000 to 10,000 feet per acre. "If you & Will own this 15 years I predict that it will be worth at least $3 pr M or—$3,525.000—It may, & probably will be worth much more." [75] Sage remained convinced of the value of these lands despite the fact that the first optimistic reports of the stumpage were drastically revised by reexamination in 1889, when 6,000 feet per acre were found to be more nearly the average. Sage's plan was to hold the lands from ten to fifteen years, during which, he

[72] Report, Henry M. Sage, President, to the stockholders of the Sage Land & Improvement Co., 1924, HWS.

[73] Sage to Dean Sage, Aug. 16; to H. A. Emery, July 28, 30, 1888; Land Book (1887–1904), entries for Aug. 1888, HWS.

[74] Sage to Colin Campbell, Aug. 6; to Dean Sage, May 1, 1888, HWS.

[75] To Dean Sage, Aug. 8, 1888, HWS.

assured Emery, the property "will *grow*." [76] In the meantime the administration of these lands required the constant attendance of an agent working in the area, the cost of whose services Sage hoped more than to recoup by the systematic purchase of additional tracts of land. He was interested also in buying strategic river frontage where mills must be located in the future.

Sage's federal land purchases in the South were made at the last possible moment. The end of cash sales meant that the old method of federal government entry was largely displaced by bargaining with private owners. State lands, especially school and tax-delinquent lands were still placed on the market, however, and Sage's agents were awake to the opportunities these offered. Large compact purchases made after 1888 were made at advanced prices. In 1889, 1,320 acres were purchased through Spencer and Berry in Mississippi at $1.75 an acre. But in the following year 7,491 acres were bought of the Alabama Land and Development Co., the land organization of the Mobile and Ohio Railroad, at $2.00 per acre, and for 12,000 acres Sage paid as high as $2.75 per acre.[77] There is some evidence that Sage allowed his agents in the South to buy homesteaders' claims which had not yet been proved up although he had rejected this practice in Washington. The pressure exerted by the prohibition on cash sales at a time when he had a large investment to protect may have induced Sage to change his mind. Ripley was given permission "to buy of the Homesteaders about as you suggest—so that good stumpage wont exceed 2/ pr M if you can safely do so—taking deed in name of HW Sage & paying Govt 10/ pr acre, and the settler what you agree to." Ripley was urged, however, to "make no mistake—run no risks—Get title in hand before you pay any above Govt price." [78]

After 1890 the pace and price of Sage's purchases in Mississippi and Alabama were greatly reduced for a few years. In 1891 and

---

[76] June 10, 1889, HWS.

[77] W. H. Sage to M. F. Berry, May 31, 1889; to L. V. Ripley, May 9, 1890; to W. W. Stone, Dec. 4, 1890, HWS.

[78] Sage to L. V. Ripley, Feb. 1, 1889, HWS. 2/ stands for 2 shillings.

1892 Sage had no one actively purchasing land in the South. When Emery returned there in 1893, he concluded that large, choice tracts could no longer be purchased for much less than $5.00 an acre. From 1893 many of the purchases made for Sage were in small lots of 80 to 320 acres from settlers except for an occasional windfall of state lands. In this way Emery bought 998 acres in Clarke County, Alabama, in 1893 at about $1.50 per acre for the joint account. Emery reported: "The only cheap land is owned by settlers and small owners. This is being gathered up into blocks and offered for sale and it will not be many years before it will be all gathered up and held by speculaters." Emery was very careful to get secure titles when he bought from settlers. He hired a man "to go among the settlers (who knows them) and get options," while he proceeded cautiously: "I will take options for 60 days   In the meantime I will learn what titles are good and buy such as we want." [79] Between 1888 and 1893 the Sages acquired, in addition to their initial purchase of 123,000 acres, 22,961.97 acres at a cost of $57,908.81, about $2.50 per acre on the average.[80] These 146,295.92 acres represented the inventory of southern lands turned over to the Sage Land & Improvement Co. in 1893.

Emery's illness and death in 1893 meant that a new agent was necessary for the southern lands. Martin Van Heuvel, a land-looker, was recommended by L. V. Ripley and accepted by the Sages to take Emery's place. Van Heuvel appeared to be shrewd and industrious. Valuable contacts had already been established by Emery which Van Heuvel made good use of. Massey Wilson, clerk of the probate court at Grove Hill, Alabama, had been employed by the Sages to take care of tax assessments in that state. Wilson evidently helped Van Heuvel to get hold of at least 600 acres of state tax lands at $1 per acre, for Wilson took a one-fourth interest in these lands which was subsequently purchased by the Sages.[81]

[79] H. A. Emery to H. W. Sage and Co., Feb. 21, March 25, April 5, July 9, Aug. 3 and 30, 1893; Jan. 29, 1894, HWS.

[80] Report, H. M. Sage to stockholders, 1924.

[81] W. H. Sage to M. V. Heuvel, May 26, 1894; Alabama Tax Lands Jt A/c Van Heuvel 1/2, Land Book (Ala., Miss.), p. 77, HWS.

Wilson may also have helped Van Heuvel to acquire 718 acres of state swamplands in Washington County, Alabama, at 25 cents per acre—swamplands which had previously been surveyed by Van Heuvel for pine. However, Van Heuvel seemed to need very little help in making his bargains. Although he had been authorized to spend up to 75 cents per acre for these lands, he reported, "By makeing some propositions with other parties that were biding on lands not to interfere with each others choice I managed to get it at 25 cts per acre." [82] Unlike Emery, Van Heuvel had no interest in lands he bought for the Sages other than state and school lands, lots of which he picked up periodically and in which he retained a one-fourth interest which was ultimately purchased by the Sages. In the nine months from December 1893 to August 1894 Van Heuvel purchased 3,200 acres in Alabama at a cost of $3,155. Aside from tax lands and swamplands he bought small lots from settlers at prices ranging from $1.00 to $1.25 per acre. Massey Wilson, too, was buying forties for the Sages at about $1.00 to $1.25 per acre on a commission basis.

Van Heuvel had a knack for finding friends in crucial places. In 1894 he reported, "Am having school land sold which I expect to get at 1$\underline{^{00}}$ per acre with a little extra to the men who work it through for me." What this remark means exactly is difficult to determine. The men he speaks of may have arranged the sale or perhaps provided him with inside information on the bidding. He acquired 280 acres "according to law The SL & I Co being the highest bidders. being at 1^{00} per acre." Throughout the nineties Van Heuvel continued to purchase several thousand acres each year in small lots at $1.25 to $2.00 per acre. He maintained caution in acquiring settlers' titles: "I got a deed from Murphy & sent it to Grove Hill to be recorded. it is all right. we take no chances in the matter knowing that Murphy complied with the homestead law." In 1897 he paid as high as $3.00 per acre for 4,000 acres of railroad lands in Mississippi. This large purchase was complemented by smaller lots acquired from settlers in the area, again

[82] To S.L. & I. Co., Dec. 8, 1893, HWS.

with caution: "we have about all we will get now for a while as there is a great many homesteads that have not nor will not make final for some time."[83] It would seem that the repeal of the preemption act in 1891 slowed down to some extent the process of consolidating timber holdings.

After Henry W. Sage's death in 1897 the Sage Land & Improvement Co. more than doubled their southern holdings. One of the purposes of organizing the new company had been to include Henry Manning Sage, Dean's eldest son, in the management of the lands, and in the early nineties the younger man began to take over the supervision of the southern lands. Between 1893 and 1913, 247,250 acres were added to the original southern lands' inventory of the Sage Land & Improvement Co. at a cost of $841,226.[84] The advance in prices had been considerable; the average price per acre was almost $3.40. But the profits were to be enormous. In 1893 and 1894 Henry W. Sage broached for the last time the question of going into manufacturing once more, this time near Mobile.[85] Again his proposal met with no enthusiasm from his sons and was dropped. The profits were to be made solely from the rise in stumpage value.

The business organization which located and administered his lands resembled the venture-type merchant enterprises of Sage's early career. Sage depended upon the services of a landlooker or cruiser to locate and enter lands. The latter was generally a semi-independent agent working for the joint account of himself and Sage, the capitalist backer. Very rarely the cruiser was a salaried employee. Sage supplied the capital, stipulated the type of land he desired, the prices he wished to pay, and the area in which the cruiser was to operate. Occasionally it was the cruiser who took the initiative by locating a desirable tract and then negotiating with Sage to provide the capital to enter the lands. The cruiser would either sell his minutes for a stipulated sum per acre or

83 *Ibid.*, Sept. 22, Oct. 1, 1894; April 7, 1895; July 31, June 5, 1897.
84 Report, H. M. Sage to stockholders, 1924.
85 To Dean Sage, Jan. 21, 1893, Feb. 8, 1894, HWS.

obtain an interest in the land. The landlooker's interest was very often left undivided until the entire tract was sold. During this period Sage paid all the expenses of the land charging the other party interest at the rate of 5 to 7 per cent. Sage rarely made formal contracts with landlookers. Agreements were made and revised by letter and in some cases orally. In view of this it is remarkable that only one major suit was instituted involving the interpretation of such an agreement.

Since Sage dealt so widely through independent men with large interests of their own outside the area of Sage's concerns, there was a persistent element of suspicion in his relations with them. In most cases such suspicion was looked upon as normal to business transactions. Occasionally, however, suspicion was voiced gratuitously and embittered relationships. Ripley testified in his suit against the Sage Land & Improvement Co.:

Mr. Sage was always very friendly to me, and his son Dean was always very friendly, but Will, for some reason or other, would seem to have it in for me. That is, when I came down, Will would say, "Mr. Ripley, I suppose you are getting a lot of pine land in Wisconsin," meaning that I had a lot of lands I had selected out, and entered in my own name while working for them.[86]

The men through whom Sage worked were all of them vigorous and enterprising, lacking only capital. A. P. Brewer was an independent lumberman prior to and during his association with Sage and McGraw. Despite numerous joint ventures in land and logs, Sage seems not to have trusted Brewer very far. Nor was Sage on his part scrupulously honest with Brewer. When Driggs entered 4,000 acres for Sage and McGraw on the basis of minutes left with the register by Brewer's crew some years before, Sage was careful to keep the news from Brewer, although he asserted that it had been left up to Sage and McGraw whether or not Brewer was to have an interest.[87]

[86] *L. V. Ripley v. Sage Land & Improvement Co.*, Circuit Court of the United States for the Western District of Michigan, Northern Division, 1912, p. 112, HWS.

[87] To John McGraw, Aug. 24, 29, 1871, HWS.

W. S. Patrick did much of the early locating for Sage, McGraw in Michigan and Wisconsin. In the early sixties he had charged 20 cents an acre for his work, but in 1867 he seemed anxious to have an interest in the lands. Reputed to have accumulated "vast quantities of state and other lands" during the construction of the Mackinaw State Road,[88] Patrick was probably land poor. Unlike most of Sage's landlookers, Patrick was active in finding purchasers and closed out his joint interest account in relatively short order. The independence of the landlooker sometimes proved a disadvantage to the capitalist. On at least one occasion Patrick simply disregarded Sage's orders to locate farm lands apparently because his own major interest was in the more easily convertible pinelands.[89] Despite occasional friction Patrick did very well by Sage and McGraw as well as for himself. Mayor of the city of Flint, founder of a bank at Stevens Point, Wisconsin, stockholder in the state bank at Bay City, Michigan, co-owner of the John Larkin lumber mills at Midland, and part agent, part owner of some 100,000 acres of pinelands, Patrick was indeed a successful man.[90]

Hiram Emery was the most trusted of Sage's landlookers. Lacking the aggressiveness and drive of men like Patrick and Brewer, he was perhaps the more valuable to Sage. At the time of Hiram's last illness Sage evaluated the man: "The quantity in him is not very large but the *quality* in sound integrity, and the faithful use of all in him *very superior.*" [91] Hiram and his brothers, Temple and John, had worked for Sage as stockers and millwrights. In 1877, with Sage's help, Hiram and Temple purchased the W. G. Grant mill in East Tawas,[92] which Sage held on default of mortgage payments. None of Hiram's ventures succeeded in providing him with ready cash, but, unlike Patrick, Emery was willing to allow his share—usually one-third to one-fourth—of lands located for the joint account to remain undivided. It was not until three

---

[88] *Lumberman's Gazette,* IX, 69.
[89] Sage to W. S. Patrick, Aug. 14, 1867, HWS.
[90] *Lumberman's Gazette,* VII, 411; IX, 69.
[91] To Dean Sage, Nov. 2, 1893, HWS.
[92] *Lumberman's Gazette,* IX, 229.

years after Emery's death that his interest in Sage lands was purchased by the Sages.

One man who did locate a considerable quantity of land for the Sages on a salary basis was L. V. Ripley. Ripley began work for the Sages in 1880 as a member of a cruising crew, and for several years thereafter he was employed at about $1,200 a year to locate and examine lands in Wisconsin, Michigan, and the South. He did acquire a one-fifth interest in 20,000 acres in the Upper Peninsula and one-half interest in about 3,000 acres in Wisconsin. In 1902 he was manager of the North Wisconsin Land Syndicate of Eau Claire. As he himself described the situation, "In my deals here I furnish the experience & have 18 partners to do the chewing, among them all the Bank Cashiers in town." [93] Because Ripley was a genial, hearty person who often invited the Sage grandsons on fishing and hunting trips and seemed genuinely fond of them, it came as a real surprise when in 1912 he sued the Sage Land & Improvement Co. for breach of contract with regard to his one-fifth interest in Upper Peninsula lands. After the sale of these lands, the Sages had computed Ripley's one-fifth of the profits by charging the cost of one-fifth of the lands against his account and then charging compound interest against this amount and the amount of taxes and other costs carried by the Sages on Ripley's share. Ripley contended that his one-fifth of the purchase price had been canceled in consideration of the labor of locating and entering the lands, and that simple interest had been agreed upon. Unfortunately the letter which constituted the agreement was not clear upon these points, and Henry Sage's death meant that the only other person party to the agreement could not speak. It does seem to have been a general practice to cancel the purchase price of the looker's share in payment of his services. The courts found for Ripley.

Often the landlooker was also an administrator of a portion of the Sage lands. Emery and Van Heuvel in the South and Simons in Wisconsin, Oregon, and California had some share in the lands they administered. Actually the difficulties which would seem to be in-

[93] To H. W. Sage and Co., Oct. 3, 1902, HWS.

herent in the administration of a widely scattered estate were rarely apparent. The Sages kept a master set of books at the home office. Painstaking bookkeeping correlated with examination and reexamination reports kept them aware of the costs and value of each tract of land. There was a rough division of the lands, and a kind of subadministrator usually residing in the area was responsible for taxes, trespass cases, and sales.

The lands of the Lower Peninsula of Michigan, which had been purchased originally to service the mill, were directly under the management of the Sages and the mill manager. In the eighties, when sales of timber appeared to be more profitable than lumbering, Sage employed George Frost, a commission dealer, to sell certain of the Michigan lands. Major sales in this area were also made by Sage. Taxes, trespass cases, and small sales were generally left to the mill superintendent's care.

Sales of the cutover pinelands to farmers had begun as early as the seventies, and continued at an increasing pace throughout the eighties and nineties. After the mill was shut down in 1892, one of the major functions of Frank Pierson, the mill superintendent, became the sale of cutovers in Michigan. Settlers bought largely in 40-to-80-acre tracts; the usual practice was for the settler to make a down payment and take over the responsibility of paying the taxes. The settler generally contracted to pay the balance in two to four annual payments on which interest was collected at 6 to 7 per cent. Title was retained by the Sages until the contract was paid in full.

The price was made up by charging for whatever timber remained on the land at the going rate of stumpage and adding this to a per-acre figure for the land itself depending upon the classification of the land as it appeared on the landlookers' reports. Pierson was further instructed not to "accept a lower down payment than enough to cover the entire value of timber." [94] Depending largely upon the amount of timber left on the land, prices ranged in the nineties from $7 and $8 to $12 and even $17 per acre.

Very often the actual price to the settler was even higher,

[94] W. H. Sage to H. W. Sage and Co., West Bay City, Feb. 9, 1894, HWS.

since much land was sold through men who might be described as land jobbers. These varied from local grocery-store owners, tavern keepers, and lawyers anxious to supplement their income or to "settle up the neighborhood so that we can get a school" [95] to professional land colonizers, who occasionally aided in the development of the area. One such proposed company was prepared to offer a percentage of the profits to a church and school fund.[96] Sage was more anxious to sell directly to the settler or the dealer than to give the dealer the agency of his lands. He occasionally did give agencies, however, first setting the price for the land. Sales made below this price did not earn a commission.

Although he was often urged to do so, Sage was unwilling to join other lumbermen and speculators in organizations designed to sell the cutovers of a specific area to settlers. His characteristic fear of corporations and possible exclusion from the "first table" operated in this sphere also. In 1885 D. P. Simons asked Sage to join in a land company to which all the landowners in a certain township proposed to deed a half interest in their lands to promote a town site. Sage replied: "We do not like putting ourselves into the hands of a corporation, but freely believe in the wisdom of all parties in interest uniting forces to build up a Town—If the property can all go into your hands we are ready to join." Ultimately Sage sold Simons the land in question, protesting again that he did not wish to become involved with a corporation and urging Simons to keep control in his own hands.[97] Sage was generally skeptical of projects for developing the cutovers whether in Michigan or Wisconsin. Such projects usually called for donations in cash or land which were to be used to build roads, temporary homes, and in one case a mill which would "enable the settlers to get some money to live on while they clear up the land." [98] Sage's concern was to get money out of the land rather

[95] J. J. Donnelly to H. W. Sage and Co., Jan. 21, 1884, HWS.

[96] Conley & Stanton to H. W. Sage and Co., Feb. 20, 1892, HWS.

[97] July 8, Sept. 3, 1885, HWS.

[98] D. M. Estey to S.L. & I. Co., March 23, 1895, HWS.

than put money into it, and his skepticism extended to all schemes of giving away lands to attract settlers or attracting settlers who would then require support.

Schemes for colonizing Land are little good [Sage wrote his agent in Wisconsin] unless it can be done with men who have something and are willing to put it into the Land from the start—A colony of Poles or any other nationality who have nothing and seek nothing but a Home on some ones Land are far from a profitable adventure—If we could find 50 or 100 Families who want to settle on Land—who can pay say $2 pr acre down—& besides that build rude homes would after a time pay in full for their places and create Homes—Men below that grade of capacity are hardly worth wasting time on, and lands may as well be unoccupied as to have the care & trouble of unproductive men added to them.[99]

In accordance with this philosophy, Sage was rarely willing to allow individuals to move onto the land before they had made a down payment, although it was pointed out that many wished to begin working the land during the summer and allow the fall harvest to provide the down payment. However, once the down payment was made, Sage permitted liberal time extensions. Many land contracts in this area ran from two to five years beyond the date of expiration. This time allowance was made in cases where the settler was making efforts to improve his land, fence and clear it. Such improvements secured Sage's interest, and the settler usually managed to keep up the tax payments.

Related to Sage's unwillingness to give land away to attract settlers was his almost stubborn conviction of the inherent value of the land. He boasted that he had never abandoned an acre once he bought it. Subsequently it was decided to abandon some of the Sage lands in Wisconsin rather than pay taxes upon them, but a good deal of this was still later rescued and sold, thus confirming Sage's faith.

The Wisconsin cutovers were more difficult to sell and brought much lower prices than those in Michigan. Simons, the agent for

[99] To D. P. Simons, Jan. 31, 1895, HWS.

these lands, was engaged largely in other affairs, and from 1898 on spent most of his time on the west coast. Therefore, a good many of the sales in this area were made through subagents. From January through July of 1900 some 5,000 acres were sold in tracts of 40 to 240 acres at an average price of $2.83 per acre; from 1900 to 1901 prices ranged from less than $1.00 to $5.00 an acre, most sales being made at about $2.50 to $3.00 an acre.[100] That sales even at $1 an acre were considered profitable is testified to by the fact that abandoned lands were reclaimed for such sales. The major profit had of course already been obtained from the sale of pine.

In Wisconsin, H. C. Putnam was the first agent for the Sage lands. Putnam, despite the fact that he was officially only a clerk, controlled the land office at Eau Claire, a situation which proved advantageous to Cornell University and the Cornell-associated investors, Sage, McGraw, and Dwight.[101] Working under William Woodward, Putnam had done the major part of the work in locating the Cornell University lands; he remained agent for the University's lands until 1875. Like most of Sage's agents, Putnam evidently lacked capital and was anxious to work through others. Sage came to know Putnam especially well through their organizing and lobbying activities in behalf of the Chippewa Valley and Lake Superior Railroad. That company, representing Cornell-associated investors as well as various other landholders of the valley, was organized in 1870–1871 in an attempt to gain all or a part of the St. Croix land grant. Sage, McGraw, and Dwight were extremely enthusiastic about the project for a time and worked to promote it in the Wisconsin legislature and in Washington. Characteristically Sage was anxious that he and his friends "have complete control of the organization," [102] and as more and more people began to claim a share of the control and the grant his enthusiasm waned. Ultimately the efforts of this group to acquire the grant were frustrated, but in the process Sage evidently came to appreciate Putnam's

[100] Simons–S.L. & I. Co. correspondence, *passim;* see especially July 26, 1900, HWS.

[101] Gates, *Wisconsin Pine Lands,* pp. 91 ff.; see especially pp. 93–94, 116.

[102] To John McGraw, Aug. 29, 1871, HWS.

capacity for large operations. Sage appreciated also the opportunities that Putnam's inside information could open to a man of capital, but the more he dealt with him the less he trusted Putnam.

When Putnam proposed to purchase tax certificates with funds supplied by Sage, McGraw, and Ezra Cornell, with which he would then buy about 3,200 acres of tax-delinquent lands, much of it well timbered, Sage and the others eagerly agreed. There followed a period of about three years during which the capitalists could learn nothing of their investment. In December of 1875 Putnam sent on a deed from the Union Lumber Co. for 480 acres. The Union Lumber Co. had gone into bankruptcy by this time; Sage did not recognize the Union Lumber Co.'s share in the transaction, nor consider its quitclaim deed of much value. "The whole thing is a swindle," he wrote McGraw.[103] Putnam's practice of settling trespass cases on Sage's and Cornell University's land without authorization and for what appeared to be much less than the damage and his carelessness or duplicity in allowing some of the Sage lands to be sold for taxes,[104] offered enough excuse to dismiss him, even without the tax-certificate incident which so enraged Sage. After 1875 both Sage and Cornell University took the agency of their lands from Putnam's hands. It is interesting to note that despite his anger Sage did not make so great an issue of his dismissal of Putnam as to close further contact between them. Indeed he urged the University treasurer to keep the matter of Putnam's dismissal and the reasons for it as quiet as possible.[105] Although he seems not to have taken part in any more of Putnam's ventures, Sage left the way open to hear of them, and in the nineties loaned Putnam and his partners $50,000—on sufficient security, however.[106]

[103] Dec. 23, 1875, HWS.

[104] Sage to H. C. Putnam, Sept. 8, 1875; to J. W. Williams, Nov. 29, 1876, HWS; and W. C. Russel to A. D. White, Nov. 30, 1876, ADW. Russel commented, "What a pity that Tweed never knew Putnam!"

[105] To J. W. Williams, Oct. 20, 1876, HWS.

[106] W. H. Sage to D. P. Simons, Jan. 3; Sage to H. C. Putnam, Jan. 5, 1891, HWS.

D. P. Simons, originally a cruiser for McGraw and others, and somewhat later the agent for W. J. Young & Co., proved to be somewhat more satisfactory than Putnam. In 1880 Sage sold Simons a one-fourth interest at 50 cents an acre in the Chippewa County lands bought through David Miles. The proceeds of all sales were to go to H. W. Sage and Co. until Simons' share was paid for. Simons had charge of all the Sage lands in Wisconsin, arranging for taxes, protecting against trespass, making sales.

Professor Paul W. Gates has told the story of the activities of Putnam and Simons with regard to gaining tax reductions for their clients.[107] In combination with other investors and their agents these men constituted an effective lobby, harrying local officials with lawsuits, pressuring for the organization of new counties and towns where the effect would be lowered taxes, occasionally stepping over the boundary of strict legality in their efforts. These efforts were very largely successful. Rarely did assessment approach the real value of the lands to their owners.

Sage's own experience had resolved the problem of taxation for him so that it resembled a tug of war. On the one hand were ranged the Tweeds, whether of Tammany Hall or the Saginaw Valley, corrupt local officials, and their friends who expected to line their pockets from the public treasury; on the other side were the investors whose profits depended upon maintaining low assessments on their lands. Lost completely from view were the legitimate needs and interests of local government. As a result Sage pulled hard for lower assessments and lower tax rates. The first step taken by Sage's agents was to ascertain that taxes were uniform as between resident and nonresident lands, and among lands of the same type held by different owners. The next step was to gain a reduction in the uniform level or from the uniform level. At times Sage attempted to work with a larger group in winning tax reductions. This was done in Wisconsin through the organizing abilities of Putnam and Simons. J. M. Longyear organized a Taxpayer's Association to protect landholders in the Upper Penin-

[107] Gates, *Wisconsin Pine Lands,* ch. viii; see especially pp. 143–164.

sula of Michigan against "abuses of the tax system, . . . illegal assessments and the corrupt expenditure of money raised by taxation." [108] Sage joined but discovered that ferreting out the abuses was not enough; he withdrew from the organization because of its ineffectiveness in aiding owners to recover. This was one of the few occasions on which the Sages actively urged the strengthening of an organization which they did not control. In 1888 they suggested that the members "pay their taxes through the Association—It would put you in a stronger position & ought to work to the advantage of members." [109] Longyear, incidentally, was the first and perhaps the only one to suggest to Sage the idea of a perpetual timber crop in these Michigan lands. He was interested in preserving a forest of 300,000 acres owned in the Upper Peninsula by six men, including Sage. "By being handled in large contiguous tracts and by taking a crop from the land each year, the yield may be made perpetual and more and more profitable." [110] Sage was interested but wary: "There are many difficulties in organizing such a plan as you suggest—It could be made a joint stock affair were the lands of equal value—But they *are not.*" [111] Apparently the Sages did not pursue the idea further. The stumbling block was their doubt that businessmen could indeed work together for their mutual benefit.

In Michigan the Sages relied most heavily upon the personal pressures exercised upon local officials by Pierson. A regular feature of Pierson's duties was his annual trip through Michigan, Lower and Upper Peninsulas, to visit the tax assessors and boards of review. In some cases the Sages instituted lawsuits to set aside taxes. After one such case, Pierson reported:

We had the good fortune to find one . . . who was acquainted with the Judge & Pros Atty. & by getting them together & this man telling what he knew of the facts, satisfied Judge & later on the Pros Atty. As we had learned by examination that the District Board had written

[108] J. M. Longyear to Sage, July 22, 1886, HWS.
[109] W. H. Sage to J. M. Longyear, Jan. 11, 1888, HWS.
[110] Nov. 23, 1895, HWS.   [111] Dec. 23, 1895, HWS.

up a record that would on the face of it, cure the defect, we did not want to send for any of them or their record & it would have cost $6 to $8 at least. We also found in visiting with the Judge that he thought our grounds of objection to tax in 21—4E sufficient to warrant setting that too aside. Although the Township had written up the papers to correct the defects apparently. So we had both taxes wyped off & set aside. . . . We took pains to be friendly & entertaining to the officials & think we are well paid for the effort.[112]

The savings in this case amounted to $744.44, hardly an enormous sum, but Pierson's efforts were directed at gaining reductions at all levels. In some cases the taxation issue was reduced to a battle of wits. In 1896 in Iosco County the board of review agreed to Pierson's special pleading and reduced the Sages' taxes. Afterwards, however, "the board reduced a large share of the roll, so that relatively we were worse off than before." [113]

The arguments used before local officials usually centered on the assertion that the lands were valued for taxation purposes much above their cash value. It was an assertion only, since Sage was insistent that his estimates were not to be shown to the tax assessors. These men, equipped with little accurate knowledge, often repeated only that the Sage lands were known to be the best in the area. The tax assessors were in a difficult position. The investor contended:

Companies holding timber for future posterity and who will pay taxes for a number of years to come should be taxed leniently so that the burden of carrying the lands might not be excessive, while Companies who are cutting & slashing the timber and who will pay taxes for the present only, should be taxed accordingly.[114]

The slashers of timber, however, contended that, because they were producers who brought employment and prosperity to the community, their tax burden should be light. And finally the owners of the cutovers maintained that their lands were next to

[112] To S.L. & I. Co., April 14, 1898, HWS.
[113] F. Pierson to S.L. & I. Co., Dec. 22, HWS.
[114] E. J. James to S.L. & I. Co., Jan. 10, 1913, HWS.

valueless and should be taxed lightly. When then was the community to regain in taxes any portion of its forest wealth? Residents of the community argued that only while the timber was still standing or the mills still in operation could the community hope to share in the wealth created initially by public resources. "If the millions of dollars which these pine forests are worth, are ever to be taxed for public improvements, in the towns and counties where they stand, it must be before they are removed in the form of logs and lumber." [115] "As the pine timber is removed, the owners reduce the valuation, by swearing it down, and the long timber, logs, etc., evade taxation for all time to come, being quietly floated beyond the jurisdiction of the townships where it grew." [116] Pineland holders retorted that county and local governments "in new and sparsely settled portions of the State" hardly required extravagant improvements and extravagant taxation.[117] It was in essence Sage's own, old argument against Wenona's sewer project.

It is difficult to make any precise generalizations about the effectiveness of the lumberman's methods of beating down taxes and the general effect of these methods on the lumber industry. County and township taxes varied widely, and even within the same township the taxes on several 40-acre plots all located for pine often differed considerably. Within the pine counties of Wisconsin and Michigan there seems to have been in very general terms a gradual increase in tax rates on lands held by Sage until the lands were lumbered. In the years when cutting was going on a drastic drop in taxes occurred. Then began a gradual increase again, corresponding presumably with the arrival of settlers and their demand both for lands and services. Within this admittedly very general framework there is room for many unexplained and at this point unexplainable increases and decreases in tax rates.

In absolute terms Sage reckoned his taxes on Michigan timberlands in the early eighties at about 20 cents to 28 cents per acre.[118]

---

[115] *The Leader,* quoted in the Bay City *Morning Chronicle,* March 14, 1874.
[116] *Iosco County Gazette,* March 22, 1876.
[117] *Lumberman's Gazette,* IV, 67.
[118] To Dean Sage, April 28, 1882; to H. W. Sage and Co., Dec. 20, 1884, HWS.

He recognized certain anomalies in taxation: "With less than 2 millions Timber in 30.1 Taxes are . . . more than 44¢ per M ft. . . . With 50 millions in 30.2 . . . the Taxes are . . . 22¢ pr M"; but he was unwilling to reveal his own estimates to provide a more equitable tax base. "Both are excessive—but nobody should know our Timber estimates." [119] In Wisconsin one of the highest taxes paid on a 40-acre tract, $56.63, still kept taxes at a level of only $1.41 per acre, and this tax was exceptional, occurring in only one year, 1889. In the hardwood belt of the Upper Peninsula taxes from 1882 to 1892 appear never to have exceeded $3.31 on a 40-acre tract, and this was the outside limit rather than the average rate.[120] Certainly taxes do not seem to have cut into profits appreciably, with the possible exception of taxes on the cutovers. This was the only area in which abandonment of lands took place and much of the abandoned land was subsequently reclaimed.

As in the Great Lakes region, Sage's agents in the South spent a good deal of their time exercising pressure upon assessors and tax commissioners. Again, as in the Great Lakes states, there was a considerable drive to lay the weight of taxation upon nonresident lands. Since the rate of taxation was held uniform for resident and nonresident lands, it was the assessment process that was under constant watch. In Alabama there was a public tax assessor, but Massey Wilson, clerk of the Probate Court at Grove Hill, advised Sage to hire Wilson to draw up Sage's assessment list. Wilson warned that the tax assessor was paid in commissions and therefore sought to raise valuations as high as possible.[121] Wilson was a lawyer, nephew of the judge of the Probate Court of Clarke County, and soon to become clerk of the state House of Representatives. Van Heuvel reported that "his influence with state officials may be considered worth a great deal to us here." [122]

Wilson assessed Sage's Clarke County lands at $1.25 an acre

[119] To H. W. Sage and Co., West Bay City, Dec. 20, 1887, HWS.
[120] Land Books, H. W. Sage and Co., *passim*, HWS.
[121] To H. W. Sage and Co., Feb. 22, 1889, HWS.
[122] To H. W. Sage and Co., June 6, 1894, HWS.

in 1889, the rate prevailing before Sage's purchase of them. The tax assessor, however, refused at first to accept this evaluation, since he had learned that Sage paid $1.75 per acre for the lands. Wilson insisted that the important fact was that none of the adjoining lands were assessed at more than $1.00 per acre and seems to have argued that the assessor was basing his evaluation on the fact that Sage was a nonresident. Wilson pleaded his case before the commissions court and won, earning for himself a $50 fee. The same battle was fought all over again in 1891, when the tax assessor fixed evaluation at $2.00 per acre; Wilson contended for $1.25 and finally settled for $1.50 an acre. In Washington County he succeeded in maintaining a $1.00 per acre assessment. In 1893 the rate of taxation was raised but not the evaluation. In 1894 Van Heuvel took over the payment of taxes. He seems to have had little trouble in maintaining the assessment figures set by Wilson, and indeed went on to get reductions where he could claim damages by cyclone and boxing. In 1895 Van Heuvel got the assessor to agree to an evaluation of $1.18 per acre at the same time that other large owners in Washington County were assessed at $2.00 per acre.

In Mississippi, Sage employed M. F. Berry of Pachuta to arrange tax matters. Despite Berry's efforts, the evaluations made in 1888 by Ripley were raised considerably by the auditor. Each year despite Sage's efforts valuation seems to have increased. In 1892 the increase over the 1888 figure ran from 50 cents to $1.00. The evaluation figures remained somewhere between $1.50 and $2.00 throughout the nineties. The actual taxes in the South, however, were extremely low, considerably lower than in Michigan and Wisconsin; they ranged from 9 to 15 mills and very rarely to 17 mills in the period from 1889 to 1895.[123]

The southern lands presented from the outset special problems which called for detailed and constant surveillance. The southern pineries were dotted with settlers, largely squatters who desired to file homestead claims only after Sage had entered their lands. Within the first year of Sage's purchases innumerable contests

[123] Land Book, S.L. & I. Co., *passim,* HWS.

were commenced against him by these settlers. Early in 1889 Sage wrote, exasperated: "We have on that Miss land—Houses—cotton plantations, churches grist mill—for all which I am sorry—They will be sources of trouble I am sure." [124] Settlement of any kind within the pineries was dangerous to the timber owner not only because of the usual risk of fire and timber trespass, but also because southern pine was easily tapped for turpentine, and turpentine was as easily converted into cash or supplies at the local store. Boxing of the trees to get the turpentine resulted in permanent injury to the timber unless the gashes were promptly filled in.

Sage tried to meet the problem by selling the settler or squatter his cleared and fenced land, while Sage retained all timber. Sage set the price at $1.60 an acre, which he felt would cover all his costs including interest. Not all settlers, however, were anxious to buy of Sage the lands they occupied. Emery reported that Alabama law provided that ten years' residence or peaceable possession of land gave title, thus giving substance to the settlers' contention that Sage had no right to land they were living on.[125] In contests with squatters Sage found that the register's and receiver's decision invariably went in favor of the settler who "was living on the land when you made the entry, which is not allowed by law." Despite his threats to "have a 'shaking up' in the Jackson Land office," Sage received little satisfaction in these contests.[126] In 1890 he tried instead to pass on the problem by providing in contracts to purchase land that the seller be responsible for settling all claims in the lands, and for all damages resulting from such claims. However, this did not solve the problem in the large 50,000-acre tract he had bought in 1888. To protect himself Sage, at Emery's suggestion, had printed a number of leases, or rather tenant-at-will contracts, which squatters on the Sage lands were persuaded to sign.[127] These provided that the tenant be allowed to reside on

124 To Dean Sage, Jan. 18, 1889, HWS.
125 To H. W. Sage and Co., Aug. 11, 1893, HWS.
126 Sage to L. V. Ripley, March 29, 1889, HWS.
127 "The Sage Land & Improvement Co. of Ithaca, N.Y., in consideration of the promise of —— to live upon and protect from depredation, and to

the land at the discretion of the Sage Land & Improvement Co., thereby obviating the difficulty implicit in the ten-year residence law. At the same time the tenant's promise in writing to protect the timber and commit no depredations upon the land would presumably help in collecting damages or in forcing evictions upon violations of the lease.

In cases where simple trespass was the issue, the difficulty lay in apprehending the offender and then in gaining a conviction and collecting damages. As Sage's agents pointed out in their reports, it was not only settlers who were responsible for tapping but also distillery owners, who trespassed themselves or induced settlers to do it for them, and groups of men whose business was the systematic tapping of trees and who had no intention of settling or farming. In some cases, particularly where the offenders had trespassed because of ignorance of the lines, the agent was able to persuade them to fill in the boxes with earth and thus prevent complete destruction of the tree. It was almost impossible to collect damages, since the settlers had no cash and judges and juries were reluctant to find against them. It was evidently difficult also to comply with the Alabama law which required trespass suits to be filed within a year of the damage.

The reports of Ripley, Emery, and Van Heuvel mention repeatedly threats of violence against Sage's agents. At one point in 1892 Sage contemplated selling some 7,000 acres in Washington County, Alabama, because it proved impossible to stop trespassing. In 1893 Van Heuvel reported 60,000 boxes. Ripley was advised that the trespassers could not "be punished nor drawn off. They will outswear all comers—and should a Jury convict the Judge will clear them." [128] Lawyers in Mobile warned Emery that back-country juries would not dare to convict. They advised instead the use of in-

---

commit no waste of timber, or of any kind; has rented and leased unto —— the following land, to-wit: —— as a tenant at will, —— to remain upon the said land at the pleasure of the said The Sage Land & Improvement Co., its successors or assigns," HWS.

[128] Sage to Temple Emery, June 25, 1895, HWS.

junctions. Constant surveillance plus the use of the injunction and repeated attempts to prosecute, some of which were successful despite threats of violence, seem to have made some inroads on the trespassing. By the close of 1896 Will Sage was able to write a prospective buyer, "We have educated the natives up to a proper respect for our lines, which are clearly run, so that there is practically no attempt to trespass now." [129]

The profits [130] from the investments in Michigan and Wisconsin lands which Sage had made in the sixties and seventies provided the funds in turn not only for securities investments and for liberal gifts to Cornell University but also for the second and third rounds of land investments in the eighties and nineties. The profits of these later land investments were not to be gathered until after Henry Sage's death; they represented the major part of his legacy to his sons and grandchildren.

The 95,319 acres of land in the Lower Peninsula which were turned over to the Sage Land & Improvement Co. in 1893 had all been lumbered for pine by that year either by H. W. Sage and Co. or by other firms to whom the Sages had sold at an ever increasing stumpage valuation. In the early eighties $4 to $5 for white pine and $2 to $3 for Norway prevailed. By 1887, however, $6 for white pine was the average figure. Despite the fact that the major profits had already been earned from the sale of the pine, between 1893 and 1924 the Sage Land & Improvement Co. gleaned from these lands additional profits of $87,322.32, largely on account of sales of hardwood and farming land.[131]

Of the 162,856 acres in Wisconsin and Minnesota turned over to the Sage Land & Improvement Co., the majority were also cutovers, and some were hardwood lands. The Wisconsin lands, too, had already earned large profits for the Sages through the sale of pine. In the early nineties stumpage prices here were put up to

---

[129] To W. J. Young, Dec. 30, 1896, HWS.

[130] The S.L. & I. Co. calculated profits after deducting for taxes, interest charges, and the costs of buying and administering the land.

[131] Report, H. M. Sage to stockholders, 1924.

176

$7 per thousand feet by the Sages. One purchaser commented that this was $1 "more per M . . . than the highest price we have ever paid for timber." [132] From 1893 to 1924 these lands showed an additional profit of $613, 323.96.[133] Sale of 1,981 acres in Minnesota owned by the Sages and Simons took place in 1899. These lands which had cost $3,003 in 1881 were sold at a net profit of $47,829.33, three-fourths of which went to the Sage Land & Improvement Co.[134]

The 105,368 acres located in the Upper Peninsula largely for hardwood and farming land were first lumbered for pine in the nineties on the basis of $6 per thousand feet. Later the hardwood and the lands were sold. The profits on the whole amounted to $646,123.47.[135] The 20,000 acres in which Ripley had a one-fifth interest were sold in 1902 and 1905 for $195,248.59 or approximately $9.75 per acre.[136] They had been entered in the early eighties for $1.25 per acre, approximately $25,000

On 1,611 acres entered by Emery in Washington Territory in 1887 the Sage Land & Improvement Co. subsequently made a profit of $23,519.10, and on a few hundred acres located by Ripley in Arkansas a profit of $1,010.19. On the whole list of lands exclusive of those in the South the profits amounted to $1,371,299.04. An additional profit of $1,085,207.69 was made from interest charged on joint accounts and from interest collected on notes for land and timber.[137] The showing was a handsome one. Henry W. Sage might possibly have been disappointed with the profits of the Upper Peninsula lands which averaged only about $6 to the acre. Nevertheless even this represented a profit of about 500 per cent.

The southern land account provided the most spectacular profits. Stumpage values in Mississippi and Alabama had begun to rise slowly in the last years of the nineteenth century. In 1899 the

[132] Eugene Shaw to H. W. Sage and Co., Dec. 31, 1891, HWS.
[133] Report, H. M. Sage to stockholders, 1924.
[134] Memo: Minn Lands Jt A/c Simons, HWS.
[135] Report, H. M. Sage to stockholders, 1924.
[136] *Sage Land & Improvement Co. vs. Lucien V. Ripley*, brief, p. 11.
[137] Report, H. M. Sage to stockholders, 1924.

Sages calculated prices on the basis of $1.75 to $2.00 per thousand feet; in 1900 the figure was raised to $2.00 to $2.50; by 1902 to $3.00. By 1908 $3.00 to $5.00 was the common price in both states.[138] The Sages' first substantial sale was made in 1899; by 1903, 78,497 acres had been sold for $1,172,234.75—

more than the total amount ever invested in Alabama and Mississippi. . . . Our last lands were sold in 1916, and the result of the entire operation was a profit actually received over all charges (not counting interest received on land notes of over $1,050,000) of $8,031,505.05, or about 700% on our total investments.[139]

In the first years of sale per-acre prices had ranged from $10.50 to $15.00. The average per-acre price of all sales was approximately $20.00. The Sages' southern investments had indeed paid handsomely.

In 1902 the Sage Land & Improvement Co. became interested in the Far West as an investment area. The Sages communicated with D. P. Simons, who had been engaged for two years previous to this in buying timberlands in northern Washington for a Weyerhaeuser company. Simons discouraged the Sages from investing in Washington. Stumpage prices had risen, he reported, from 38 cents, at which he had bought for Weyerhaeuser, to between 55 and 75 cents. Moreover the choice tracts had been located already. Weyerhaeuser and others of the timbermen had preceded them in Idaho, too, and there "the best of the surveyed lands are gone." [140] Simons suggested instead the Nehalem Valley of Oregon which, though somewhat remote from transportation lines, was reputed to be the area in which the Northern Pacific would build an extension line. Evidently its isolation had saved it from speculators up to this time. Simons was able to buy for the joint interest—Simons retaining a one-fifth interest—13,528

---

[138] U.S. Bureau of Corporations, *The Lumber Industry* (Washington, D.C., 1913), pt. I, pp. 195–196.
[139] Report, H. M. Sage to stockholders, 1924.
[140] To S.L. & I. Co., Jan. 20, Feb. 26, 1902, HWS.

acres, largely in quarter sections, at an average cost of $9 per acre or 25¾ cents per thousand feet of fir timber. These lands were held a relatively short time. In 1906 they were sold for $283,500. Their cost, including taxes, expenses, and interest up to the time of sale amounted to $122,169.67.[141] The total profit then was considerably more than 100 per cent. The profit to the Sages alone was $143,198.78.[142]

The major investments of the Sage Land & Improvement Co. in the twentieth century were made in California. The Bureau of Corporations Reports in 1913–1914 listed the Sage Land & Improvement Co. as one in the third ranking group of major redwood holders in the Mendocino Valley.[143] Investment in California redwood involved a large outlay of capital. Between 1905 and 1912 the Sage Land & Improvement Co. purchased 60,459 acres of redwood in Mendocino and Humboldt Counties at a cost of $2,135,529.14.[144] Most of this was located by D. P. Simons, who took a one-tenth interest in the lands. Prices ranged from $20 to $60 an acre, although the average was $35. Stumpage costs ranged from 75 cents to $1.50. These figures were high when compared with Michigan and Wisconsin investments in the sixties and seventies or even with the investment in Washington Territory in 1887.

After Simons' death the Sages employed E. J. James as their agent. James planned to consolidate the California holdings by selling or exchanging all lands not in the vicinity of the major tracts and by filling in the major holdings in Mendocino and Humboldt Counties. Acting on this plan the Sage Land & Improvement Co. purchased, up until 1927, 106,000 acres at a cost of $5,307,801.47. In the thirties several large sales were made, four of them to the Save-the-Redwoods League; in 1940 the holdings of the company in California were 85,678.57 acres containing

---

141 D. P. Simons to S.L. & I. Co., July 4, 1902; May 14, July 13, 1906, HWS.
142 Report, Olaf Holter to stockholders, 1940.
143 U.S. Bureau of Corporations, *op. cit.*, pt. II, 107.
144 Report, H. M. Sage to stockholders, 1924.

2,648,515,000 feet of redwood and 811,730,000 feet of fir.[145] The company continued throughout as a family firm.

In terms of acreage the holdings of the Sages in 1940 were very substantially smaller than they had been at the time of Henry W. Sage's death in 1897. They were acquired at a significantly higher cost. Just over one million dollars had paid for the entire southern inventory, nearly 400,000 acres. Proportionately the vast tracts in Michigan and Wisconsin had been acquired even more cheaply. In California, the last major investment area, it took over five million dollars to pay for 106,000 acres. Moreover, new lumber frontiers in which profits might be reinvested were no longer in evidence. The frontier was closed; the public domain had been alienated. The California holdings had been purchased from private holders generally as had a great part of the southern lands. Indeed there was a final irony implicit in the situation as of 1940 when the government was looked upon as a prospective buyer of redwood lands.

The truly remarkable aspect of Henry W. Sage's acquisition of an empire in timberlands was the limited number of times—in the age of the robber barons—he felt compelled to break the law consciously and deliberately. The purchase of Indian reservation timber before the lands had been patented constituted one such occasion. The purchase of homestead claims in the South through fraudulent application of the preemption privilege before 1891 might be considered another infringement of law. But by and large the enormous profits of investment in timberlands were made possible by a government policy which ostensibly aimed to encourage and protect the homesteader and effectively promoted the interest of the speculator. Sage's major investments in government lands were made with agricultural college scrip at considerably less than the minimum government price and by simple cash entry.

It is perhaps only to be expected that after twenty-five years of experience with the government practice—practice in default

[145] Report, Olaf Holter to stockholders, 1940.

of policy—of giving away timberlands for a token payment, Sage was not seriously disturbed by the repeal of the cash-sale law in 1889, nor by the suggestions voiced about that time that timberlands be reserved from entry and sold at prices approaching their true value.[146] If the government intended to strike at the investor in timberlands by forcing him to compete at auction sales, the latter would simply resort to the tactics of the "ring," employed so successfully in other areas. He would combine, not compete. "No harm can follow—except possibly that under a new plan there will be combinations of purchasers & prices may be no higher." [147]

Sage's analysis of the proposed government action, an analysis which ignored the positive aims of the program—the protection of homestead opportunities, more adequate compensation for the alienation of the public domain, and possibly conservation of forest resources—was perhaps only realistic. The operation of the homestead law in timbered areas had merely made speculators of ostensible homesteaders. When the public domain in the South was indeed closed to cash sales, no reservation was made of timbered areas, and Sage, as we have seen, continued to build up his timberland holdings by purchasing homesteads and before 1891 preemption rights. The latter operation was of course open to the charge of fraud, but all the legal requirements were carefully adhered to and the practice itself was sanctioned by custom. That the government should be adequately compensated for the surrender of natural resources to private exploitation was again a foreign notion to Sage, who did not identify government and public in any meaningful sense. He accorded to government only the very limited functions of protection and promotion of private property. He was prone to characterize government officials very generally as "Tweeds," open to corruption and eager for personal aggrandizement. That there was a decided correlation between

[146] E.g., Report of W. A. J. Sparks, Commr. General Land Office, *House Executive Document 2541* (Washington, D.C., 1887), pp. 168–169; John Ise, *The United States Forest Policy* (New Haven, 1924), pp. 113–114.

[147] Sage to M. F. Berry, June 6, 1888, HWS.

these two aspects of his definition of government and that his attitude and those of his business contemporaries not only aggravated but created the situation, he did not apparently consider.
Conservation of forest resources was again an aim that Sage could
not appreciate. In his own lifetime there was always a new lumber
frontier waiting after the exploitation of the old. The stripping of
forest resources, despite the claim of overproduction, was identified with progress. Neither active promotion of settlement in the
cutovers nor appreciation of the function of the taxpayer seemed
vital to Sage's picture of himself as a contributor to the development of natural resources.

Sage nevertheless betrayed a certain measure of sensitivity to
the growing attack upon investors or speculators. The present
plan, he asserted, "leaving everyone at liberty to buy, and interesting private enterprise in the development of the country's resources" was as good as any that might be devised. The disparity
between buying for purposes of development and buying to gain
the unearned increment of advanced stumpage values was slurred
over, as indeed was the effect of advanced stumpage prices as a
result of private engrossment upon the price of lumber, the end
product of the development of this resource. "There may be
abuses of the privilege—and some men may profit by the investment—but what if they do?—The same may be done with everything in the market as merchandise." [148]

Investment in timberlands was not what Sage himself termed
a speculative enterprise. Speculation, a word he used with some
contempt, referred, for example, to the manipulation of watered
stock, or the rapid turnover of vacant city lots in boom times,
enterprises in which profits were accumulated as the result of
prevailing optimism, rather than from the appreciation of real
values, of rolling stock and track mileage, of ore and timber.
Timberlands counted as real value; indeed as an ever increasingly
valuable asset. Investment in timberlands was based on the scarcity

[148] *Ibid.*

created not only by rapid exploitation of forest resources but also by rapid private engrossment of the public domain. Sage argued that only when the timbered areas of the South were substantially concentrated in the hands of a limited number of owners would stumpage prices rise: "It will be in Alabama as it was in Michigan & Wisconsin—there will be no strong advance in price of stumpage till the bulk of the land is in strong hands and no considerable quantity is available at very low prices." [149] This process he regarded as inevitable. A near-monopoly situation would create monopoly prices. And he was able and willing to wait for this situation, a situation he had first taken advantage of in Michigan. From Michigan one of his sales agents had written in the eighties:

We . . . believe as you do, that stumpage, where it is wanted, will in the future bring higher rates than the price of lumber will warrant. We have observed that Saw Mills are hungry concerns, and where the provender gets scarce they are inexorable, and *must have* that which alone can sustain life. For this reason we agree with you in asking all that can be obtained for standing timber.[150]

Yet Sage measured his own growth in terms of his role as a producer. The personal satisfactions inherent in entrepreneurial functions counted heavily in Sage's interpretation of the good life. Again and again he urged a new manufacturing enterprise on his sons and for the benefit of his grandsons. During the course of his forty years as a lumber manufacturer Sage had arrived at a satisfactory rationale of his business activities and those of his associates. The unseen hand, derived in part from classical economics, in part from the conviction of progress, worked through the businessman, regardless of the latter's personal motivation, toward the greater productive capacity of the nation. Moreover, in the wake of this increased wealth came a general uplift in culture and refinement. This explanation has a surprisingly current ring.

[149] To H. M. Sage, Jan. 24, 1894, HWS.
[150] George S. Frost to H. W. Sage and Co., Aug. 26, 1886, HWS.

Nineteenth-century industrial statesmanship has been interpreted today as the persistent effort to produce more goods more cheaply and efficiently. Nevertheless the logic of profit, the underlying motive of expanded and more efficient production, seems to have directed H. W. Sage and Co. from production to speculative investment.

Chapter VIII

Investor

SAGE'S earliest investments, in 1836 and 1837, were in real estate; they were speculative, made in anticipation of a rapid turnover which did not materialize. From 1845, when he once more began to buy property in the Ithaca area, until the seventies Sage's major outside investments continued to be in real estate. Perhaps in this also he was modeling himself on the success of the Williamses. A smaller amount of his investment funds went into local Ithaca enterprises: plank roads, railroads, a waterworks company. Undoubtedly this investment pattern reflected as much the habits of a small-town merchant capitalist as it did the limited resources available to the investor.

There was evidently a correlation in Sage's mind between settling in a community and becoming a substantial property holder in it. In 1857, the year he moved to Brooklyn, Sage purchased a number of city lots there for $17,500.[1] The panic of 1857, the crisis of 1861, and the fear of investing in land because of war taxes seem to have deterred Sage from further real estate ventures for some time. By 1864, with John McGraw, he was reinvesting lumber profits in a new mill in West Bay City and in Michigan timberlands. In 1868, however, Sage and McGraw bought jointly 43½ lots in Brooklyn's ninth ward for $143,400—in cash—ample testimony to the new mill's success.[2] Subsequently Sage continued to buy Brooklyn property. Unfortunately the ninth ward did not develop as rapidly as he had anticipated. In 1884 Sage calculated

[1] Deed from Wendell to Henry W. Sage, April 1, 1857, HWS.
[2] Deed from Russell Adams to Sage and McGraw, Dec. 19, 1868, HWS.

his losses on Brooklyn real estate in the previous fifteen years as $175,000.[3]

Yet other similar ventures had been successful. In 1869 Sage had purchased 160 acres of land in Detroit for approximately $14,000. He held the land until 1885, when he sold for $250 an acre. The land had been inventoried at $20,000, and rents had "more than paid taxes." Now, however, Sage calculated, "If we can get 6 pr ¢ for the cash it will give us 2400 pr year." [4] By the eighties the Sages had become securities-oriented.

By 1867 at the latest Sage was accustomed to maintaining reserve funds in government bonds, and by 1872 he was taking advantage also of the call loan market for investment funds. Call loans offered substantial interest rates and the advantage, usually, of rapid conversion. Sage also bought privately commercial paper at interest rates from 9 per cent to 12 and 15 per cent. Mortgages and long-term loans to private firms provided other outlets for investment.

Until 1873 a large part of the profit on lumber was reinvested in pinelands, and throughout the decade Sage's gifts to Cornell University required considerable sums. Nevertheless he acquired a few stocks and bonds. His characteristic anxiety to "get in on the ground floor" and for "a seat at the first table" was to be modified in time by successive disappointments with "original" enterprises. Given the inadequate sources of information available to the investor, Sage had to rely largely on the word of acquaintances or friends who might be presumed to know the reliability of securities. Occasionally the enthusiasm of these friends, whether innocent or interested, proved misleading. Nevertheless, even after he came to depend upon brokers, Sage continued to invest on the advice of friends. He undertook a number of ventures, few of them entirely successful but all ambitious, with a group of New York and Brooklyn businessmen including A. S. Barnes, H. G. Bond, and E. C. Litchfield. In Ithaca as well as in West Bay City

[3] To Dean Sage, Feb. 1, 1884, HWS. [4] *Ibid.*, Jan. 21, 1881.

there were also small circles of local capitalists with whom he habitually invested in local enterprises.

Investing as a group did not necessarily imply mutual confidence. Sage was well aware of the opportunism prevalent in the business community. In every enterprise he looked fearfully for "a Fisk or Tweed" and all too often found one. Group investing was a weak form of insurance; yet it seemed to offer a measure of support for the individual investor through a nucleus which might attempt to control policy.

Sage's first investment in Brooklyn's elevated railroads was typical of his investment pattern in the seventies in so far as the initial capital required was small, the anticipated profits enormous. His fellow stockholders included Litchfield and S. B. Chittenden, with whom he early proposed to share control of the organization. As in many of his later investments, Sage understood that what appeared to be a simple business operation involved not only political opposition but conflict with rival business organizations.

Sage's interest in Brooklyn steam railroads began in 1875 with the purchase of stock certificates in the Brooklyn Steam Transit Company, whose sole asset at this time was a charter to build an elevated railroad line. Sage, president of the company, was anxious to undertake the project. A very minor Machiavelli, he wrote a fellow stockholder:

As to the men named by me whose influence I thought desirable in influencing popular favor for the project, and through that, stock subscriptions, whatever may be chargeable to them as inconsistent with honest purposes they *are* to a great extent directors of public opinion in this city—They control the press, and, more or less—Political organisations—I think their good will for this project can be had for the asking because it is in line with their interests—This could do no harm, while their opposition might *kill*.[5]

However, in the next three years little was accomplished. An attempt to sell the charter to General Fremont and his associates

[5] To Joseph White, Nov. 18, 1875, HWS.

failed. In 1878 the charter holders were forced to build a mile of road to maintain their privileges and to test the validity of the charter. At once rivalry with surface railroads and other charter holders came into play. Sage had attempted to circumvent opposition by gaining a general railroad incorporation law through the state legislature. He specifically asked Erastus Brooks "not to make public the particular road I have named, as it might arouse local opposition." [6] Sage was not loath to use what influence he had in the state legislature, where he enlisted S. D. Halliday as well as Brooks in his interest; he advised Halliday: "Mr. Alvord of the RR Comm is an old friend of mine and I think it could do no harm to tell him that I have a personal interest in this Bill." [7] Sage wrote his son, "Our charter & its uses *mean conflict* with every Rail Road enterprise in Brooklyn." [8]

An injunction stopped the construction of the test mile, and David Dudley Field was employed to argue the case for Sage and his associates. Through 1880 litigation in the courts and maneuvering in the legislature continued to no apparent conclusion. Field's insistence that the charter was valid was answered ultimately not by a court decision but by a consolidation of the Sage interests with a rival organization, the Kings County Elevated Railroad Company, headed by H. G. Bond: "If B & his friends decide so we shall then go on together and one charter or the other will doubtless be maintained." [9] Sage bought 400 shares in the new company, which also had no assets except its charter, and he again entered into the controversy, more pessimistically this time: "The $20 M it has cost me is not badly invested if I learn henceforth to invest in enterprises that are already born. . . . Let others take all with which the duties of midwife have not ended." [10] He was not, however, to abide by this lesson.

A further reorganization took place in 1882, in which the man-

[6] April 5, 1878, HWS.   [7] April 18, 1878, HWS.
[8] To Dean Sage, June 17, 1878, HWS.
[9] Sage to W. H. Sage, Nov. 21, 1879, HWS.
[10] To H. G. Bond, Nov. 16, 1880, HWS.

agement of the road passed into the hands of Judge Shea of New York and Edward A. Abbott of Boston. In December 1884 no road was in operation, and Bond wrote unhappily to Sage, "I see no way of getting any money out of the business unless we can at the next annual meeting take control again, and negotiate with someone for what of a franchise we have." [11] At this juncture Sage held $\frac{1}{12}$ of the stock with a face value of $80,000. In 1885 a syndicate of stockholders was formed, which raised the funds for construction and in return received all of the bond issue of the road "and seventy five per cent of all the stock to be issued, after two miles of the road are completed." [12] Sage hesitated about joining: "I have doubts *now* of everything except profit in syndicate—That will probably be sure—but payt of intst on bonds without creating a floating debt I dont consider sure for the next three years." [13] Presumably the only certain profits would be made from construction, and the construction of the road was not yet in sight. The New York Court of Appeals did not confirm the charter of the company until the spring of 1887, and not until 1888 was any portion of the line in operation.[14] Sage did not join the syndicate in 1885, and two years later when the court sustained the company he tried to recoup his loss through the lawyer, William C. DeWitt, charging fraud in construction expenses and stock watering. His avowed object was not to expose the syndicate but to defend his "right to be let into this syndicate upon equal terms with its other members." [15] The DeWitt inquiry evidently was forceful enough to precipitate an offer for Sage's stock. Sage received $90,000 of the railroad's first mortgage bonds as collateral for Shea's note endorsed by Abbott for $72,000. Since Sage had been willing at earlier stages to sell his stock at 35 and 40 per cent of par, he came out with a fair margin to his credit, but without the enormous profits he contemplated in the seventies. It would be straining a

[11] Dec. 4, 1884, HWS. [12] W. C. DeWitt to Sage, May 11, 1887, HWS.
[13] To Dean Sage, Dec. 14, 1885, HWS.
[14] *Poor's Manual of Railroads*, 1888, p. 177.
[15] W. C. DeWitt to Sage, May 11, 1887, HWS.

point to say that Sage's hesitation to join the syndicate initially was based in moral disapproval. The arguments he presented his son were based in risk and profit calculations: "A chance to be in the syndicate may have value—But *the bonds* we can buy if we want to much below par. (I think 40 pr ¢) within next 5 years if we desire." [16] Sage also feared his minority position in the syndicate. Later it is probable that Sage made his accusations about the syndicate's operations to buy his way out rather than in, and again it was his fear of the shakiness of the organization as well as of its hostile control that seemed to determine his decision.

Sage took an interest also in the Prospect Park and Coney Island Railroad of Andrew R. Culver. For a few years all went well between the promoter and the stockholder. When the Brooklyn *Eagle* attacked Culver, Sage offered to help through a local politician— "I gave him *material aid* to assist in his election." Sage urged expansion of the line to take in all the popular beach areas:

Above all we should have connection with any system of rapid transit in the City of Brooklyn—we should, if possible, prevent any of which we are not a *part,* by being connected with it—Brighton Beach interests will certainly destroy ours if they can, & the new project *is* Brighton Beach substantially. . . . I am quite sure we are just now in danger of being surrounded & cut off from our base of supplies—the great currents of travel.[17]

Railroad promotion was a kind of warfare, indeed, war of all against all, for Dean Sage was given permission to invest in a new elevated project for the joint interest although in his own name since Henry Sage might have to fight the new project in the interest of the Culver line.[18]

It was with expansion in the form of consolidation that difficulties began. In 1881 the East River Bridge and Coney Island Steam Transit Company was formed by merging the Prospect Park line with a new company represented substantially by E. C. Litchfield

[16] To Dean Sage, Dec. 14, 1885, HWS.
[17] To A. R. Culver, June 10, 1880; Feb. 8, 1881, HWS.
[18] Sage to Dean Sage, Feb. 9, 1881, HWS.

and Allen C. Washington. Henry Sage and Dean Sage each subscribed for $25,000 of the stock.[19] Construction of a road which
was to be the product of the new company precipitated a battle
for control. Sage had a proposal all worked out to deal with the
financial arrangements. But Culver evidently had made arrangements of his own and suggested that Sage put his stock in the company "into a pool to be disposed of in the same way and upon the
same terms" as Washington's and Culver's stock. Sage protested
immediately that he wanted to be fully informed of all activities:
"I am a joint stockholder with you." [20] More information evidently
convinced Sage that he might trust at least a semiblind pool, for
he accepted 25,000 income bonds, 25,000 in common stock, and
50,000 first-mortgage bonds. The last he sold sometime before
1887. Between 1883 and 1887 Sage lost any control he might have
had in the policies and disposition of the road. His sole source of
information was *Poor's Manual*: "I have seen no report to stockholders—have had no notice of stockholders meeting in years."
Given his knowledge of his fellow stockholders and his conception
of business management, he assumed that Culver had been running the line "in the interest of Culver & his friends." [21] William
C. DeWitt was hired to investigate. The case dragged itself out
into the nineties. Culver sold the P.P. & C.I. road to the Long Island
Railroad, and Sage's lawyer wrote bitterly:

Culver is now among the retired aristocracy of our country. He has
attained wealth without honor and idleness without rest. Passing his
summer at our best resorts he is none-the-less, morose, troubled and as
much out of place as a wild boar in the cage of a Menagerie! Alas!
What a keeper is conscience! [22]

After a long-drawn-out suit, which finally enabled Sage's lawyers
to examine the firm's books, no evidence of fraud was discovered.
From the books it appeared that the road had been insolvent for

[19] Sage to A. R. Culver, April 12, 1881, HWS.
[20] May 13, 15, 1882, HWS.
[21] To W. C. DeWitt, April 22, 1887, HWS.
[22] W. C. DeWitt to Sage, Sept. 12, 1895, HWS.

years before its sale and had been "kept in operation . . . only through the self-sacrifice of Culver and Washington in not drawing their salaries, interest and rents." There was no means of judging whether Sage's contention that Culver had been milking the line was correct. In 1896 DeWitt closed the case by selling the $50,000 of stocks and bonds owned by the Sages for $16,000.[23]

These discouraging ventures did not permanently dampen Sage's investing spirit, nor did they keep him from investing in similar enterprises, enterprises which entailed considerable of the midwife's talent. The lure of extraordinary profit was compelling. In 1881 Sage became involved in the affairs of the Tehuantepec Interocean Railroad Company. He was dubious of the enterprise from the beginning, his fears ranging from the character of the Mexican people—"Fuertes says the people there are about worthless"[24]—to the competition "Lesseps' Canal" would provide. But Dean Sage was insistent, and A. S. Barnes and George S. Coe, prominent New York businessmen, were associated with the project. Sage ultimately took 80,000 of the bonds of the road, along with which went $\frac{1}{60}$ of the "parts" or stock control of the organization.[25] He immediately began to regret the decision and, although Dean Sage was made a director, distrusted the managers of the project, and began again on a familiar tack, to gain control of the road for the debt holders, including himself and Barnes. His object was not to realize the project but to insure what had already been invested. To do this Sage relied on the promise of the Mexican government either to subsidize the road or to buy it upon the completion of forty miles by the company. In 1888 he received the last of his share of the payments made by the Mexican government, which had agreed to purchase the bonds of the road. Sage collected in all $63,012.27 on his $80,000 investment. His loss may have been smaller than these figures indicate since it is possible he

[23] *Ibid.,* March 2, 1896; telegram, March 7. Since Sage had paid only $12,500 for these securities, the "loss" is somewhat overstated.

[24] Sage to Dean Sage, Feb. 12, 1881, HWS.

[25] *Ibid.,* Nov. 25, 1881; Feb. 18, 1882.

did not pay par for the bonds. Nevertheless for a period of six to seven years this considerable sum carried no interest for its owner.

The unsuccessful outcome of these investments was not typical of Sage's investments as a whole. The incidents themselves are significant because they describe the investing scene as Sage saw it, risky, chaotic, unscrupulous. Sage accepted the terms of investment with some protest, but accepted them nonetheless. He resented loss of effective control over his funds but he was attracted by high profits. He tended to rely on the reputation and his own estimate of men almost as much as he did on the assets of the project in which he proposed to invest. Moreover, it was not so much absolute losses as losses in terms of extraordinary expectations that seem to have been sustained.

Through the seventies Sage seems to have kept $20,000 to $25,000 in the call loan market, and about $25,000 in government bonds. Railroad stocks and bonds, the most conspicuous type of security in the market, began to figure in the Sage portfolio at this time. In the late seventies Sage began to use the services of Wood and Davis, New York brokers, and, to a limited extent, to play the market. In 1879, for example, Sage thought he recognized the tail end of a stock market boom and began to sell with the idea:

In any pressure which may occur on very short notice speculative stocks will tumble *fast*—& they will drag good ones a considerable way—If we can use cash on call at near the price these securities are paying now I think the chances are that we can invest in the same securities, if we want to, at much lower prices.[26]

Presumably the proceeds of the sales went temporarily into the call loan market, which continued into the early eighties as an attractive alternative to the securities market.

The limited investments of the seventies became more and more extensive with each year after 1880. Lumber and timber sales in the eighties provided funds more rapidly than they could be reinvested in timberlands. In 1880 Sage paid more than $80,000 for

[26] *Ibid.*, Oct. 23, 1879.

securities. In February 1881 Sage drew up an inventory of some of his productive securities. These were largely railroad securities and included United New Jersey; New York Central; Lake Shore; Chicago, Burlington, and Quincy; Kansas Pacific; and Harlem. Sage estimated their current value at $412,020 and his income from them as $23,980 or "5½% on present value." At the same time Sage's portfolio contained enough "unavailable" or "speculative" securities to make him uneasy. Better than any railroad securities, he advised his son, would be "choice lots of lumber": "Within 4 months they will pay us 10% profit." [27]

Nevertheless, in April of 1881 Sage's securities portfolio was inventoried at $615,099, and in the succeeding sixteen years, 1881–1897, the Sages bought approximately six million dollars of securities (see Table 2). Railroad stocks and bonds accounted for more than four millions, while township and county bonds, industrials and utilities, government bonds, and bank stock made up the remainder of the list (see Table 3). To these investments were added almost $400,000 in western mortgages over the years 1883–1896. With the major exception of 1889, when heavy investments in southern lands were being made, these years of investment activity coincided with a period of relatively small timberland purchases by the Sages. On the other hand during the eighties and nineties high profits accrued to the Sages from sales of stumpage and timberlands in Michigan and Wisconsin. Moreover, until the mill was closed in 1892, sales of manufactured lumber brought considerable income to the Sages. A great part of the profits from lumber and timber sales, then, was being channeled into securities and mortgage investments.

Alternatives to this kind of investment were certainly possible. The Sages might continue and expand the manufacturing end of the business, and the elder Sage continually urged this course upon his sons; or they might increase even more their holdings of timberlands. To the latter alternative there was at least one major objection. Until they were sold, timberlands, as they were ad-

[27] *Ibid.*, Feb. 19, July 29, 1881.

Table 2. Purchases and sales of securities 1881–1897

Year	Recorded purchases of securities at cost to Sage *	Recorded sales
1881	$151,600	
1882	34,100	$ 20,000
1883	361,138	
1884	224,660	19,600
1885	192,400	17,500
1886	119,590	
1887	520,910	37,950
1888	646,629	357,568
1889	569,300	21,600
1890	477,632	177,152
1891	235,454	216,800
1892	510,290	145,548
1893	427,188	86,330
1894	152,548	41,680
1895	212,333	42,310
1896	256,079 †	122,540
1897	380,631 ‡	554,433
Totals	$5,472,482	$1,861,011
Inventory, April 1881	615,099 §	
Total purchases	$6,087,581	
Minus sales	—1,861,011	
Inventory, 1897	$4,226,570	

* These do not include more than $339,000 in bonds, par value, the cost of which was given, and at least 690 shares of stock whose cost was not given. Figures have been culled from the correspondence over these years. Undoubtedly some transactions escaped notice.

† This includes $32,000 in shares in names of Sage's grandchildren.

‡ This includes $52,000 in bonds in names of Sage's grandchildren and $8,182 in shares in names of Sage's grandchildren and Mrs. Dean Sage.

§ H. W. Sage and Co. Day Book, April 1, 1881, pp. 770 ff., HWS. There is an overstatement of approximately $25,000 in the 1881 figure, for securities purchased in the first four months of 1881 and thus included in the inventory.

Table 3. Recorded purchases at cost to Sage *

Year	Railroad bonds	Railroad stocks	County & township bonds	Indus- trials & utilities	Bank stock	Govern- ment se- curities
Inven- tory 1881	$280,222	$209,672		$107,905	$17,300	
1881	105,200					$46,600
1882		34,100				
1883	289,000	51,628	$20,000			
1884	111,410	53,250	10,000	10,000	40,000	
1885	126,450	46,300		19,650		
1886	105,180		14,410			
1887	54,315	231,775	233,420	1,400		
1888	359,125	174,804	28,500	34,200		
1889	437,950	47,350	52,000	17,000	15,000	
1890	287,340	81,080		93,400	14,812	
1891	137,954		87,500	10,000		
1892	235,274	112,000	154,856	8,160		
1893	152,915	149,850	75,053	49,370		
1894	132,928	12,900	6,720			
1895	150,200	36,100	10,163		15,000	
1896	60,100	21,389		111,090		50,000
1897	136,080	123,691		120,860		
Totals	$3,161,643	$1,385,889	$692,622	$583,035	$102,112	$96,600

* The figures have been obtained from the Sage correspondence during these years.

ministered by the Sages, provided no income but rather represented a continuous drain for taxes and upkeep. The administration of more than half a million acres—the approximate size of the Sage landholdings in 1895—might also create serious problems for necessarily absentee landlords. More than profit-and-loss considerations came into play when the Sages thought about continuing as manufacturers. Sage's sons were obviously reluctant to commit themselves or their sons to the routine and the risks of a manufacturer. Undoubtedly the initial investment in plant and equipment would be higher and profits less spectacular than when Henry Sage had begun his milling career in Michigan. Tied to these factors was the apparent lack of desire to meet the challenge of manufacturing under these changed industrial conditions and a lack of interest in a business requiring constant attendance.

Whether investment in securities was in fact "safer" and more profitable than manufacturing for the Sages, it is difficult to determine. It is clear that in the long run the Sages not only collected a substantial income but indeed "broke even" on their investments, which was no mean feat given the chaotic state of the securities market. At the time of Henry Sage's death in 1897, H. W. Sage and Co. had accumulated securities inventoried at more than four million dollars. In that year the net value of the securities inventory appreciated slightly. In seven of the fifteen years from 1883 to 1897, however, the net value of the inventory was depreciated, in years like 1885 and 1894 severely—it appeared to the Sages, disastrously. In the course of these years the Sages sustained losses of almost one and a half millions (see Table 4). Although appreciation of their total inventory compensated for such losses, it was, nevertheless, immediate losses, whether absolute or in terms of expectation, that seem to have dominated the Sages' state of mind as investors. Their correspondence mentions continually railroad reorganizations, panics, outright fraud, and the collapse of uncertain enterprises, in all of which they saw themselves as victims.

Henry Sage habitually distinguished between a "speculation" and an "investment." The bases for this distinction were not always clear, but in a general way they were the difference between an enterprise already established and one in process or in the proposition stage. Whether or not an enterprise might be termed speculative depended also on who were its controlling figures, men who might be presumed to have a sincere interest in the prosperity of the enterprise or those whose reputations indicated that they would be interested only in "milking" the organization. Often enough to make him apprehensive Sage discovered that an "investment" had become a "speculation." Not that Sage steered clear of speculative propositions. In the seventies and early eighties he was attracted to several ventures which by his own definition were speculative. By 1885, very roughly, there was a noticeable slackening of interest in this type of investment, however. The year before Sage calculated the firm's losses "in business we don't understand, and in speculative securities" as $407,500. These included $30,000

Table 4. Annual inventory value *

Year April 1	Inventory of 1881 + annual purchases — annual sales	Gain in value	Loss in value	Net value of inventory
1883	$780,799	$8,500	$69,000	$720,299
1884	1,081,437	28,877	92,660	1,017,654
1885	1,222,714	11,491	213,611	997,612
1886	1,172,512	182,940	22,750	1,332,702
1887	1,452,292	96,485	22,211	1,526,566
1888	2,009,526	102,832	94,059	2,018,299
1889	2,307,360	135,582	45,367	2,397,575
1890	2,945,275	106,272	62,025	2,989,529
1891	3,290,002	152,915	0	3,442,917
1892	3,461,571	119,006	99,572	3,481,005
1893	3,845,747	34,435	91,017	3,789,165
1894	4,130,023	48,468	217,754	3,960,737
1895	4,071,605	68,865	112,971	4,027,499
1896	4,197,522	120,000	167,233	4,150,289
1897	4,283,828	335,681	105,500	4,514,009
Totals		$1,552,349	$1,415,760	

* The inventory of 1881 is used as the base figure to which purchases are added and from which sales are subtracted annually. The figures for gain and loss in value of inventory are from H. W. Sage and Co. Day Book, *passim,* HWS.

in Wall Street notes, $50,000 in a cement company, $70,000 in Tehuantepec, $130,000 in miscellaneous securities which had depreciated since the Sages' purchase, $50,000 in the Ithaca Organ Company, $7,500 in the Oregon & Transcontinental, and $70,000 in the notes of Beecher and Silliman, the men to whom the Canadian mill had been sold. Despite the fact that some of these losses were at least partially recouped, it was an impressive warning. Sage dutifully checked the items on the list for which he was especially responsible, leaving to Dean Sage, by inference, the responsibility for the Tehuantepec, Oregon & Transcontinental, and the miscellaneous securities failures. The analysis of the failures is interesting, because it throws the burden squarely upon the Sages themselves. The cement and organ companies were "business we could not attend to ourselves and did not understand"; Tehuantepec, Oregon & Transcontinental, and the call loan notes were "pure speculation," while the loans to Beecher and Silliman resulted from "a mixture of sentiment and poor judgment." [28] There is no charge of fraud, of duplicity, of lack of faith among businessmen. These were constants in the securities market as Sage knew it, but ranting against them was reserved for the moment when the loss was recognized. After the initial exasperation and anger, Sage accepted the terms of investing. Relationships between stockholders and managers were undefined; self-interest was undiluted by personal attachment to the fate of the enterprise itself; the interest of minority stockholders was rarely consulted, that of the public never.

In 1885, when negotiations were underway for the sale of the Beech Creek, Clearfield, and Southwestern Railroad Co., an enterprise to which the Sages had subscribed $50,000, Dean Sage became enraged. He contended that the sale profited only the Vanderbilts, chief stockholders of the road. Dean charged Charles Langdon and General Magee, through whom the Sages had come to make their investment, with favoring the Vanderbilt scheme, which ignored the interests of the minority stockholders, and even went so far as to suggest that Magee had made large and presumably unwarranted profits out of the construction of the road. Victorian sensibilities were outraged and, as often was the case, answer was made by referring to the letter of the law:

The Messrs Vanderbilt agreed to sell their interest . . . and I assume that they had as much right to do it as your son has to sell his lum-

[28] *Ibid.*, Feb. 1, 1884.

ber. . . . We acted as an intermediary party in presenting the proposition of the Penna people to the parties in interest.

The elder Sage acted as mediator, acknowledging the "legal right" of the Vanderbilts to sell but protesting that "the bases upon which we subscribed has not been respected." Sage's advice to his son indicated a mellow appreciation of power relationships in business, more characteristic than his occasional tempers and expressing more profoundly his attitude about the world he worked in.

Your estimate of Magee is about right—Langdon you estimate too low —though it is not at all strange that both pay some deference to the Vanderbilts from whom they have received liberal treatment heretofore, and with whom they now have, and expect to have mutual business relations. In judging of men *always* some forbearance must be used (when they seem in conflict with our interests) in consideration of their established relations to others.[29]

Sage recognized, without cynicism, that the principle of self-interest regulated his world, a world which he did not after all desire to see radically altered.

Typically Sage had been interested in the Beech Creek securities by a man he considered a neighbor if not a friend, Charles Langdon of Elmira, whose reputation as a businessman Sage respected. Sage was aware from the beginning that "the small holders will be covered by Vanderbilts many times deep!" but a personal interview with Langdon reassured him. The Beech Creek was to be a coal line with an affiliate company, the Clearfield Bituminous Coal Company, headed by Langdon; the subscriber to one enterprise was automatically a member of the second and received securities in both. By Sage's own definition this was something of a "speculation" but it had seemed also a proposition for "a manly, productive business." [30] Undoubtedly Langdon had assured Sage that he would sit down at the first table to a large share of pie. In

[29] G. J. Magee to Sage, Nov. 9; Sage to Magee, Nov. 10, to Dean Sage, Nov. 14, 1885, HWS.
[30] Sage to C. J. Langdon, April 11, 1883; May 4, 1886, HWS.

addition to $50,000 first-mortgage bonds in the railroad enterprise Sage received for his $50,000 subscription an equal amount of stock in the road as well as stock in the coal company. The subsequent lease of the road separated the road from the coal mines, thus reducing their value, and began a series of reorganizations of both enterprises in the process of which the Sage holdings were gradually devalued. In 1889 the Vanderbilts offered to buy the stock of the Beech Creek Road at 40 per cent and 90 per cent of par, and Langdon urged, "That is all that the stock is worth, so long as the Central RR control it and stand in the way of further extension of the line." [31] When in 1891 the Sages sold the Beech Creek stock and their common stock in the coal company, Sage commented briefly, "We have doubtless made another considerable contribution to the Vanderbilts." [32] Later the coal company underwent reorganization, and the Sage interest was reduced to less than half, their $10,000 in 5 per cent bonds exchanged for $5,000 in 4 per cent bonds, guaranteed by the Beech Creek Road.[33] At about this time Sage requested information about the Beech Creek Road from Langdon, who replied, "I have nothing now whatever to do with the Co—except that to please Mr. Vanderbilt, I consented to remain on the Board, but I am simply a figure head used to make up a quorum." So much for the responsibility of the promoter. At a later date Langdon indirectly acknowledged some concern by arguing with Sage that the original investment had shown profit.[34] Presumably whatever the Sages had made on their Clearfield securities and on the stock of the Beech Creek was considered by Langdon an "extra" dividend while the Beech Creek bonds, which the Sages valued at 92 per cent of par in 1891, represented the "normal" expectation from their investment. On the other hand the Sages anticipated, when they joined the enterprise, realizing on the whole of the securities they were offered. The

[31] To H. W. Sage and Co., June 17, HWS.
[32] To Dean Sage, Jan. 31, HWS.
[33] Sage to M. E. Olmsted, April 23, 1891, HWS.
[34] C. J. Langdon to Sage, Oct. 25, 1891; Nov. 2, 1892, HWS.

difference between expectation and realization accounts for Dean Sage's sense of outrage as well as for his father's milder resentment of the situation. This type of situation continually arose during the Sages' investing career. The crux was not absolute losses but losses in terms of what had been expected. It formed the picture father and son shared of the business scene; individualistic or selfish, dishonorable or fraudulent were the terms both men applied depending upon the temper of the moment, though the father was generally less choleric perhaps because he had made his own successful way.

The Detroit, Mackinac, and Marquette Railroad was still another venture that disappointed the Sages. Again it was not a matter of absolute loss but of failure to measure up to their expectations of gain. The complaint was that "we have not been anywhere on the inside—have had no benefit of bond issues & construction Co⁵—nothing to do with management." [35] As with the Beech Creek investment Sage was confident that he was to "be at the first table & on a basis sure to be right" when he agreed to invest in the proposed road. Sage relied particularly on the land grant of the road to see the enterprise carried through and the original subscribers profitably rewarded. He paid $70,460 for securities carrying a par value of $207,950,[36] on which he confidently expected to realize. By his estimate and presumably that of the promoters the road could easily be built with the funds already paid in, leaving the land grant and the profits of the road when completed to pay the subscribers handsomely.

In 1884 the D.M. & M. defaulted; its managers offered no explanation to the bondholders, and Sage suspected that the land grant was "so tied up that it will be difficult to untie it." In 1886 a scaling down of the debt of the road and consolidation with the Duluth, South Shore, and Atlantic Syndicate were proposed. Sage not only protested on the score of being kept ignorant of the business transactions of the road but also, after reviewing what little he had been told, suggested fraud: "The question will come to my

[35] Sage to Dean Sage, June 6, 1889, HWS.   [36] *Ibid.,* June 8, 1881.

mind where has the money gone?"[37] The sale to the D. S.S. & A. was completed; Sage accepted in place of $45,000 first-mortgage bonds $30,000 of the D. S.S. & A.; $29,000 of the old income bonds were exchanged for an equal amount of preferred stock in the new organization; $46,150 of common stock in the old were replaced by $55,440 in common stock; and a bonus of $45,000 in preferred stock was also received, presumably to make up for the loss in mortgage bonds.[38] Although this appeared, superficially, an equitable transfer, Sage's disappointment was keen. Not only were the bonds scaled down but $29,000 of them had been replaced by stock, and railroad stock, Sage had cause to believe, was worth only what the road's managers cared to make it worth. From the new management he was even further divorced than he had been under the old arrangements. Fear of these managers led the Sages to sell the land-grant bonds, although Henry Sage felt this move would "prove one of the greatest mistakes we have made although it lets us out whole on the original investment."[39] From complete confidence that they were getting in on the ground floor, investing in a railroad project at the best possible moment, when the profits of construction were to be divided, and with the best possible security, a land grant in the rich Marquette and Menominee iron ranges, the Sages were reduced to complete skepticism. They had been kept in the dark as to expenditures and receipts; they feared fraud; their wishes had not been respected with regard to the sale of the road and exchange of securities; their expectations of profit had been disappointed. When their protests as members of the "original syndicate" went unheeded, the only recourse was to resolve once more "to keep our capital out of new enterprises when we are outside of their management."[40]

Sage discovered again and again that the voice of an investor went unheard during the manipulations of the great railroad

[37] E. F. Drake to Sage, Oct. 31, 1884; Sage to Drake, Nov. 4, 1884; May 11, 1885; to J. McMillen, Oct. 6, 1886, HWS.

[38] W. H. Sage to Central Trust Co., Nov. 19, 1886, HWS.

[39] Sage to Dean Sage, May 5, 1887, HWS.   [40] Ibid., June 6, 1889.

magnates. During the West Shore–New York Central maneuverings Sage appealed in vain to both parties for information. To the chairman of the West Shore reorganization committee he wrote, "We dislike to pledge ourselves to act with any others in this matter without more knowledge than we have of their definite purposes." Taylor's reply was, however, "either very cautious or insincere," and Sage applied to Vanderbilt for information. "We own near ¾ million of 'Vanderbilt' securities and desire to act in line with them unless there is sound reason why we should not." [41] Ultimately Sage deposited his $60,000 New York West Shore and Buffalo bonds with Drexel Morgan to be used in the reorganization proposal, but more because he was resigned than because he had been enlightened. Sage was caught once more in the Nickel Plate–Vanderbilt conflict. Controlling $170,000 of Nickel Plate bonds of his own and $50,000 of Cornell University, he toyed with the idea of acting independently of a proposed bondholders' committee. He had "no faith in Vanderbilts good faith to Friends or Enemies," but expected that they would not allow the proposed bondholders' committee to wrest control of the road from them. He was right, but neither did the Vanderbilts propose to settle with the Nickel Plate debt holders on a par basis. Ultimately Sage was willing to accept, under protest, a "villanous" compromise, "robbery" by "the Lake Shore People." [42]

Accurate information concerning railroad securities whether new or old was difficult to obtain. Typical were these complaints: "I have been trying to look up UP affairs—but they are such a wilderness of Roads, stocks, Bonds that it would be a life work to understand them." And again, "I have tried to learn from *Poor* the exact condition of the Lext Av extension . . . ie—the length of road, the amount of Bond &¢ and the conditions surrounding it — But I can get no clear idea of it." [43] Although Sage was in his

[41] To F. Taylor, June 29; to C. Vanderbilt, July 1, 1885, HWS.

[42] Sage to H. Sanger, Oct. 15, 1885; to Wood, Heustis and Co., Dec. 8, 1885; to Dean Sage, Feb. 25, 1887, HWS.

[43] Sage to Dean Sage, Feb. 24, 1894; Jan. 18, 1895, HWS.

eighties by this time, he was far from senile; it was not his fault that he could not follow railroad finance.

Despite these persistent complaints—and the correspondence was bound to reflect losses and fear of loss more than safe investments—the greater part of Sage's railroad investments did earn a steady income throughout the eighties and nineties. The underlying causes of the uncertainty and pessimism of the Sages as investors in railroad securities were of course the overcapitalization, the wasteful construction, the reckless and fraudulent manipulation of railroads. As early as 1888 one observer of the financial scene, Henry Clews, had pointed out a tendency of railroad bond premiums to fall to 4 and 4½ per cent.[44] This was a result of competition between new roads and older, more wastefully organized ones. The "water" was being "squeezed out" of railroad investments generally to the disadvantage of the bondholders. Successive reorganizations after foreclosure or upon the threat of foreclosure forced bondholders to accept a scaling down of debts.[45] The bankruptcies of 1893 accentuated the trend. Occasionally Sage could be philosophical about losses: "Possibly when we become reconciled to the *inevitable*, 3 to 4 perc on money, our future verdict will be, 'It has proved to be wise.' "[46]

But a philosophical temper was difficult to maintain as his investment portfolio was being depreciated. The results of the panic brought to a head if they did not resolve the conflicting purposes of Henry W. and Dean Sage. The father had consistently favored investment in "our own projects, organized & carried out by ourselves & wholly in our own control." The panic of '93 seemed to confirm his opinion of securities investment. It was not only a loss in monetary terms that they had suffered, Sage contended, but as well a loss of "nerve, fibre, force, skill, capacity" in the process of "getting *all we have* into securities the value of which depends on

[44] Henry Clews, *Twenty-Eight Years in Wall Street* (New York, 1888), pp. 476 ff.

[45] William Z. Ripley, *Railroads: Finance & Organization* (New York, 1915), p. 108.

[46] Sage to Dominick and Dickerman, Sept. 13, 1894, HWS.

the wisdom & management of men we dont know." Sage feared particularly for the young men of the family. These men lacked "the best of all teachers—necessity." [47] Like many another self-made and long-lived man, he had so long and so well dominated the family fortunes that his grandsons and indeed even his sons would probably find it difficult under any circumstances to prove their competence conclusively. The decision not to engage in manufacturing after the Michigan mill was closed was probably the only major policy decision which was carried through against Henry Sage's wishes. Its results seemed to him in 1894 and 1895 disastrous, and brought almost to the surface a sneaking suspicion that his easy-circumstanced sons and grandsons were not as "manly" as he had been.

Indeed one of the few times in their long years of business association that Sage lost his temper bitterly and expressively with his older son occurred in 1895 when Dean forbade further "investments in Mortgages in Western States—while looking with favor upon automaton Weighing machine—and any other security offered us by operators who press their sale." Sage continued angrily: "I have yet to learn that it is or *ever has been* your habit to personally *see* and carefully investigate the securities you buy. . . . Our *largest* losses have been those taken because some one has commended them." While there would be some losses on western mortgages, Sage contended emphatically that these were "not subject to RR reconstruction." [48] Sage regretted his strong language almost immediately and within a few days apologized to Dean. Nevertheless the accusation had been made that if Dean were not lazy or uninterested he was at least gullible. Sage estimated a loss of $154,000 on seven investments alone. Most of these had been purchased on the advice of W. H. Male, president of the Atlantic Trust Company, of which Dean Sage was a director. When the panic stripped these securities of value and reduced as well the value of the stock of the Atlantic Trust Company, Dean

[47] To Dean Sage, Aug. 10, Nov. 21, 1889; Oct. 26, 1894, HWS.
[48] *Ibid.*, Jan. 5, 1895.

Sage characteristically turned on Male, accused him of bad faith, resigned from the board of the Trust Company and prepared to withdraw the Sage accounts and sell the Sage stock in the company. Henry Sage tried to restrain Dean's rashness. He sought more information from his easily moved son. What had led to Dean's resignation? Was it wise to sell the stock at this low point? How much did Dean *really* know about the value of the company's assets? Some months later Sage again urged:

We can learn about *value* of the stock more than we now know— They have some of our securities in charge. . . . They have also a lot of uncollected coupons—If we finally decide to sell our stock & move let all be cleared up before we do it—*Then* I think it not advisable to sell at auction before offering it to inside parties—Let us leave them in a friendly way. . . . The men there—have some good qualities— Male even—and its not certain that he is wholly unworthy of confidence.

Then, with some show of irritation, Sage turned the argument on his son by referring to "the apparently unswerving faith that his codirectors have had in him [Male], and their neglect to use their own judgement instead of accepting his." [49]

The Sages' experience with industrial securities duplicated their experience with railroad investments. The largest number of these investments were made in utilities: gas, water, and electric companies. Smaller sums were invested in enterprises like the American Automaton Weighing Machine Co. and the Celluloid Manufacturing Company. The Sages dabbled also in Western Union and Adams Express Company securities, relying occasionally on "inside" information from Alonzo B. Cornell on the prospects of Western Union. In 1888 the Sages made their first investment in Standard Oil stock and by 1893 they held 500 shares at a cost of approximately $83,600. This proved up to the time of Henry Sage's death one of their most profitable investments paying regularly a 12 per cent dividend in addition to an extra dividend of

[49] *Ibid.*, April 29, Oct. 16, 1893.

5 to 10 per cent during the year. In 1896 the stock was quoted at
250; the highest price Sage had paid was 171, the lowest, 157⅝
Characteristically, however, the Sages found themselves "in the
dark as to the cause for the big rise in price" and were tempted to
sell.[50] In the late nineties the Sages began to invest in other industrial securities, the Pullman Railroad Car Company, the American Tobacco Company, the American Sugar Refining Company.
Again a rise in the price of these stocks proved just as disconcerting
as a drop in value. When the Sages applied for information from
their brokers, W. B. Dickerman replied: "Of course, it is difficult
to give an opinion upon the stock of a Company whose books are
not open to the public, and whose statements never appear. We
believe, however, that Sugar will continue to pay dividends as
heretofore." [51] The basis for investment was still misty not to say
mystic.

Many of the industrial securities which Sage felt had shown
losses had been taken on the advice of W. H. Male. When reorganizations and devaluations began to be the order of the day,
Sage was sure that he and his son were once more on the outside
looking in and were less well treated in the process than inside
rings. Nevertheless he maintained, "The *wonder* is that we (with
some right to use our own Judgment) fell such easy victims to
his." [52] Sage had become wary not only of reorganizations but also
of mergers of industrial concerns; when the American Automaton
Weighing Machine Co., which had paid regular dividends since
the Sages had acquired shares in it, proposed to take over the lease
of the National Automatic Machine Company he sold his stock.
Perhaps the fact that W. H. Male was interested in the new organization influenced Sage. There was also Sage's belief that such con-
solidations resulted in the divorce of management and ownership,
were indeed a "conspiracy against legitimate management" aiming

[50] W. H. Sage to Dominick and Dickerman, Feb. 11, 1896, HWS.

[51] June 30, 1896, HWS. W. B. Dickerman was president of the New York
Stock Exchange, 1890–1891.

[52] To Dean Sage, Feb. 21, 23, 1893, HWS.

at monopoly profits for the promoters and inevitably tending toward failure. This was not a principle which Sage held to consistently. In 1890–1891, for example, he continued his interest in the Celluloid Manufacturing Company after its consolidation with similar organizations. In fact it would be difficult to point to any principle which Sage abided by in the business of investing. The investing scene was too chaotic, the basis of upturns and downturns in the fortunes of individual securities too obscure and, as he viewed it, too dependent on personal and corporate manipulation for him to have much faith in himself as an investor. The bases of value in securities investments—land grants, plant capacity, market opportunities—seemed to disintegrate before his eyes.

Very rarely he did show enthusiasm for an investing project. In 1893 the Niagara Falls Paper Company was organized by three young men whom he knew personally. The Sages invested in it very cautiously. Moreover Sage advised Dean not to become one of its directors, "at any rate not before it has capital enough to be on a safe basis—& dont need you to bolster its credit—*That* is what you are wanted for now." The more profound basis for hesitation Sage had noted some weeks earlier:

Were I 60 years younger I should not fear to enter upon the whole of it—But I am not—and I dont see that we now have in the Family men with trained experience enough—with vigor and force enough—and *necessity enough,* (the greatest lack of all) to warrant the risks of the enterprise.[53]

But Sage continued his interest in the project, advising the young men of the firm on how to estimate costs, urging caution on them, and seeing in the enterprise a parallel with his own milling experiences. Clearly this was the type of enterprise he found most "worthy" and expected most profit from. Again and again in the last two decades of his life he attempted to introduce his sons and grandsons into this sphere, and "were he 60 years younger, or 50,"

[53] *Ibid.,* Sept. 23 and 6.

he would have undoubtedly undertaken again something of this sort. In this area he felt himself competent.

As an investor he doubted himself:

I have spent all the time I could for two days past trying to find safe & satisfactory investments—& dont succeed yet—Some outside things that seem good pay 6—but we have been so beaten in investments the past few years that I have less confidence in my own judgement than I once had—Money in the concrete is dangerous stuff to handle.[54]

The 1893 collapse made clear Sage's concern for his investments. A significant portion of them were taken on the personal recommendation of individuals: friends, bankers, or brokers. The character of these men might be sound but their judgment was not always infallible. Statistics, particularly for railroad investments, were plentiful, but their basis was doubtful. Neither membership in an "original syndicate" nor representation on a board of directors was a guarantee of accurate or "inside" information. Undoubtedly much that troubled Sage on the investment scene was beyond his control. Investing was a peculiarly risky business in an era that recognized few legal restrictions. Sage attributed much of the evil to the divorce of ownership and management: "See . . . the recent explosions in Industrials—Most of these—let alone to be managed by original owners would *pay*—but take away the management by their builders, remit it to speculative boards of directors—and the tendencies inevitable will be to failure." [55] He recognized, as we have seen, the "inevitable" decline in interest rates in the last half of the century. He recognized also the widespread fraud in investment procedures. "Rings" and *"conspiracies against legitimate business management"* were constants of the business scene. But it is significant that Sage rarely blamed the state of the market or other relatively impersonal forces for his losses. Ultimately he blamed the Sages; when the Louisville, St. Louis & Texas road began to forecast losses and urged reorganization, Sage noted this as "another case where we were 'manipulated' to give up abundant security for a loan and take Bonds—But

[54] *Ibid.*, Feb. 18, 1892.   [55] *Ibid.*, May 6, 1893.

that fault was our own—we elected—poor security for good." [56]

Never did Sage contemplate government regulation of business as a partial solution. Even so staunch a defender of the honor of Wall Street as Henry Clews was led to suggest limited government supervision of railroads,[57] but never Sage, though again and again he found himself without recourse and without the chance so much as to investigate when he suspected fraud. The politics of the postwar era would probably not have inspired confidence in government regulation in a more progressive mind, and Sage was not—even in business—cast in a progressive mold. He never fully understood the possibilities of the corporation or accepted the idea of a responsible division of management functions. Unified ownership and management had become for Sage more than a business principle; as a moral principle it was linked with the virtues of "manliness" and industry. Given this peculiar bias, the corporation itself as well as its abuses became "wicked." Undoubt-edly there was much in the objective scene to reinforce this view, but the subjective elements cannot be dismissed. These explain not so much Sage's failures as an investor—and we have already said that in the long run his losses were more than made up—but his fears of failure, his deeply based insecurity with regard to investments. Long used to controlling his own affairs completely, Sage resented loss of effective control in corporate enterprises. Although the Sages relied on personal recommendations in securi ties investment, they ran the gamut from trust, that occasionally appeared to be gullibility, to universal suspicion, depending upon the market reports. True of Henry Sage, this attitude was aggravated in Dean. Neither man worked well with others, but Dean lost his temper, made accusations of fraud against Victorian businessmen, and lost whatever influence he might have had. (Both the Sage sons lost their heads in '93; their father, more restrained, urged them against selling all their railroad stocks at the low point

[56] *Ibid.,* Dec. 8.

[57] Clews, *op. cit.,* p. 251. Henry Clews was a prominent investment banker whose views on finance and financiers were publicized not only in his books but as well in a weekly circular distributed by his firm.

of the market.) Equally resentful of investment losses, equally suspicious of fraud, Sage rarely voiced his suspicions outside the family circle. Alternating between anticipation of high profits and disillusionment, the Sages saw themselves fairly consistently being pushed away from the "first table." Their explanation was personal, whether they blamed others or themselves.

Since Sage's first alternative to investment in railroad and industrial securities was decisively rejected by his sons, he urged that they invest in another type of security, in western farm mortgages. "Farms on which owners live," he felt, were safe. "The security in such loans remains if wisely placed—and they are much safer & pay better than corporate investments which depend on corporate management." [58] As early as 1883 Sage had begun investing in western mortgages through the Kansas Loan and Trust Co. of Topeka, Kansas. In 1887 alone he placed about $130,000 in such loans. Up until 1888 and 1889 the prevailing interest rate on Sage's Kansas loans was 7 per cent. However, as this investment area grew more settled and funds more plentiful, there was a tendency toward a 6 per cent rate. Sage was reluctant to submit to the decline in rates and occasionally was able to bargain with the loan companies to buy 6 per cent mortgages at 97 and 98. But by 1890, 6 per cent at par was the best that could be obtained on Kansas mortgages, and shortly thereafter 6½ per cent gave way to 6 per cent in Nebraska. Typically Sage was a latecomer to the western mortgage field. In the sixties, when Kansas mortgages were bringing 12 per cent,[59] for example, Sage was making his disastrous investments in Brooklyn real estate. In the seventies, when 10 to 12 per cent might have been obtained, Sage was dabbling to little profit in elevated roads. He did not, then, profit from the period of highest interest rates. When he did start to invest in mortgages, Sage was looking for a "safe" investment in reaction from his speculative disappointments, and even a 6 per cent rate of return seemed attractive. These loans were above all made on property the value of which Sage presumably knew, and not on the good

[58] To Dean Sage, Dec. 21, 1893, HWS.
[59] Allan Bogue, *Money at Interest* (Ithaca, N.Y., 1955), p. 47.

faith and judgment of men. This was at any rate the premise on which Sage termed western mortgages "safe."

Sage was not quite as safe as he thought. Unlike shrewder investors, he did not initially refuse loans on city property; loans on such property later accounted for the largest part of his losses on mortgage investments. Following the pattern that had been set up by Sage and others for Cornell University's investments, Sage bought his mortgages through loan and trust companies located in the Middle West. Until 1890 Sage experienced comparatively little difficulty with his investments. In that year interest payments on $46,000 in loans taken through the Kansas Loan and Trust Company were in default. These loans, representing 100 mortgages had been made to one individual, "a speculator in city and country property" who was "overloaded." By 1891 out of a total list of $221,750 in loans taken through the K.L. & T. Co., $98,000 were in arrears for interest.[60] For some time the company had evidently been paying interest and taxes on loans in arrears without informing the holders of the mortgages. The loan company then demanded not only the sum advanced but 7 per cent interest on that sum before releasing their liens on the property. Despite complaints on this score from the Sages, the practice was continued until 1894, when the Sages withdrew their business from the firm. At that time $126,250 in loans were in process of foreclosure; only $84,690 were considered "live" loans.[61] However, Sage's estimate of eventual loss was $50,000 at the most. And in 1895 Sage pointed out to his son that on Cornell University's investment of a million and a half in western mortgages "in six years our defaults on intst have not been *one percent*—Our losses nothing." [62] Indeed where Sage had abided by the rule of loans to farm owners living on their property—and these were generally small loans of $1,500 to $2,000—he did not fare badly. Of 35 of such small loans, $67,000, taken through the Stull brothers in Nebraska in the nineties only three were behind in interest payments in July 1897, while 18 out

[60] Sage to Dean Sage, Feb. 5, 1890; to G. M. Noble, Jan. 13, 1891, HWS.
[61] W. H. Sage to K.L. & T. Co., Feb. 27, HWS.
[62] To Dean Sage, Sept. 22, 1894; Jan. 5, 1895, HWS.

of 37 had been in arrears the previous summer. Ultimately only one of these loans was foreclosed, and the sale of the land paid all costs. Similar loans made in the eighties through the Central Loan and Land Company were also almost all paid in full. Of 14 loans, $30,300 taken from the Central Land and Loan Company of Emporia, Kansas, between 1884 and 1889, only one, for $5,500, was behind in interest payments in 1893. Most of the others had been paid in full by 1891. It was Sage's preference for large loans that led him into difficulty. Such loans were offered generally by owners of city property, often not yet developed, or by "overloaded" speculators. Undeveloped city properties overvalued during boom times were like wild lands bought for speculation, subject to drastic devaluation when the boom burst. On this type of investment made through the Kansas Loan and Trust Company Sage expected to suffer losses.

From 1883 to 1896 the Sages purchased at least $392,935.68 of western mortgages, approximately $23,500 of which had been paid in full before 1898: [63]

Year	Western mortgages purchased
1883	$ 7,500.00
1884	43,075.68
1885	
1886	56,300.00
1887	129,700.00
1888	74,550.00
1889	29,000.00
1890	
1891	
1892	7,500.00
1893	
1894	21,860.00
1895	19,650.00
1896	3,800.00
Total	$392,935.68

[63] These figures were compiled from the Sage correspondence.

During the probate of Henry W. Sage's estate the value of good mortgages was given as $126,751.88, the value of mortgages in arrears and in litigation as $10,241.20.[64] Presumably the discrepancy between the figure given for mortgage holdings in the probate of the estate and the sum total of mortgages taken by the Sages is accounted for by payments made on mortgages up to that time and by foreclosures. Since foreclosures provided some hope of ultimate recovery of all or a part of their investments, there was some basis for Sage's insistence that western mortgages were safer than securities. In the nineties, however, he added to this rule of thumb the qualification that such mortgages be taken on farms under cultivation by their owners, and expressed the desire that they be placed personally by one of the Sages. Such investments would prove safe if the Sages themselves managed them.

For in mortgage investment also the Sages had suffered disillusionment with their agents. Will Sage, to whom management of mortgage investments for the firm had been assigned in the same rough way that securities investment had been made Dean's province, was exasperated and angered by the handling of delinquent mortgages by the K.L. & T. Co. When the lawyers to whom the Sages entrusted the K.L. & T. Co. litigations suggested that there were not sufficient grounds to prosecute the firm, Will suspected them, too, of duplicity. Sage had again to mediate with a son.

I dont want to think they lack good faith—but rather that they try to manage affairs with KL&T Co to serve our interests best—But you may be right. . . . The fact is, it is a terrible hard time to press collections in Kansas now—There is no cash there—men cannot pay—municipalities cannot pay—and they do & will resort to all sorts of expedients to avoid being forced to pay—We are in the nip with them and must take our place in the procession—Time will make them better—and we must learn to be patient.[65]

[64] The figure given for value of good mortgages represents the aggregate of principal due less 5 per cent; 50 per cent was deducted from the face value of the mortgages in arrears and in litigation (Proceedings of the Surrogates Court in the estate of Henry W. Sage, Tompkins County Court House, Ithaca, N.Y., p. 15).

[65] To W. H. Sage, Nov. 24, 1894, HWS.

The elder Sage's patience in this instance may have been encouraged by his general faith in the value of the property he had had to foreclose. Perhaps his faith in mortgage loans was also prompted by the fact that he had been their main sponsor among the Sages.

In the effort to get away from railroad and industrial securities Sage interested himself largely in the bonds issued by western towns and counties, as well as in western mortgages. These bonds were generally issued for school improvements or railroad aid. From 1883 to 1897 the Sages bought at least $692,622 of these securities. Cornell University had purchased an even larger quantity, and the examinations undertaken in behalf of the University had proved eminently satisfactory. In 1887 Sage wrote his son: "From all the consideration we are able to give them *they are good* —Boardman has carefully examined the legislation & we all conclude that there is nothing lacking to make them sound security. . . . There has never been a default or defence." [66] Dean may have been disturbed by the large amount the firm had taken; at least $233,420 in 1887 alone had been paid for such bonds. Within a few years his alarm began to seem justified. In 1889 defaults in interest payments were suffered, and though most of these were paid up in short order they began again in 1891 with less successful results. Between 1891 and 1898 interest was defaulted on bonds amounting to $267,500. Not all of this sum represented permanent loss, although total losses did occur in some areas. From 1890 on the Sages had difficulty in collecting interest on $22,000 Leoti City, Kansas, bonds. Nor were the town's officials sympathetic. In 1892 E. C. Shelton, treasurer of Leoti City and proprietor of its Hoosier Grocery, wrote: "From the tone of your letter you must have imbibed too much of the prevailing hot weather. . . . I have enough funds to pay out on July '91 & Jan '92 coupons." To the Sages' reluctance to send their coupons to the Bank of Leoti City for payment, he replied: "I am not a mule and only want what is right—Other holders of bonds have adopted this plan and have

66 To Dean Sage, Dec. 24, 1887, HWS. Douglass Boardman was a trustee and legal adviser of Cornell University.

no kick coming." [67] In 1893, however, interest payments were once more in default. Leoti City's population had dropped from 1,000 when the railroad aid bonds were issued to 250 in 1894. "People mostly left—starved out by poor crops etc. . . . The way out I dont see." [68] In 1897 negotiations were still in process to gain a compromise plan which would permit the survivors of the city to pay some of its debt.

Kiowa County, Kansas, attempted to repudiate its bond issues, $46,000 of which Sage held, on the grounds that their issue was not constitutional. In 1896 the circuit court upheld the county, declaring unconstitutional the exceptional law which allowed Kiowa County to issue bonds before a year had elapsed after its organization. But E. O. McNair of the Bank of Warsaw, New York, through whom Sage and Cornell University had purchased these bonds, continued to press the issue, and in 1897 wrote the Sages that the order of the circuit court had been "modified" and a judgment obtained for the coupons. [69] In a similar case the Sages were unsuccessful. When Cimarron Township in Kansas repudiated its railroad aid bonds, $20,000 of which the Sages held, the courts found for the community, alleging that the bondholders must have known when they accepted the debt that the township had been organized less than a year. [70] And indeed there is some evidence that Sage did realize that the bonds were not secure. When default in interest first began to occur, Griswold and Gillette, who sold the Sages these securities, noted, "At the price you bought them, it was a gamble and a low price, and when you bought them *you* said *you were willing to gamble on them at the price.*" [71]

In one other case, *West Plains Township, Meade County, Kansas, v. Sage et al.,* the court again found for the bondholders. Here the bonds had been issued ostensibly to care for the indebtedness of the community but actually to subscribe for the building of a sugar refinery. The "mill was never completed & has since been

[67] Sept. 19, 1892, HWS.   [68] Sage to Dean Sage, Oct. 25, 1894, HWS.
[69] Oct. 29, HWS.   [70] *Sage et al. v. Fargo Township,* 10 7F 383.
[71] To H. W. Sage and Co., March 27, 1890, HWS.

torn down & moved away"; [72] the township as a result attempted repudiation. The bondholders on the other hand held, with legal justification, "As to the question whether the Township received full value for their Township bonds, is something the bondholder has nothing to do with." [73] Nevertheless the opinion of the dissenting justice in the court of appeals suit was perhaps closer to the sentiments of most Kansans in the distressed years of the nineties.

Not one of the principal cities in this circuit could sell its bonds to any dealer . . . until he had examined . . . the statutes of the state and the ordinances and records of the city relating to their issue. . . . It is therefore only dishonest and corrupt officers and disreputable dealers . . . that profit by the business. . . . The effect of the doctrine of the majority of the court in this case is to give validity to fraudulent bonds.[74]

It is interesting to note in this connection that just about two weeks *after* the Sages had taken the bonds, Griswold and Gillette, through whom they purchased, "noticed" in newspaper reports the circumstances of their issue.[75] In 1896 an attempt was made to compromise with the Sages on behalf of the township. It was argued that the indebtedness of the community would reduce its population, and that the Sages would not be able to collect despite legal decisions in their favor. The threat of repudiation, the loss of income in the preceding years, the litigations he had undertaken undoubtedly all entered into Sage's reply:

We have no doubt that the people in that country have had hard times —All people do in new countries—but nothing is so certain to make hard times perpetual as the spirit of repudiation—& disregard of all moral obligations to pay honest debts. These seasons of crop failure are doubtless at an end—or nearly so—They will raise new crops— new openings for foreign shipment via Galveston etc will give more

[72] Len Follick, County Treasurer, to Griswold and Gillette, July 30, 1891, HWS.
[73] J. A. Blair to Griswold and Gillette, Aug. 4, 1891, HWS.
[74] *West Plains Township v. Sage et al.*, G 9F 943.
[75] Griswold and Gillette to H. W. Sage and Co., Dec. 14, 1889, HWS.

value to all they raise. . . . The debt to us, extended through thirty years *can be paid* if the people *try*.[76]

"Hard times" in Kansas with its complicated history of optimism and Populism was reduced in effect by this analysis to a moral question. Despite the fact that their losses in county bonds were nowhere as great proportionately as in railroad and other securities, the Sages experienced in this investment area, also, disillusionment and uncertainty. Still, between 1892 and 1895 they paid at least $246,792 for bonds of this type, largely in Minnesota, Idaho, and Utah.

Perhaps as a result of his own lack of confidence as an investor, Sage does not seem to have played so forceful a role in the management of Cornell University's investment funds as he did in other aspects of University management. The absence of a large volume of correspondence with regard to the University's investments would indicate that he did not assume major responsibility in this area. In certain investment areas, indeed, his own portfolio seems to have been guided by the success of University investments. This is true particularly of western farm mortgages and township bonds. Occasionally an entire issue of township or county bonds was taken by the Sages and the University. In railroad and other securities there was some duplication of portfolios, and where difficulties arose Sage spoke not only in his own behalf but also as the representative of the University. In some investments the University undoubtedly followed the Sages. For the most part, however, it appears that the University's investments were handled by its treasurer, for many years E. L. Williams, and its legal adviser, Douglass Boardman. Whenever Sage did mention investments taken by the University, he almost always prefaced his remarks with a reference to the examination of the value of the investment by all three men.

By the time of Henry Sage's death it was clear that the proceeds of the lumber trade were to be channeled into investments both in timberlands and securities. H. W. Sage and Co. had become an

[76] To J. T. Herrick, Feb. 3, 1896, HWS.

accounting convenience and indeed was dissolved upon the death of Dean Sage. The determination not to invest energy—Henry W. Sage's "personal service"—in managing a manufacturing establishment was apparently not challenged by the uncertainties of securities investment. Apparently also sufficient income was derived from this source and regarded as "safe" to eliminate the factor of "necessity." The trials and tribulations of investing did not affect the wealth of the Sages so much as their sense of security; these trials and tribulations reinforced their conception of the business world as an individualistic and selfish society, a thing of rings and conspiracies. In investing they saw themselves as "outsiders" and victims of the inside rings even more persistently than in their careers as manufacturers and merchants.

Sage came to investing late. He was fifty-six in 1870, and for twenty-two years more his most intensive energies were given to land and lumber. These he knew intimately, and in the management of these aspects of his business he was the undisputed leader. Working with others had always proved difficult for him, working through others where he was not at the same time the ultimate decision maker, impossible. These aspects of temperament taken together with the objective facts of an unregulated securities market conditioned his lack of confidence in the new business arrangements. The ideal picture of business as he drew it represented an individual producer managing his own concerns to his own profit and, by a leap of faith, to the profit of society. Even when his experience belied this picture and he saw himself as a victim of unregulated and unscrupulous business management, the concept of public regulation remained alien and repugnant.

Chapter IX

Trustee of Cornell University, 1870-1897

HENRY W. SAGE expected, with some justification, that the individual's successful pursuit of wealth would be accompanied by national "elevation and refinement." [1] His own generous philanthropy was directed to this end. For more than a quarter of a century he devoted a major portion of his time and energy, and a substantial part of his fortune, to the development of Cornell University. The opening exercises of the University, highlighted by Andrew D. White's emotionally charged tribute to Ezra Cornell —at which point White himself broke down—called forth an immediate and warm response from Sage's Victorian sensibilities. His attachment to good works, his enthusiastic appreciation of a major undertaking, drew him to the University. So also did the community of friends who had already identified themselves with the University: Ezra Cornell, John McGraw, Judge Francis Finch, Josiah B. Williams. Through these connections the University became at once a familiar and personal project to Sage.

The principles which guided Cornell University's early development were in significant part those of Andrew D. White: "the idea of education based on the needs of our land and time—of equality between honorable pursuits;—and professions 'learned' and 'unlearned'—of freedom from sectarian trammels." [2] Such principles

---

[1] Waterman T. Hewett, *Cornell University: A History* (New York, 1905), I, 687.

[2] A. D. White to W. C. Russel, Dec. 26, 1873, ADW.

commanded at least superficial concurrence from Sage. Himself a manufacturer with some inkling of the momentum, the increasing complexity and increasing dependence upon science, of the industrial process, Sage could appreciate White's insistence on a modern, technical education for the "captains . . . of industry." [3] Moreover, it was difficult to resist these ideas while White clearly demonstrated his enthusiasm for the activities of the industrial magnate. After a trip to Wenona, for example, White noted in his diary: "About his [Sage's] great mills. Wonderful enterprise and noble man." [4] Nor was Sage preoccupied with narrow religious distinctions, although he was a thoroughly conventional church-goer and church supporter. Sage's religious experience, particularly at Plymouth Church under Henry Ward Beecher's tutelage, had neglected dogma and strict orthodoxy in favor of a broad, senti-mental, uncritical Christianity. White's emphasis on secular con-trol of university education was not intended, as he protested re-peatedly, to create a "godless institution"; the warfare of science and religion was not a war to the death but an attempt to free sci-entific inquiry from the taboos of orthodoxy and to subject dogma, not faith, to rational tests. Thus White rejected in disgust an "old fashioned 'hell fire' sermon," but found a sermon by Lyman Ab-bott the "best and most useful . . . I ever heard," for "dogmas were made nothing of" and Herbert Spencer, Arnold, Renan, and John Stuart Mill were cited "to lead men to Christian life." [5] On the broad bases then of "practical" and largely secular education the first President of Cornell and the future Chairman of the Board of Trustees could agree, although in the less sophisticated Chris-tianity of Sage and in White's more sophisticated understanding of the educational process lay the seeds of future conflict.

Sage brought to the analysis of White's ideas on education very little in the way of formal training. His brief instruction in botany

[3] Walter P. Rogers, *Andrew D. White and the Modern University* (Ithaca, N.Y., 1942), p. 112.

[4] Diary of Andrew D. White, Nov. 7, 1873, Cornell University Library.

[5] *Ibid.*, Dec. 5, 1875; Jan. 10, 1897.

under Dr. Church and his early interest in phrenology were, as we have seen, quickly superseded by years devoted almost exclusively to business. Business success had provided not only wealth but also prestige, had indeed accounted for his ability to play a major role at Cornell. Above all, business success had lent assurance to Sage's conviction that it was the businessman, the man of "affairs" as distinguished from the "Professional and Literary or Artistic," who was most influential in determining the course of "mankind through its commerce, manufactures, Legislation" and as well through its "Religion, Education in all its breadth." In advising his niece on the education of her son, Sage pointed out that, although formal education along technical lines, as engineering, was desirable, if a man were to enter the realm of "affairs" he would manage as well if not better without college training.

I am sure there are no scientific researches, operations, or inventions, conducted with more positive accuracy than are the plans & details of men wielding successfully the management of large affairs—No education is more valuable none produces larger or better results in this age.[6]

In the same vein Sage advised a young man who had not the money for college, "Don't get in debt for your education & come out half starved & with a mortgage on you." He urged instead that the young man earn his living—"*Go in* with all your might to build your own foundation,"—and study the while under the direction of a minister or "some wise, sensible Lawyer." [7] Advanced education was clearly something in the nature of a luxury. For those who could not afford luxuries it must be analyzed in terms of its contribution toward winning success, where success was measured largely in financial returns. Sage's was at best an unimaginative conception of the function of education.

Closely related to his idea of education as an "extra" if elegant accomplishment was Sage's occasionally undisguised contempt for

[6] To Alice Kelly, Sept. 26, 1888, HWS.
[7] To W. S. Menough, Jan. 9, 1890, HWS.

the practical abilities of the college professor, regarded as a distinct type. Sage maintained sincere and long-lived friendships with a large number of the Cornell faculty. Nevertheless a patronizing tone appeared more than once in his comments on the professorial breed. Of the installation of water power in the new law building, he wrote, "Like nearly all Professors work it has to be done again by somebody who *knows how*." Again in rejecting his sons' suggestion that they take an interest in a concern outside their field, Sage commented, "We are no more fitted to properly care for and manage it than a College Professor to manage our Michigan Lumber Trade." [8] Such casual slights could perhaps be dismissed as an unthinking resort to the cliché if it were not that their inference tended to color Sage's estimate of the value of a professor's opinion whether that opinion related to current political or economic problems or the affairs of the University. It was easier to reject *without consideration* the views of the group which Sage came to identify as "the liberal element" on the faculty, if such views could be put down to the woolliness of the professorial mind; easier also to reject the faculty's wish to participate actively in deciding University policy if the general charge of impracticality could be attached to the faculty. These considerations strengthened Sage's effective view of the faculty as hired employees of the trustees.

And yet, after these limitations of imagination and sensitivity have been detailed, there remains the impressive record of Sage's contributions to Cornell. Not only more than a million dollars in buildings and endowments and gifts stand to his credit, but also twenty-seven years of persistent and resourceful attention to the strengthening of the University. There is much of paradox but nothing of hypocrisy in Sage's sponsorship of advanced education. Undoubtedly the factor of prestige was involved. And in this connection it is interesting to note that Sage's own grandsons attended not Cornell but the older, more conservative, and tradition-conscious Yale, that some of them at least were subjected to liberal doses of Greek and Latin, that is, the old-fashioned and nonvoca-

[8] To W. H. Sage, Aug. 29, 1892; to Dean Sage, May 1, 1884, HWS.

tional curriculum. But the reason that being benefactor and Chairman of the Board of Cornell was prestige-worthy, is perhaps more to the point than the prestige itself. Sage and a significant number of his contemporaries, notably business contemporaries, cherished a sentimental and altogether fortunate regard for Education; the word was capitalized in Sage's mind. His early years in Ithaca, when lyceum and church, self-improvement and social striving were vital experiences, were undoubtedly the basis for this regard. The fostering of education was identified, almost in a religious sense, as a noble work. Sage's reaction to White's speech in 1868 sets the proper emotional background for his attachment to education and Cornell. He turned to McGraw "with tears in his eyes, and said: 'John, we are scoundrels to stand doing nothing while those men are killing themselves to establish this university.' " [9] He saw White and Cornell bound together in a Christian endeavor.

"Christian" is used advisedly since it is a key word in analyzing Sage's thinking about the University. In 1889 Sage declared:

No man can know the depth of my love and purpose in trying to lay solid foundations for this institution. . . . I have tried to save it from financial peril—have tried to make it a Christian University resting at all points upon bases which God Himself would approve.[10]

Sage's description of the foundations of a university was clearly different from White's, but on the other hand it was not that of the sectarians whose presses damned Cornell throughout the seventies. Sage was undoubtedly sensitive to such attacks; by his own report the gift of Sage Chapel was intended to crush finally all charges of godlessness.[11] Nevertheless White successfully urged a visiting preachership rather than the minister in residence included in the original plans for the chapel as Sage and Dean Sage conceived them. For many years Sage continued to suggest a minister in residence on the ground that this would provide "the

[9] Andrew D. White, *Autobiography of Andrew Dickson White* (New York, 1905), I, 399.

[10] To Prof. Andrews, June 21, 1889, HWS.

[11] To Ezra Cornell, Sept. 24, 1872, HWS.

power of consecutive Building," but ultimately he seems to have accepted White's idea: "The plan adopted is a larger one. . . . It interests large numbers in our work as a whole, and the entire absence of sectarian bias gives real as well as apparent breadth to all we do." [12]

Sage's object in endowing the Chair of Christian Ethics was avowedly "to secure to Cornell for all coming time the services of a teacher who shall instruct students in mental philosophy and ethics from a definitely Christian stand point." [13] The Susan Linn Sage School of Philosophy which developed out of this chair was endowed by Sage for similar reasons. He felt that up to this time Cornell had done "little, very little . . . for the topwork of man's structure and development, the crown of his character and achievement through his moral and religious nature." [14] Though there was implicit here an absolute standard of values, it was broad enough to escape the charge of sectarianism. The breadth was real as well as apparent, for under Jacob Gould Schurman, the first incumbent of the chair and first dean of the school, and a layman, these became the basis for scientific philosophical study. In the announcement of the school of philosophy, courses in psychology, physiology, and contemporary philosophy were offered along with the history of religions and ethics. Although Sage's understanding of current trends in these sciences was limited—he suggested that Schurman explore the remains of the work of those favorites of his youth, Gall, Spurzheim and Combe [15]—he was excited by their possibilities and recognized their relationship to his concern for Christian ethics. His confidence in the Christian orientation of Schurman meant that this scholar and educator was given a free hand despite the fact that Schurman attached "no importance to denominational distinctions." [16]

Sage's conception of the Christian institution largely revolved

---

[12] To A. D. White, Aug. 20, 1894; to Thomas Slicer, Dec. 8, 1880, HWS.
[13] John Selkreg, *Landmarks of Tompkins County* (Syracuse, 1894), p. 558.
[14] *Ibid.*, pp. 6–7.   [15] May 31, 1890, HWS.
[16] Selkreg, *op. cit.*, p. 558.

around the character of the faculty and the governing board. His method of implementation, if method it was, was insistence upon the need for unity of purpose among the faculty and departments, looking toward the molding of Christian men. Unity of purpose in this sense could be measured only by subjective and consequently arbitrary tests in a university which remained nonsectarian and devoted to scientific inquiry. Sage singled out of the faculty a group on which he "relied" to give the University its Christian orientation.

> The group of soundly Christian men of which he [Prof. E. D. Andrews] is one, with yourself [Prof. Moses Coit Tyler],—Schurman, Wheeler, Babcock—Williams, Thurston & some others I have looked upon as a nucleus, from which we could radiate sound character and influence in all directions, and help to build up Cornell as a great, noble, Christian University.[17]

In the same way he occasionally singled out others who did not pass his tests, and created for himself a reputation as the tyrannical Chairman of the Board, "our Millionaire master" in White's phrase.[18] But by and large he was satisfied with the character of the scholars and teachers who built Cornell, satisfied that Cornell was or was becoming a Christian university.

It was on this basis, sentimental and highly personal, that Sage contributed to the growth of the University. Sage had been interested in Ezra Cornell's project while it was still in the formative stage. As early as 1865 he had advised Cornell in the location of the agricultural land scrip which was to comprise the bulk of the University's endowment. Although not yet a trustee, he came from Brooklyn to attend the opening exercises of the University in 1868 and picked up the hints of White and Cornell with regard to the education of women, pledging to help with that project when it became feasible. In 1870 he was made a trustee of the University; in 1875 upon Ezra Cornell's death he became Chairman of the

[17] June 23, 1889, Moses Coit Tyler Scrapbooks, Cornell University Library, VII, 229.
[18] Diary of A. D. White, May 5, 1892.

Board and effective manager of the University lands.[19] With John McGraw he had purchased 50,000 acres of the University's pine lands in Wisconsin, and he had pledged himself to return all profits of this transaction to Cornell. In the seventies Sage had already begun to make good that pledge; the building of Sage Chapel and of Sage College in 1873 added impressively to the plant of the University.

By 1890 Sage estimated his gifts to Cornell University at $1,177,000.[20] Sage College had cost, with endowment, equipment, and greenhouses, $267,000; Sage Chapel, $31,000; the Chairs of Ethics and Philosophy, $261,000; the library building and endowment, $560,000. Additional gifts included a $20,000 contribution to the floating debt of the University in 1874, a $3,000 contribution toward the grading of University paths in 1876, a $2,000 contribution toward the establishment of the new department of history and political science in 1881, and $15,000 for a botanical laboratory and greenhouses in 1881.[21] Sage seems to have given also $20,000 in 1878 simply on account of profits made on the land contract with Cornell.[22] This would bring the total up beyond the $58,000 in miscellaneous gifts he remembered in 1890. Subsequent gifts included casts and equipment for the archaeological museum.[23] The gifts of Sage's sons are not included in this list. Dean Sage supplied the funds for the endowment of the visiting preachership at Sage Chapel and for the building of Stimson Hall. In 1903

[19] Sage's superb handling of the lands has been detailed by Prof. Paul W. Gates in *The Wisconsin Pine Lands of Cornell University* (Ithaca, N.Y., 1943); see especially p. 243.

[20] To H. W. Parker, Dec. 17, 1890, HWS.

[21] Sage to G. W. Schuyler, Dec. 18, 1874; to A. D. White, June 21, 25, 1881, HWS; and Sage to the Trustees of Cornell University, Aug. 1, 1876, Executive Committee Minutes, Cornell University Archives.

[22] Sage to A. D. White, July 2, 1878, ADW.

[23] Selkreg, *op. cit.*, pp. 7, 467. Selkreg's "List of Benefactions" is evidently the basis of President Schurman's estimate of Sage's contributions to the University, $1,155,000, quoted in Sage's obituary notice, Ithaca *Daily Journal*, Sept. 18, 1897. It seems to be an understatement by at least a few thousand dollars.

Will Sage gave $150,000 toward a pension fund for professors.[24] His sons donated Henry Sage's home to the University; the mansion is still used, as part of the Cornell Infirmary. Sage had then, from the very beginning of his association with the University, a heavy investment in Cornell, and although he did not expect cash returns from this investment he would hardly consider relinquishing his interest in its management.

Sage's most absorbing concern was centered naturally enough in the "practical" aspects of the University's management. The development of physical plant, the husbanding of its financial resources, the expansion of the student body were the tests of the University's success as an investment. New construction on the campus attracted him powerfully; in the summer of 1890 he described with warmth his daily trips up the hill to the site of the library he was building for the University. He would "watch the growth there, and try to forecast the future, and see through my imagination what will be there when the men who now try to give form & substance to it have passed away." [25] But insistence on the primacy of the institutional aspects of the University, its physical growth and financial health, led to conflict with the educator's concept of a university. Sage opposed "practical" considerations to what he referred to impatiently as the "theories" of White. For example, Sage opposed what he considered unnecessary extravagance in architectural adornment and took little notice of White's contention that beauty in building was itself an educational experience. Sage's use of the financial argument as a last resort in winning his point was extended to other cases in which Sage's conservative prejudices seemed also to be an issue. This was apparent in his long struggle against White's theories on coeducation. Sage had eagerly volunteered to aid in the establishment of coeducation at Cornell, and had indeed provided the funds to make it possible. But his sponsorship of advanced education for women on an equal basis with men did not imply a conviction that women were

[24] *Cornell Alumni News,* Jan. 21, 1915.
[25] To M. C. Tyler, Aug. 24, 1890, Tyler Scrapbooks, VIII, 17.

equally capable with men of regulating their own lives or handling the work of the world. His sponsorship of coeducation was roughly parallel to his dedication to Education in so far as he held both separate from the real world of accomplishment, which he recognized as a man's world and a businessman's world. It was again a fortunate sentimentality that made Sage a sponsor of coeducation. Vagueness of purpose enabled him to dismiss White's "theories"— "Woman is the equal of man in intellect, morals and prudence. We (at Cornell) trust men and put them upon their honor to act as men with little or no restriction or rule. We should not restrict women when men are free" [26]—without further consideration than that which saw in them the reason for the small number of women students enrolled. Sage commented in the course of his pleas for a system of "protecting" the young women at the college in a manner that would win the approval of their parents, "Cornell has not done justly by me nor toward women, in the method of administering my gifts for the education of women." [27] Clearly he felt that the University had incurred an obligation in accepting his gifts, his investments, to accept also his direction in their management. Sage favored the Oberlin system of regulation and supervision of women students by a lady-warden, predecessor of today's housemother, and in 1884 a lady-warden was introduced at Sage College.

It was in the seventies that Sage's economy arguments told most effectively, for the depression following on the panic of 1873 not only cut down student enrollment but also made unavailable Cornell's major asset, the pinelands. At the same time Ezra Cornell's death and White's absence on diplomatic missions abroad created a vacuum which Sage's dominating personality came more and more to fill.

Initially there had been no provision made for a division of administrative and policy-making functions at the University.

[26] To Stewart L. Woodford, characterizing the theories of White and former Vice-President Russel, July 12, 1883, HWS.
[27] *Ibid.*

White had spoken of his desire to encourage faculty participation in policy making, but the charter of the University did not formalize such participation.[28] Nor did White and his successors provide for this lack. As the University faculty increased and President White became absorbed in his diplomatic career, the gap between faculty and President grew. Charles Kendall Adams, White's successor, was reluctant to admit the faculty to a share in decision making even in the crucial area of faculty appointments and promotions. And Jacob Gould Schurman, Cornell's third President, considered the faculty incapable of handling practical affairs because of the "immense fund of critical explosibility" characteristic of any academic community.[29]

The alumni, like the faculty, were more or less excluded from significant intervention in University policy making, except in so far as they were represented on the Board of Trustees. In the eighties substantial criticism of Cornell's administration was voiced in alumni circles, particularly in the alumni association of New York. The crux of the criticism was the power wielded by a minority of the trustees, namely the Executive Committee, whose chairman Sage was from 1875 to 1897. The dismissal of Vice-President Russel by the Executive Committee in 1881 and the choice of Charles K. Adams as a successor to White were the occasions of widely publicized alumni opposition to the Board. However, attempts of the alumni to widen the locus of power at Cornell in their favor made little headway. Bills which would have increased alumni representation on the Board did not pass the legislature, where Erastus Brooks, a fellow trustee, and Governor Cornell were called upon by Sage to defeat them.[30] Sage strongly seconded the comment of Judge Amasa J. Parker, also a trustee: "The alumni should learn that they have nothing to do with the government of a college beyond choosing the Trustees that rep-

[28] Hewett, op. cit., I, 142, 144.

[29] Jacob G. Schurman, A Generation of Cornell 1868–1898 (New York, 1898), pp. 39–40.

[30] E.g., Sage to Erastus Brooks, Governor Cornell, March 14; to Erastus Brooks, March 25, 1882, HWS.

resent them," and added on his own account, "Attempts to control the action of the Trustees by mass meetings of alumni are simply vicious and impertinent.[31]

Academic administration then remained the exclusive province of the President and the trustees. With Sage's assumption of the chairmanship of the Board in 1875, it was commonly acknowledged that the power of the Board rested with him. A scrupulous administrator, Sage neglected no detail of University life. Whether it was the reprimanding of an instructor who had stayed beyond the appointed hour at the young ladies' college or the investment of millions of dollars of the University's funds, Sage gave the matter his personal attention. His thorough command of the University's affairs earned the respect of his fellow trustees, and given the fact that many of them, including especially the ex officio trustees, regarded the University as a minor interest, his leadership was easily accepted. Both friends and enemies paid tribute to that leadership.

But Sage was a jealous as well as an able administrator. Never having learned to work in harness, sincerely dedicated to the University's interests, and utterly convinced that he understood best the "practical" concerns of the University, he inevitably precipitated a painful rivalry with the University's presidents, White and Adams, both of them capable administrators, far-seeing educators, and equally jealous with Sage of their positions at the University.

No serious problem arose out of the question of ultimate authority at Cornell until White accepted a diplomatic assignment abroad without resigning the presidency of Cornell. White left as Vice-President William C. Russel,[32] a man of undoubted integrity, dedicated to the principles on which Cornell had been founded, but more obvious than White in his attack on sectarianism and religious orthodoxy, less cautious in his speech, less diplomatic in

[31] To A. J. Parker, July 10, 1885, HWS.
[32] This discussion of the Russel incident has benefited by talks with Gould Colman, who has studied Russel's role at Cornell.

232

his relations with the trustees. Russel early alienated John McGraw by supporting the treasurer's request that McGraw pay his contract obligations to the University on time. Russel was acting within his legitimate sphere, but it was hardly wise to embarrass McGraw before his fellow trustees. Russel was fearless not only before trustees but also before sacred clichés. On one occasion he urged White "not to say anything about Christian Ethics. Christ's Ethics had nothing new in the practical part of them—and in the new part such as turning one's face twice and selling all we have for the benefit of the poor, nothing practical." [33] The analysis may have been apt, but scarcely could have found favor with the new Chairman of the Board, who was subsequently to donate a Chair of Christian Ethics.

The Executive Committee of the Board gradually adopted a policy of ignoring Russel. Russel himself attributed some of its hostility to the demands for expenditure he felt compelled to sponsor in the teeth of the Board's determination to retrench.[34] White's continued absence increased the trustees' irritation with Russel. Sage wrote his son,

R has many good qualities besides his undoubted capacity in learning and experience—His defects are many, as to methods—personal bearing towards Professors & Trustees—and most unwise expression of intellectual beliefs, which he has a perfect right to have; but which need not and should not have imprudent utterance.[35]

In 1879 White accepted the office of minister to Germany. That act intensified Sage's dissatisfaction with both Russel and White. The insistence of the trustees on White's return or resignation resulted in July of 1880 in White's resignation.[36] Sage recognized that it was probably White's embarrassment rather than his desire to relinquish the post that prompted the resignation: "The action of the Trustees has touched him, perhaps wounded him, for he is

[33] Nov. 15, 1876, ADW.
[34] To A. D. White, April 11, 1878, ADW.
[35] To Dean Sage, March 29, 1879, HWS.
[36] To W. H. Sage, July 26, 1880, HWS.

sensitive as a woman." [37] The resignation was kept a close secret and finally withdrawn in September 1880. Yet in January 1881, after White's intention to return had been established but before he did return, the Executive Committee asked for Russel's resignation as Vice-President and as professor. The trustees refused to present any tangible charges to Russel or indeed to White. Sage's first communication to White on this matter contained by way of explanation only this sentence: "The final conclusion was to act squarely upon our convictions in the interest of the University." [38]

Russel's letter of resignation precipitated a heated controversy in the press and agitated faculty, students, and alumni. Protest petitions based their argument on Russel's removal as professor.[39] While, they contended, the trustees might possibly have removed Russel from an administrative post, his removal as professor required explanation. Editorials pointed out that White had not been consulted, nor had the full Board of Trustees made the decision. Security of tenure for professors was held to be violated, and the question of religious orthodoxy was seized upon as the proper explanation. Abuse was aimed particularly at Sage. Indeed one story, which seems to have had its origin in Russel's desperate search for the charges against him, was circulated to the effect that Russel's opposition to Henry Ward Beecher's preaching at Cornell had so enraged Sage that he sought Russel's removal.[40]

The more violent the attacks of their critics, the more autocratic became the tone of the Executive Committee. Sage wrote trustee Hiram Sibley, "We have given no reasons to the public for our action assuming that it was our concern not theirs." [41] And when what Sage referred to as the "liberal" element of the faculty protested on Russel's behalf, Sage suggested that they fire the entire

[37] Sage to Dean Sage, July 28, 1880, HWS.   [38] Jan. 4, 1881, HWS.

[39] E.g., *Cornell Era*, XIII, 281, 295; *Cornell Sun*, April 20, 1881; and Alumni of the instructing body of Cornell University to A. D. White, April 16, 1881, ADW.

[40] W. C. Russel to A. D. White, Jan. 4, 1881, ADW; *Cornell Era*, XIII, 293–294; Sage to E. B. Morgan, May 11, 1881, HWS.

[41] May 5, 1881, HWS.

faculty and then re-elect "only such as we know we can work with." [42] The controversy conclusively demonstrated Sage's autocratic, almost proprietary, attitude toward the University. The President of the University, the faculty, the alumni, the full Board of Trustees had not been consulted before the action was taken, nor were the President, the public, or the subject of the action himself permitted to question the decision. With the beginning of widespread agitation of the matter, Sage's only concession was to contact other board members through private channels to gain their assent.[43] Certainly at this time there was no appreciation among the trustees of the concept of security of tenure. White himself after much private soul-searching accepted the decision. The tenure issue had been raised, but was scarcely even acknowledged by Sage.

The reason for the action, deliberately left obscure, was vigorously debated. Most comment centered in Russel's charge, clearly spelled out in his letter of resignation, "Many will ascribe your action to an abandonment of the original idea of those who founded the University and to a plan of bringing it into line with the popular theology." [44] Undoubtedly Russel's religious iconoclasm had made him personally obnoxious to Sage. Dean Sage, ever given to hasty judgments and more conservative than his father, identified Russel's attitude with atheism. Henry Sage warned his son: "I fear you have said too much to Parker about R's atheism— What we could prove about that I dont know—We have been very careful about raising the religious issue." [45] It was clear, however, that Sage was disturbed by Russel's irreligious reputation particularly as he considered it related to the University's reputation. On the other hand Russel's charge was clearly unfair in so far as it implied a concerted plan to substitute sectarianism for free inquiry at Cornell. Russel's militancy in the face of religious cant, which Sage accepted with sentimental naïveté, not only alienated

[42] To A. D. White, May 10, 1881, ADW.

[43] To Judge Francis Finch, April 25, 1881, HWS.

[44] To the Executive Committee of the Board of Trustees, March 31, 1881, Trustees' Minutes, Cornell University Archives.

[45] May 16, 1881, HWS.

these men from each other but also exaggerated the difference between White's statement of the principles that should guide Cornell's development and Sage's acceptance of those principles. It would be difficult to believe that Sage had been moved to contribute handsomely to an institution whose basic orientation he disapproved. The dismissal of Russel was part of a plan only in the sense that Sage openly and repeatedly asserted his intention of imbuing Cornell with a Christian foundation, which, given his own lack of appreciation of dogma, cannot readily be confused with sectarianism.

Hostility to Russel among the trustees seems to have had a broader base than the religious issue. A persistent source of conflict at the University was the ultimate distribution of power between the President and the trustees, and particularly the Chairman of the Board. In this conflict Russel may have suffered as White's partisan. Many years later in replying to criticism of his treatment of Russel, Sage commented, "Poor Russel suffered not wholly for his own wrong—but more for the position he took to serve a Friend." [46] White's absence during the period of the University's severe financial trials had given Sage the opportunity to consolidate his power. It was a time when the reasons for lack of growth at the University were anxiously sought. Sage found such reasons in the irreligious reputation of the University, in White's absence, and in the "theories" of White, theories supported by Russel.

Resentment of White's absence was expressed in many quarters. Dean Sage was evidently especially harsh in his judgment of White. Characteristically the elder Sage cautioned his son to moderation and reminded him that White "has given *Ten* of the best years of his life to the University without pay, and fully $100 M in cash besides." But Sage judged also that White's course had been determined by "conflicting motives"; his loyalty to Cornell had been deflected by his desire for a political career.[47] White's hesitation

[46] To Susan Phelps Gage, June 26, 1895, HWS.
[47] March 29, 1879; July 28, 1880, HWS.

did not spell security for Sage's investment, and his impracticality Sage considered disastrous. With this picture of White in his mind to serve as reason and as rationalization, Sage resisted firmly on White's return the latter's reassumption of the power he had wielded so completely in the early years of Cornell. The removal of Russel may have been a first move in the campaign waged on a power and personality basis against White. Goldwin Smith's report, "The only reason assigned to me by Sage for the dismissal of Russel from the *Professorship* was that he would have too much influence in the Faculty meetings," [48] would suggest that the power struggle was uppermost in Sage's mind.

A series of petty conflicts with Sage marked White's last four years at Cornell. They argued largely about finances, but more and more their conflicts took on a highly personal tone. Thus after a meeting in which White felt his dignity had been assaulted he wrote contemptuously: Sage's "remarks were simply those of a 'good businessman' as utterly blind to the realities of the case as to the beauties of a sonata of Beethoven." [49] And Sage shortly after reported to his son about an article in the New York *Sun:* "Reporter had a long interview with White and White is duly accredited with being the author of CU, through his suggestions to EC—*That* is characteristic—Cornell is dead!" [50]

The Russel dismissal had undoubtedly embittered White, and the McGraw-Fiske suit, in 1883, found Sage and White again on opposite sides of a question of major importance to the University. Jennie McGraw Fiske had bequeathed the greatest part of the fortune her father left her—some two million dollars—to Cornell University for the building and endowment of a library. But during and after the settlement of the estate the trustees, particularly Sage and Douglass Boardman, deeply offended Willard Fiske, Jennie's husband and the University's librarian. Fiske joined members of the McGraw family in bringing suit against the

[48] To A. D. White, May 22, 1881, GS.
[49] Diary of A. D. White, Nov. 8, 1882.
[50] To W. H. Sage, Dec. 19, 1882, HWS.

University, and after seven years of litigation the court ruled in their favor on the grounds that the University in accepting Jennie's bequest had exceeded the charter's express limitations on endowment.

Throughout the controversy White maintained that a compromise with Fiske was essential and that only the intransigence of Sage and Boardman made it impossible.[51] On the other hand Sage contended that Fiske's demand for a measure of control in the administration of his wife's bequest was equivalent to a demand that the trustees violate their trust, that it was indeed a "frivolous" excuse for contesting the will.[52] Sage refused to give an inch. "White sails today [to see Fiske who had taken up residence in Italy]—He goes without any authority to suggest or receive proposals—I much regret that he goes at all, as I am quite sure that no good can result, unless it be by the miracle of a complete surrender on the part of our late Friend." [53] Early in the proceedings Sage promised to build and endow a library for the University himself should the case be lost. Undoubtedly the blunt insistence by Sage and Boardman on their rights and duties as trustees ignored the sensitivity of Fiske. It ignored as well the financial benefits which might accrue to Cornell through Fiske and which they risked. An objective observer, Goldwin Smith, reported some years later:

As a most intimate friend of Fiske I believe I heard all about it. My impression has always been that Mr. Sage and Judge Boardman did nothing, as men of business, to which exception could fairly be taken, but that they missed the opportunity of securing by a little deference to feeling, a great accession of wealth to the University.[54]

Evidently it was unwillingness to share with others the power of the University that played the major role in Sage's intransigence.

[51] Diary of A. D. White, June 12, 13, Dec. 20, 21, 1888; Sage to Dean Sage, May 23, 1890, HWS.
[52] To A. D. White, July 27, 1883, HWS.
[53] Sage to Douglass Boardman, July 25, 1883, HWS.
[54] To J. G. Schurman, Feb. 6, 1905, GS.

Sage explained, with some exaggeration undoubtedly, that the controversy resulted from Fiske's "strenuous efforts to get sole control of his wife's bequest":

[These efforts were] resisted and defeated because the trustees had no legal right to vacate their Trust and give him control. . . . He demanded $25M in cash to take to Europe for Periodicals when there was no cash in CU's treasury—when Boardman had no cash from Mrs. F's estate—It was denied for that sufficient reason.[55]

The request for funds for periodicals for the Cornell library, Fiske's desire to have some voice in the disposition of the McGraw-Fiske mansion, and other similar incidents seem to make up the substance of the charge that Fiske sought "sole control" of the bequest. Inevitably the quarrel became personal, and petty questions of how much cash Fiske had at Jennie's death and what of her personal possessions he took from the mansion were raised. Sage insisted on dedicating the library he ultimately built to the "Memory and in behalf of Jennie McGraw; that Pure and Noble woman whose purposes, thus far thwarted and defeated, yet begin to bear the Fruit which she tried to plant," and a plaque to that effect was placed in the entranceway of the new library.[56] White evidently objected that this would alienate Fiske further and perhaps cut off hope of future gifts from him to the University, but Sage was adamant. He stood obstinately by his early position, "If he [Fiske] succeeds in wresting from us the legacy of our friend and then chooses to return to us any portion of it *as an act of sincere penitence,* & without conditions, I would vote for its acceptance." [57] His unwillingness to compromise with Fiske ultimately helped to lose for the University a sum considerably larger than the $560,000 Sage devoted to the library building and endowment. Still later

[55] Sage to J. G. Schurman, May 31, 1890; see also Sage to Dean Sage, May 26; to A. C. Barnes, June 3, HWS.

[56] Sage to Dean Sage, Oct. 31, 1889, HWS. The wording of the plaque, implying somewhat immodestly that Sage acted as God's instrument in fulfilling Jennie McGraw's wishes, has been a source of amusement for generations of Cornellians.

[57] To C. K. Adams, Dec. 19, 1888, HWS.

the bitterness aroused by official University participation in the ceremonial burial of Fiske in the memorial chapel at Cornell and the acceptance of his bequests to the University was the occasion of the resignation of both William H. Sage and Henry M. Sage from the Board of Trustees; [58] after this the Sage family largely severed its connection with Cornell.

The University lost the case, and although Sage built the library in memory of Jennie McGraw Fiske, White was seriously alienated. Sage was convinced, with some justification, that newspaper censure of himself at the close of the controversy was directed by "the Friends of Fiske inspired and led on by Andrew D. White." Characteristically he interpreted the Fiske incident in the light of a long-standing rivalry with White: "Our differences began long ago—when Russel was deposed—The bitter fight then was—with R in the front, White in the back ground, all the time." [59]

The conflict between Sage and White continued on other levels. In 1884 Sage made an effort to gain legislation which would delimit the President's powers and duties.[60] The attempt failed but is illustrative of the tack Sage was taking. In 1885 White retired from the presidency. His successor, Charles K. Adams, had been hand-picked by White, but was welcomed by Sage with a sigh of relief:

We have had twelve years of practically one man power in which theories predominated and details were almost wholly neglected—and were rapidly reaping the reward of such management till the Trustees assumed the responsibilities belonging to them and from that moment on our advances in right direction began. We have now a very different man—a man of detail and of generally wise and good purposes.[61]

Sage, nevertheless, maintained the feud with White, making a determined but ultimately unsuccessful effort to keep White out of

58 W. H. Sage to Van Cleef, Jan. 20, 1905, Cornell University Archives; J. G. Schurman to C. Shepard, Jan. 14, 1905, JGS.
59 To Dean Sage, May 23, 26, 1890, HWS.
60 Sage to J. F. Gluck, May 16, 1884, HWS.
61 To Erastus Brooks, Oct. 29, 1886, HWS.

the Board, giving as his reason the hampering effect on the new president of having his predecessor so close.[62]

Much as Sage had praised Adams, there early appeared to be friction between the trustees and the new president. Sage noted with disapproval the tendency of the President to assume to himself the task of choosing new faculty. Sage recommended that the

Presidents duties be confined to the organization and management—(under the advice of the Trustees as to general policies) of the purely educational work of the University—leaving all purely business and financial management to the Trustees. . . . I think all legislation upon improvements, additions, increase of departments should originate with the Trustees upon their own motion after consideration of recommendations if any are made by President or Faculty.

Sage then added with obvious disapproval, "Whoever is our President the tendency will always be (in the absence of clearly defined duties and powers) towards concentration of power *in him*." [63]

Adams was an able president, particularly perceptive in the choice of faculty members. But at Cornell, as later at Wisconsin,[64] he was jealous of his power, as jealous perhaps as Sage. The "old Pachyderm of a President," as Moses Coit Tyler referred to him, stimulated considerable opposition to himself among the faculty, offending even Tyler himself, an old friend. It is noteworthy that faculty members who were closest to Sage—Tyler, Thurston, Schurman—were among the most persistent of Adams' attackers.[65] The organization of the University Senate in 1890 was a direct result of the faculty's feud with Adams and provided the faculty with a share in the nominating of professors. When Tyler told Sage that

[62] To J. F. Gluck, Jan. 4; to Hiram Sibley, Jan. 21; to Hiram Sibley, Jr., Feb. 4; to Stewart Woodford, Feb. 9; to A. B. Cornell, March 4, 1887, HWS.

[63] To Erastus Brooks, Oct. 29, 1886, HWS.

[64] Merle Curti and Vernon Carstensen, *The University of Wisconsin* (Madison, Wisc., 1949), I, 571, 576.

[65] Diary of Moses Coit Tyler, Nov. 22, 1889; Jan. 19, 1890, Cornell University Library.

241

the permanence of the Senate would lead logically to the abolition of the University Presidency & the establishment of an annual Rectorship, his face became very bright, & he emphatically assented to the statement as one which he seemed to have already formulated for himself.[66]

The creation of the faculty Senate quieted, if it did not end, the controversy of the faculty with Adams, so that the announcement of Adams' resignation in the spring of 1892 was met in many quarters by surprise. Adams indicated in a letter to White that it was the trustees and Sage particularly who had forced this move.[67] The controversy with Adams indicates far more clearly than that with White Sage's anxiety to maintain personal hegemony at the University. There were in this instance, no substantial issues at stake with the exception of the power issue. Adams was a thorough-going conservative in religious as in political and economic matters.[68] In a report to one of the trustees in 1890 Adams not only pointed to substantial improvements in enrollment and standards at the University, but gave special emphasis to the improved "moral and religious atmosphere" at the University since he had taken office.[69] Sage himself had commended Adams' "practical" abilities. But Adams' aggressive administration was resented by Sage, particularly since Adams seemed to work well with, and with the approval of, White. During the battle for the University Senate, for example, Moses Coit Tyler reported after calling on Sage that Sage was "preparing for an extra meeting of the Full Board, when the square fight will be made between him & the two Presidents." [70]

Moreover Sage had almost surely picked Adams' successor, Jacob Gould Schurman, a man whom all opinion agreed was eminently suited for the post, and a man who had "no Ex[s] to hamper or control." [71] Schurman had been brought to the University in 1886 on the recommendation of White to fill the Chair of Christian

---

[66] *Ibid.*, March 31, 1890.   [67] May 9, 1892, ADW.
[68] Curti and Carstensen, *op. cit.*, I, 574–575.
[69] To Stewart Woodford, Dec. 10, 1890, JGS.
[70] Diary of M. C. Tyler, April 24, 1890.
[71] Sage to M. C. Tyler, Sept. 6, 1892, HWS.

Ethics endowed by Sage. As incumbent of this chair and dean of the Susan Linn Sage School of Philosophy, Schurman distinguished himself both as scholar and administrator. The features in Schurman that appealed most to Sage were his modesty and his great energy. Sage recognized a similarity between Schurman and himself as he had been at Schurman's age, ambitious, industrious, eager. "Schurman is a very able man—He has won his way thus far by industry & hard blows . . . . All this has failed to develope a particle of vanity or self assertion. . . . He has the power and purpose to work very much like that I had at his age." [72] The relationship between the old Chairman of the Board and the new President of Cornell is perhaps best illustrated by Schurman's first letter as President, addressed to Sage, "My friend, my father," and signed, "Ever cordially and filially yours." [73] Given this relationship, it may very well have been the rumor that Schurman was considering leaving Cornell for a more advantageous position that precipitated the forcing of Adams' resignation on the ground that he created "an atmosphere of conflict." [74]

Schurman's inauguration ended the power struggle at the University. Sage at seventy-nine was willing to allow the tactful and deferential Schurman full rein. Sage seemed "a quiet lion now, with no unsatisfied appetite gnawing him and causing him to roar." [75] Schurman's administration was long and advantageous to the University; during its course the single body of faculty was "differentiated into ten Faculties," testifying to a development along true university lines. Expansion of the University's student body, staff, and facilities called for and received a differentiation in function between trustees and academic officers. "Today the Board of Trustees have exclusive charge of business; the Faculties have exclusive charge of Education," contended Schurman.[76] The definition of business and educational functions might of course

---

[72] To C. P. Williams, May 21, 1892, HWS.   [73] June 17, 1892, HWS.
[74] Sage to D. S. Jordan, May 20; to Dean Sage, May 24, 1892, HWS.
[75] M. C. Tyler to A. D. White, Feb. 5, 1893, ADW.
[76] Schurman, *op. cit.*, p. 40.

remain the source of difficulties but not while Sage and Schurman respected and trusted one another.

Clearly Henry W. Sage enjoyed both prestige and power at Cornell University. He had sought both in every sphere of his activity, regarding them as the measure of success. The University attracted him initially as the project of his friends; he had found gratification in its work because of his own highly sentimental if limited appreciation of the function of education; he had found in the tasks of building its plant and husbanding its resources a major satisfaction for his intense energies. His determination to achieve ultimate exclusive power at the University was never directly stated, perhaps never admitted to himself, except in so far as he asserted the businessman's superiority to the college president in the appreciation of the institutional factors of success.

In 1880 he wrote a fellow trustee and a fellow businessman, "Thus far, with the important exception of what White has done the foundations of the University have been made by *business men.*" [77] In so far as physical resources were concerned this statement was substantially correct. His gratification in the situation had nothing mean in it; the situation was proof to him that the pursuit of profits ultimately benefited society. Sage's major contribution to the University was without doubt the creation of the financial basis for its success, not only by his own gifts but also through his management of its resources.

On the other hand his inordinate concern for "unity of thought and action" at a university betrayed a lack of understanding of education as experimentation, as the willingness to examine new ideas and ideas in conflict with established values. Yet this concern could be voiced and pressed because by and large his contemporaries within and outside the University did accept with him a set of standards, a system of values, a code of behavior which appeared to be not only reasonable but morally right. In the long run Sage's conception of a unified Christian orientation for Cornell University was broad enough so that, as interpreted by able

[77] To A. S. Barnes, June 2, 1880, HWS.

educators like White and Schurman, it aided rather than hampered the development of specialized, diverse, and profoundly secular education at Cornell. Cornell's experience indicates that the impetus for vocational and secular education came from the professional educator rather than the businessman trustee. The latter, who was in this period replacing the cleric-trustee at the major universities, was highly conventional, particularly in religious orientation. The businessman's lack of interest in dogma, however, gave the educator the opportunity to concentrate effectively on secular studies.

Sage's use of the power he attained at Cornell was arbitrary, highly personal. He recognized neither security of tenure for professors and presidents nor the right of the faculty to participate in policy determination. In the latter case at least presidents as well as trustees shared his conviction. Luckily the ousting of able individuals like Russel and Adams did not result in permanent injury to the University.

That Sage was willing to use his power to keep out teachers whose social and economic views did not correspond with his own is clearly indicated by his own statement in the case of Henry Carter Adams:

As you know my objection to him was not personal, for I always liked the man—It was only because some of his evidently sincere, intellectual beliefs . . . seemed to me much out of line with sound economic wisdom—*and such as I should not willingly have taught to students at Cornell*—I speak particularly of his views about the federation of Labor. . . . If his mental attitude upon the matter under discussion is as it was then I should deplore his selection.[78]

Again, such attitudes and actions based upon them did not seem to harm the University. Its enrollment grew; it retained able scholars and excellent teachers. The reputation for "soundness," for conservatism, which Sage sought to achieve for Cornell perhaps did contribute to the successful outcome of the years of struggle

[78] To C. K. Adams, Jan. 26, 1892, HWS (italics mine).

during which Cornell's future as an institution was precarious. And it was Cornell University as a successful institution rather than as a revolutionary educational force that Sage best understood.

Sage came to the office of trustee with a fixed if uncritical standard of values. To these he attributed his personal success and the very fact of his trusteeship. It was natural to expect that he should dedicate his substantial investment in time and energy to the perpetuation of these values. His attachment to the University was sentimental but sincere, personal, and ultimately fortunate.

Chapter X
Henry W. Sage, 1864-1897

HENRY SAGE was fifty years old in 1864. The most successful years of his business career were immediately before him. The new mill in Michigan was under construction. Cheap timber and high demand were to make it immensely profitable and justify his own hard labor and concentration; in his own reckoning the mill became the darling of his enterprises, the pivot of his success:

It has been built up with great care, labor and thought, and I am much attached to it. . . . Nothing would please me more than to have you and Dean appreciate its value, and the value of the labor of caring for it—as I do. . . . It won't fail if well attended to produce in any term of ten years a fortune large enough for any man.[1]

Not only the fortune the mill created but also "the value of the labor of caring for it" entered into Sage's reckoning. Competence engendered self-respect; certified by success, competence made one a man of affairs, one who earned the respect of others.

The decade of the sixties marked several significant changes in Sage's business career. Foremost was his changed financial status. By the mid-sixties Sage's business no longer required outside credit. The outbreak of the Civil War had temporarily halted recovery from the panic of 1857; 1861 marked a low point in lumber prices. Once the adjustment to wartime and postwar demand had been made, however, lumber producers experienced a tremendous boom: "Eleven fat years from 1862 on." For the first time and from this time on Sage's business affairs were liquid. When Beecher and Silliman asked that he borrow for them he replied: "I dont

[1] To W. H. Sage, July 25, 1879, HWS.

do it for myself—and I have more pride in that matter than you will understand till you live (as I did) full fifty years a constant borrower—and then, by Gods grace, being freed from the necessity, resolve never again to be a borrower." [2]

A steady high income, beginning in the sixties,[3] not only persuaded Sage to expand his milling operations but also provided considerable sums for investment in timberlands and securities. In 1881 the net worth of H. W. Sage and Co., including timber and lands, mortgages, notes, and securities, mill and lumber, amounted to $2,841,682.70. By 1893, the year after the mill was closed and the year in which the Sage Land & Improvement Co. was created to manage the land accounts, annual additions to the stock account had increased the net worth of the firm to $8,469,088.[4] But the end of the eighties marked a change in the distribution of the firm's holdings. Timberlands and securities rather than mill and lumber now dominated the inventory.

The profits of the fat years and his sons' entry into the business enabled Sage to realize his ambition of a family firm. With the dissolution of his partnership with McGraw in 1868 Sage never again took an outsider as partner in the major areas of his business. Particularly in years that witnessed depressed lumber prices Sage's sons urged the sale of a share of the mill outside the family. Sage's reply was characteristic. Immediate control and immediate responsibility were his guiding principles: "Now we control our own property—have no directors to meet—nobody to question or control—I think we should keep it so—and only part with that

[2] Sage to H. W. Sage and Co., Toledo, July 17, 1874; to Beecher & Silliman, Dec. 26, 1871, HWS.

[3] There are a few figures available which give clues to Sage's income; e.g., Sage's personal income for 1864 was valued for tax purposes, at $60,000 (receipt, U.S. Internal Revenue Tax, HWS). This represents largely the production of the Bell Ewart mill and the profits made by the New York lumber yard. The West Bay City mill in which Sage owned only a three-eighths interest at this time had only just begun operations. This does not include, of course, the income of Dean Sage, who owned a one-fourth interest in his father's Canadian enterprises.

[4] H. W. Sage and Co. Day Book, March 24, 1882, and *passim*, HWS.

business when we can close it *cleanly*, get our pay and leave it." [5] His policy was the control of the whole or the sale of the whole. The family firm meant independence to Sage, and linked to that were the solid virtues, "manliness," integrity.

He had little appreciation of the concept of the modern cor-poration, the essence of which is continuity of existence without respect to continuity of ownership. The Sage mill was to remain a large and profitable organization but it was not given the impulse to grow. Owned by one family, run largely by one man, perhaps it could grow no larger without resorting to corporate form and a more complex and responsible management hierarchy than ob-tained in the Sage organization. Yet these were conditions Sage was unwilling to meet, and expansion was not what the Sage sons had in mind when they proposed widening the ownership base. Sage's concept of the proper business form was limited to inde-pendent proprietorship or its extension, the partnership, that busi-ness organization which is the creation and tool of the owner and in which the owner's personality is the dominant factor. A partner-ship was indicated only when additional capital or services were required: "We need no more capital—and I know of no man's services *worth enough* to give for it an interest in our business." A partnership was not looked upon as a permanent arrangement, and hence involved separate accounts and interests and final set-tlements which might not prove mutually satisfactory: "I *cannot* have another general partner to get mixed up in all our affairs, involving separate accts and interests and settlements at last." [6] Sage found it difficult to make his sons understand that for him the family's ownership of the mill, an enterprise free of debt and earning profitably, was the apex of success, testimony to his per-sonal achievement.

In 1861 Dean Sage had taken a one-fourth interest in the Bell Ewart mill. Four years later William Henry Sage, upon his gradua-tion from Yale, joined his father and brother in business. Even-tually each of the sons held a one-fourth interest in all the enter-

[5] To Dean Sage, Jan. 27, 1881, HWS.   [6] *Ibid.*, Aug. 15, 1874.

prises of H. W. Sage and Co., milling, timberland speculation, securities investment. Evidently their father loaned them the capital to invest in the firm, and the loan was kept on the books of the firm until the eighties, when the balance was made over into gifts from Henry Sage to his grandchildren.

Both young men had been given impressive academic educations for businessmen of their day. In Ithaca they had been tutored by Dr. W. S. Wheeler, a graduate of Oxford and rector of St. John's Church.[7] When the family moved to Brooklyn, Dean attended Adelphi Academy, and Will the Brooklyn Polytechnic Institute. Dean went on to take a series of courses at the Albany Law School, and Will went to Yale, where he was elected to Phi Beta Kappa.

His sons' decision to join him in business was undoubtedly pleasing to Sage and undoubtedly had been influenced by him. Many years later he wrote Dean, "The policy of my whole life with regard to you and Will—[has been] to keep our interests one." [8] There was an element of protectiveness in the elder Sage's attitude toward his sons and, related to this, an element of doubt. His sons had been given opportunities he had yearned for as a young man, but were they as able, as determined, as "manly" as he? When he presented the firm's prospects to Dean in 1861 Henry Sage wrote, "Properly conducted it will develop *Manliness*—will enable you to gain an honest living—and a competent fortune by *fair production*—& positive earnings." Manliness, strength, and independence would be the necessary by-products of application, and if there were virtue and profit in the struggle itself, there was also the ability to "do a positive good every day of your life by developing the resources of the country, and furnishing to hundreds labor by which they can earn an honest living." [9] At the same time Sage feared that Dean had not the experience to command the enterprise, should something happen to himself. This doubt, natural enough in 1861, was never fully discarded. For the next thirty-five

[7] T. F. Crane, "In Memoriam—William Henry Sage," *Cornell Alumni News*, Nov. 6, 1924.

[8] Feb. 13, 1882, HWS.   [9] May 13, 1861, HWS.

years the father kept tight hold on the reins of the family business and on his sons. The sons never broke away, but neither were they given the opportunity truly to prove themselves within the family firm.

Dean particularly was a source of worry to his father. A victim of chronic dysentery, sensitive, irascible, he was high-minded but cold; he lacked the mellowness of temper of the elder Sage, who at one point urged Dean:

Go in to the social life before you and try to take a part of it—It will do you good, and break up some habits, & dislikes which you will get benefit from breaking up. . . . Wisely done, it helps to broaden experience & increase spheres of usefulness & influence.[10]

At the same time Sage consistently, and perhaps unwisely, discouraged his son from accepting duties outside the firm. Despite Dean's interest as a sportsman—Dean was the author of a treatise on salmon fishing—Sage urged him not to accept an appointment as the head of an Adirondack State Park commission: "To do the duties properly, wisely, vigorously will take all the time of a vigorous man—There's no pay in it—not much honor—Don't take on new cares!"[11] Within the firm, as we have said, the elder Sage maintained strict control. Very rarely Dean protested and precipitated a family crisis. The elder Sage tried to justify himself:

Yours 11th has caused me two sleepless nights—Have I ever done anything to provoke such a letter? In all that I have said about our business and its management look—read—decide for yourself and answer yourself! . . . I have offered to take your interest, not because I underrated your service, but because I was anxious to have you relieved if I found that to be your determination. . . .

Your assumption that I have ever tried to deprive you of personal liberty of thought and action has no truthful foundation. . . . A very few times in the past fifteen years I have made suggestions about tendencies which I feared would work you injury.[12]

[10] Dec. 20, 1886, HWS.   [11] Feb. 11, 1893, HWS.
[12] Feb. 13, 1882, HWS.

This particular crisis in family and business relationships was brought on by the question of the sale of the West Bay City mill. Invariably the maintenance of the manufacturing interest was to be the issue in conflict between father and sons. Periodically the question was raised, but until Henry Sage himself was too old to begin anew and the old mill had used up the accessible timber of its hinterland the father's will prevailed.

The picture which Sage drew for his sons of the businessman who combined self-interest and altruism, personal independence and national development in his daily affairs, was bound to clash with the actual workings of the business world in which Sage dealt. It was this clash which grated on the sensibilities of his sons, while the father apparently was able to accept the disparity between his philosophy of business and the workday world with the good grace born of long experience and personal success.

Business success was always a matter of jealous self-interest, often a matter of bargaining power in which one side was the loser despite appeals to the social function of the entrepreneur. In his dealings with partners, agents, employees, with labor, with other businessmen, with the mill town, Sage recognized the efficacy of power. The basic assumption with which Sage faced community conflicts in his role as citizen and taxpayer was that the property holder by the acquisition of property and the ownership of the means of production had proved his worth to the community and was thereby entitled to a dominant voice in its affairs. From an apprenticeship in a period when both the individual businessman and the community were "on the make," from his experience in developing an industrial town from a frontier village, Sage carried over an identification of the interests of the businessman with those of the community. The prosperity of the community became a corollary of personal profit. Expansion, growth, development, visible and material wealth were the obvious personal and community motives in the society he knew. Hence, it was the chief object of town council, state legislature, and ultimately the national Congress to promote the entrepreneur, the capitalist, the man who initiated the chain of progress. Sage sought and often obtained tax reduction and tax exemption. He urged tariff revision upward or downward as his interests dictated. Far from expecting government to remain aloof from the affairs of business, he regarded government as a useful if unwieldy tool to further the primary interest of the individual and the nation in material advance.

Similarly, he met the problem of labor conflict with the un sophisticated view that the ultimate interests of labor and capital were identical. These were an ever more abundant stock of goods, an ever expanding volume of production. The rewards of labor and capital were equally subject to the law of supply and demand, while in so far as that law required interpretation Sage felt that it was the capitalist who was best equipped and best qualified to interpret it. Sage refused to deal with his workers as a group or a separate interest. Even while joining with other manufacturers in the resolve not to raise wages or to shorten the working day, he maintained that the terms of labor were a matter to be arrived at by the agreement of the individual worker with his employer. Unions, collective bargaining, were alien concepts. Sage's thinking was the product of an economy more fluid than that which was emerging after the Civil War. For an industrious and able man to remain a laborer was unthinkable, even disgraceful. It was still more inconceivable that he should acknowledge as permanent his status as a wageworker and should organize to protect his interests on that basis. The explanation that came to hand most readily was that these men were unworthy, inferior. Their leaders were written off as irresponsible agitators heedless of the public welfare, their strikes as mob action. Yet the easy acceptance of the dogma of free opportunity for all became ever less realistic as industrialization changed the nature of the American economy, and it is difficult to see how it ever applied to the Irish canal laborer or the Polish mill hand. Sage's commitment to this premise hardly equipped him to sympathize with the demands of factory hands, whose opportunities were neither abundant nor apparent. Compromise with strikers' demands represented the surrender of principle to the mobs and the demagogues. The employer had the right and the power to determine wages; both right and power had been achieved through business success.

If Sage recognized the drive toward independent proprietorship in himself, he recognized it as well in others. The company store and the Toledo yard, for example, were run on a partnership basis. Both had been directed by salaried managers, but these men, having proved their ability, demanded and got an interest in the profits. In some cases the interests of these junior partners, partners in some one aspect of the organization, ran counter to those of H. W. Sage and Co. Yet that price had to be paid by Sage in a day when ability was measured by independence and proprietorship. It meant also that Sage's orientation in the direction of detailed attention to the affairs of his business and his commitment to individualism were reinforced by the compulsion of other able men to prove their worth by personal success.

Increasingly with the progress of industrialization, the businessman had to face the problem of relations not only with labor and the community but also with his fellow businessmen. The national market had been a direct result of the startling improvements in transportation throughout the century. Competition meant lower prices particularly during the depression of the seventies. But competition was not sufficient to force an association of manufacturers to reduce output, the goal which individual producers recognized and at least one of their trade magazines, the *Lumberman's Gazette,* advocated. After several abortive attempts the effort was given up. As far as the lumber trade was concerned, the millmen refused to surrender their prerogative, their function in a free-enterprise system, of regulating their individual outputs and selling prices. The initiative of the profit-seeking individual was the first premise on which these men operated. This did not mean, however, that they regarded competition favorably. These same millmen combined in what has been called the most successful pool of the nineteenth century, the Michigan Salt Association, to maintain the price of their product. Yet, within this organization conflicting interests, jealousy, and suspicion of the motives of various members or groups of members was apparent. The association per se was of little concern to the individual mill-man. What benefits he could achieve through it for his personal organization were of paramount interest. In the same way the boom associations characteristic of the lumber industry were the scene of repeated maneuvering to gain or maintain control. Control was essential in Sage's scheme of things to ensure protection of his interests. His goal had always been independent proprietorship and the independence of action which went along with it. Suspicion of regulation, even of cooperative regulation, was one of his marked attributes. It was not that he feared regulation for the group interest, but rather he was sure that regulation would benefit most those in immediate control. This same attitude made him hostile toward the corporate form of organization, or indeed toward any but the family-owned and family-managed enterprise.

Perhaps the only type of cooperative effort among businessmen which Sage sought without reservation was in the area of lobbying. Here and in the combination of employers as against employees, especially in periods of labor unrest, the object to be gained was limited and well defined. Moreover, the commitment to cooperative effort here was temporary and comparatively loose.

Sage's business behavior, then, was marked by suspicion and exclusiveness. He did not recognize community of interests among businessmen. That sense of being an outsider which was so apparent a part of his personal make-up in the early days of his career was evidently retained in the years of success and intensified by the conditions of business. At the same time his rationalization of business success was based on the ultimate identity of all interests in material advance. The assumption that material advance was the condition of spiritual and cultural progress was explicit. Very rarely was the paradox brought to Sage's attention, and when it was he dismissed it easily, perhaps because he did not truly understand the point. Thus when William C. DeWitt sug-

gested that the depression of the nineties was "the natural outcome of the artificial and strictly monetary prosperity of the last
twenty five years of thrift, affluence and extravagance," that the
materialism expressed in "devoting government to the enhance-
ment of business interests," in the struggle between capital and
labor for government power, was the root cause of suffering and
discontent, that what was needed was a religious and cultural revival, Sage answered confidently and not quite to the point, "Underlying *all* mans duty to himself & his family & country is the
necessity for accumulation through Industry—Hence God gave
him the *instinct to acquire.*" That instinct was subject to perver-
sion. In that case,

bad legislation—corrupt policies, will follow, and much suffering . . .
will need to be *spread broadly,* before the growth of sound virtuous
political action can begin to take root again—We are *in* a *bad way* not
because people are enterprising—industrious and accumulators—for
these things are right—but because the purely animal instincts of
men—& *not* their higher moral natures, have been (temporarily I hope)
placed in command.[13]

Widespread suffering would suffice to remind men of their guilt
and automatically bring about a better balance between the animal and the moral. It is perhaps more for the facile means on
which he chose to rely to bring about the better balance than for
the conviction that material and cultural advance were complementary, that Sage's position is subject to criticism. His complacency suggests a certain hypocrisy, unconscious though it may have
been. "The businessman had reason to prefer moral regulation to
legal regulation for moral law was remote and somewhat retarded
in its operation." [14] In so far as he sought a resolution of the conflict between self-interest and "universal good," Sage relied on
natural law, the unseen hand, ultimately on God to bring it about.

[13] Feb. 17, 20, 1894, HWS.
[14] Irvin Wyllie, *The Self-Made Man in America* (New Brunswick, N.J.,
1954), p. 93.

I dont want to see the men who know how to organize large industries (in themselves most useful to all) deprived of power, and liberty to use the faculties God has given them in their own way. They are the greatest helpers men have, and whether or not their motives are beneficent, the results of their actions are. No single influence, perhaps not *all* combined have done so much to cheapen transportation —reduce cost of living—add to the comfort and convenience of the people as the Vanderbilt roads—preserving their own interests in their own way (and that a selfish one) but Providence has so over-ruled that their work has helped their fellows (in the aggregate) much more than it has themselves. . . . I hope they may have renewal of vigor & force, and God may be trusted to direct it into channels for universal good.[15]

Again, not the "violent destruction" predicted by DeWitt, nor presumably government regulation, but the natural force of "new competition which has *always men & means* in reserve for anything which promises profit" would control the power of trusts.[16]

Sage did not spend much time thinking about economic phenomena in the abstract. His explanations were based on reactions rather than analyses. Moral law and personality rather than institutions and systems were his limiting concepts. Availability of credit, the great forest resources made easily accessible to the lumber barons were not among the items he reckoned in the success tally. Energy, ambition, ability were the positive virtues. Nowhere is this more apparent than in his comments on panics and depressions.

Never again was a panic to come so close to Sage's vital interests as in 1857. His interpretation of the business cycle, nonetheless, remained substantially what it had been in that year. The wicked and the weak were the villains of the piece. This was perhaps a natural reaction to pressure from creditors and delay from debtors. The trade itself was always regarded as sound. At the height of the '57 panic the editors of the New York *Times* were "quite sure that the money-lenders now have the ability, through a rational

[15] Sage to Dean Sage, Aug. 29, 1894, HWS.
[16] Sage to W. C. DeWitt, Dec. 11, 1894, HWS.

concert of action and a determination among themselves, to think better of mercantile credit, . . . to lend liberally, where lending will bring relief." [17] And a harassed businessman found in the businessmen's prayer meetings—a phenomenon of the 1858 revival—a measure of calm to help him face the situation in which he was placed:

One sees his property taken from him every day, by those who might pay him if they were willing to make sacrifices in order to do it, but who will not make the least effort . . . and by some who seem designedly to take advantage of the times, in order to defraud him.[18]

Will, and therefore morality, was the clue to popular economic thought. "In a climate of opinion which accepted prosperity, panic and depression as the inevitable operations of natural law, the nature and scope of men's questioning would not embrace social institutions. It would be directed towards individual culpability." [19] The very appearance of the revival which swept the business districts of New York and a number of other cities reflected the conviction that the panic was the result of guilt. Revival meetings concentrated on the individual's sin and conversion. Given his orientation, Sage could not have avoided becoming part of the throng that crowded religious meetings at noon hour and in the evenings during the troubled months of 1857.

The sensational failure of White and Co. in 1873 was attributed by Sage to the firm's officers, who had undertaken "too much for their capital—& besides that were working outside affairs—Dodge, in Politics & social life neglecting business therefor—Barnard— (the capitalist of White Co.) trying to bolster other weak men when he needed all his power to carry himself." [20] As a creditor of White and Co., Sage was probably entitled to express moral disapproval

[17] Sept. 14, 1857.

[18] William C. Conant, *Narratives of Remarkable Conversions and Revival Incidents* (New York, 1858), p. 357, note.

[19] William Greenblatt, "Some Social Aspects of the Panic of 1857," (M.A. thesis, Columbia University, 1948), pp. 102–103.

[20] To Robert Thurston, June 2, 1873, HWS.

of the lack of single-minded concentration on the firm's affairs. The continuance of depressed conditions after the sensational failures had eliminated weak and undesirable firms Sage explained by the general rule: The owners of money "will only part with it when they secure large profits—& a vast amount of security must grind out before money will go into regular channels at small profits." This was the statement of a condition, not a cure. While one waited for the natural law of supply and demand to re established a balance, irresponsibility characterized the business world. "The Bank pooling arrangement ends tomorrow and then will begin the Tragedy of 'The Devil take the hindmost.' " [21]

Sage's picture of the business cycle, a confused picture of natural law and personal weakness, left him in a dilemma as far as his own actions were concerned. Should he lend freely or should he too participate in the game of "Devil take the hindmost." Although he castigated the banks, he himself was not always anxious to endorse for others when he was in the position to be a lender. He refused with misgivings but nevertheless refused to aid further his old partner, Grant, during the panic of 1873. His rationalization was the classic one and made necessary by his friendship with Grant and Will Sage's concern. Grant, wrote Sage, was a poor manager who would not be able to work his way out of difficulties. It was for Grant's own good to get out of business, sell his property, pay his debts, and husband what was left.

Four years later Sage visited Grant, now broken and desperately ill, living in the back rooms of a house owned by his wife and rented to boarders.

I incline to the opinion that Grant is without property except what his wife has—and if he eats her bread *it* is *bitter*—Well—This is the Fruit of that Tree—such as was planted by hands not wholly idle or wasteful—but lax—inefficient—without definite purpose—vigor or industry equal to the work to be done—The fruit is legitimate—the reaping that which was sown.[22]

[21] To John McGraw, Oct. 13, 31, 1873, HWS.
[22] To Dean Sage, May 28, 1873; to John McGraw, Feb. 10, 1877, HWS.

If his symbolism was biblical, Sage's sentiment was nonetheless that of the social Darwinist.[23]

Sage became familiar with social Darwinism through the words of Henry Ward Beecher and other popularizers. He was not a "scientific" social Darwinist, but he does seem to have accepted social Darwinism at least as the latest variation of the optimism cults which had reassured him since the thirties. Beecher preached that "nature sifts and riddles everything from the lowest to the highest, and always in the direction of increasing strength, sacrificing the relative imperfection, throwing it away, and from generation to generation advancing, that by and by the average strength may be vastly increased." [24] Sage rationalized that panics, natural phenomena not subject to rational control, eliminated the unhealthy areas of the economy to permit substantial constructive growth. He dismissed the failure of Grant as evidence of Grant's incapacity, whether inherited or acquired. The parallels are not exact but they seem to demonstrate that Sage was absorbing the social application of Darwinism.

Mellow and relatively secure in 1893, Sage viewed the panic of that year without bitterness. He expected a steady decline until "the deadweight of losses & frauds by corporate & other mismanagement is squarely *earned out* and paid for & all values of corporate property go down & reconstruct upon basis of real value and availability." The panic was not even deplorable, since it served a moral function: "Debtors strive to pay—but when creditors know they cannot they are considerate and wait—So none but the very weak & the unworthy go to the wall." [25] Sage did support Governor Alger, a major debtor of his, throughout the troubled period

[23] Irvin Wyllie's position, "The success cult took its text from the Bible, not from the writings of Darwin and Spencer," seems to be based on the argument that the self-made man claimed success as the result of self-cultivated rather than inherited talents. The distinction is a fine one, perhaps too fine for the type of mind he is discussing (Wyllie, *op. cit.*, pp. 83, 34, 35, *passim*).

[24] Henry W. Beecher, "Evolution and Revolution," in Lyman Abbott, *Henry Ward Beecher* (Hartford, Conn., 1887), p. 571.

[25] To Dean Sage, Dec. 29; to W. H. Sage, Aug. 14, HWS.

and despite the opposition of his sons. Alger was a good risk, of course, a man with ample security, and Sage had at this time of his life no need to worry about immediate collections.

Sage's solution to the problems of depression remained the same. His frame of reference was in this area, too, individual action. Cut wages immediately, cut production only if that was unavoidable. "*Don't break—no use in it*"[26] was a moral as well as a business imperative. Continued operation, continued production, would keep a fundamentally sound economy going and, more important to one who customarily thought in individualistic terms, would save the entrepreneur from the humiliation and possible catastrophe of bankruptcy. Sage appreciated to a limited extent that there were unhealthy areas in the economy, but these he believed to be the result of fraud and incompetence. The incompetent and the fraud would be eliminated by the purgative effects of the panic, and all the rest would continue singing the same tune perhaps in a lower key. In essence it was not an economic but a moral problem that concerned Sage.

For those who survived it successfully a panic brought its own rewards. In 1873 Sage urged John McGraw: "John,—dont get Blue. . . . I have always had more solid satisfaction and better growth in blue times than when all went easy & there was a harvest of prosperity only—More victory—More development of power— Hasn't this been so with you?"[27] The doctrine of hard work and the cult of success were spiced by the challenge of panic conditions. A man could truly prove his worth in a crisis.

The sense of well being and power was carried over from Sage's business life in the post–Civil War decades into his personal life. The homes he built in Brooklyn and in Ithaca in this period were mansions. His last home in Brooklyn was built at a cost of $80,000 and located in one of the most fashionable residential districts, a neighborhood where "solid comfort could be found, where croquet and tennis could be played on the lawn, and where flower

[26] Sage and Grant to Latham, Tozer and Perry, Sept. 11, 1857, HWS.
[27] May 31, HWS.

gardens were cultivated in full view of the street." [28] In Ithaca his home was built on a hill midway between the town and the University; carriage house and greenhouses complemented it. Not only handsome wood paneling, as befitted a lumberman's establishment, but also imported tiles and elegant furnishings graced the house. After the death of Susan Linn Sage in 1885, her sister, Katherine Linn, acted as hostess. In Brooklyn, Dean Sage's home was close by his father's, and in Ithaca, Will Sage built on the adjoining lot. Nine grandchildren made all three households lively.

Sage was a devoted grandfather, and an exacting one. He wrote his grandchildren delightful letters describing the Indians who traded in the store at West Bay City, the turtles and alligators of Florida, the gorges of Ithaca, the more pleasant aspects of the life of the lumberjacks. And almost always his letters embraced a moral lesson: "I tell you nothing makes men happier than plenty to do, with plenty of food & clothing!" [29] He tried to impress upon them responsibility, self-control, frugality. Once he sent a box of candy for his grandchildren and entrusted Will's oldest son with the responsibility for dispensing the sweets.

You must put the Box upstairs in the dark closet where no one but yourself and Grandma know about it—and take out one Bundle at a time and put in the drawer where you can go every day and take one stick—Each of you—The days you dont go you will get none—and no more the next day—You are not at liberty to call in your friends for "treats"—but if you have a friend with whom you want to divide what you have you can do it. [30]

When the children visited him, Henry Sage tried to teach them graphically good business principles. He put young Harry to

[28] Sage to Charles Simpkins, Aug. 1, 1885, HWS; R. W. Weld, *Brooklyn Is America* (New York, 1950), p. 85.

[29] Fragment of letter, n.d.; see also letters of Sage to Henry W. Sage, Jr., 1877–1879, HWS.

[30] To Harry Sage, Aug. 30, 1878, HWS.

work in the garden at 5¢ pr day—working hours from 10 to 12—and from 1 to 4 . . . The first day fully ½ was done the 2d—a little less —the third . . . he made a partnership with Tom Clarendon—Tom to help do the work and have half the pay—The work done by *both* was less than Harrys first day alone—I have arranged with Harry to dissolve the partnership—& convinced him that *during work hours* it is better not to have visitors—& that he dont want a partner at all— as it is better to keep the money in the Family.[31]

As the boys grew older, Sage's major concern was that they be employed in work which would absorb them and prove their capacity. With the closing of the mill he evidently felt that the Sage enterprises could not provide a sufficient challenge for the young men of the family.[32] Although Sage denied it in the face of Dean Sage's opposition,[33] it is probable that one of the compelling motives behind his desire to investigate the possibilities of manufacturing in the southern pinelands was just this anxiety to create absorbing and testing work for his grandsons.

In 1866 Sage was admitted to the membership of Plymouth Church,[34] whose pastor, Henry Ward Beecher, had made it the most newsworthy church of its day. Beecher's sermons were dramatic, sentimental, topical. His "broad Christianity," as Sage termed it, had a strong emotional appeal. What it lacked in orthodoxy Plymouth Church made up in warmth and a sense of the richness and fullness of upper-middle-class Victorian living.

Plymouth Church's mission Sunday schools were equipped "not with the average Sunday-school books, but with the best English classics—Scott, Dickens, Thackeray, Hawthorne, Cooper, Howells." [35] The social parlors "were handsomely furnished and there

[31] Sage to W. H. Sage, June 12, 1879, HWS.

[32] Sage to Dean Sage, Aug. 13, 1889; May 28, 1892, HWS.

[33] *Ibid.*, Jan. 21, 1893.

[34] N. L. Thompson, *The History of Plymouth Church* (New York, 1873), p. 161.

[35] Lyman Abbott, *op. cit.*, p. 278.

every Monday evening Mr. Beecher held an informal reception. . . . The prominent members of the church were present, including such men as Messrs. Howard, Bowen, Claflin, Sage. . . ." [36] Sage, one of the "merchant princes" of the congregation, was soon made a trustee and became the devoted friend, benefactor, and protector of Beecher.

Until the time of the sensational Beecher-Tilton scandal relationships at least among the inner circle were cordial, even intimate. When the charge of adultery was brought against Beecher, Sage was made a member of the investigating committee. He was convinced almost immediately that Beecher was the victim of "a conspiracy most cunning—most malignant. . . . *I have no doubt he is wholly innocent.*" [37] Sage insisted on that verdict for the remainder of his life. It is one of the phenomena of the age that, given the nature of the charge, the suspicious and sober businessmen of the Plymouth congregation, men who like Sage regarded deviation from the Victorian moral code particularly in the area of sex as deserving the most severe anathemas, discounted the scandal and continued by and large to support Beecher. Perhaps when they entered Plymouth Church, these men consciously shed the suspicion that characterized their business dealings for the warmth of fellowship and the spirit of sentimental and righteous unity which Beecher did so much to create. To doubt Beecher might mean the shattering of the security his messages spelled.[38]

For Sage Beecher remained "the great man who has fed me for near twenty years." [39] Evidently Sage never suffered from indigestion after a Beecher sermon. Beecher's crusades were not directed against the vital interests of his congregation. He did not take up a "radical" issue like the slavery question until its popularity was

[36] Stephen M. Griswold, *Sixty Years with Plymouth Church* (New York, 1907), p. 126.

[37] Sage to A. D. White, July 31, 1874, ADW.

[38] Paxton Hibben presents a much harsher interpretation in *Henry Ward Beecher* (New York, 1927), p. 274.

[39] To S. B. Halliday, Oct. 8, 1880, HWS.

assured. His acceptance of evolution was influential [40] but not revolutionary except among orthodox theologians, whom he and his congregation had largely ignored as narrow sectarians. Social Darwinism had long been implicit in the messages that he delivered to his audience, and this brought specific comfort to the wealthy members of Plymouth Church particularly in the depression years after 1873, when wealth was subject to attack. In 1877 Beecher visited the Sage mill, and some unsanctified wretch scattered about in his path a hand bill bearing the following disreputable card: 'Don't forget that the Brooklyn Bull lectures tonight at the Opera House. All moral people are expected to attend.' "[41] Perhaps this unflattering reception was as much motivated by the subject Sage's friend had chosen to lecture on as by the Tilton scandal, for Beecher proceeded to lecture in a mill town suffering the effects of the depression "On Wealth."

> Mr. Beecher . . . proceeded to show how the virtues were developed by man's pursuit of wealth: self-denial and patient application. . . .
>
> In the conduct of the industries truth, honesty, fidelity are necessary. . . .
>
> Every man has a right to enjoy a liberal portion of what he has gained to make himself better, larger, freer. He believed in beautiful surroundings.[42]

This was a message more attuned to Sage's position than that of his employees. Undoubtedly Sage welcomed the justification of the successful businessman. He too held that the pursuit of wealth implied the positive virtues of sobriety and industry. It is doubtful that he entertained unqualified the notion that "truth, honesty, fidelity" prevailed in business circles, but it was a notion which was essential to his metaphysics. Honor and responsibility among businessmen were at least "ought" concepts. The use of his wealth "to make himself better, larger, freer" implied for Sage more than

[40] Richard Hofstadter, *Social Darwinism in American Thought* (Philadelphia, 1945), p. 15.

[41] Bay City *Observer,* Sept. 27, 1877. [42] *Ibid.*

beautiful surroundings: it included a generous philanthropy, of which Beecher himself was the beneficiary on occasion.

The assurance of Beecher's words, the charm of his personality, the warmth and optimism and sense of righteous community he fostered among his parishoners undoubtedly all contributed to the love men like Sage bore for him. Beecher was one of the few men —the others were university professors—in whom Sage was able to tolerate financial mismanagement and incompetence. His tolerance and exasperation extended to all the Beecher family: "Did you ever know a whole Family so little fitted to take care of themselves?" In the rare instances when he disagreed with a stand taken by Beecher, as when Beecher attacked the substantial businessmen and good Republicans James Joy and Governor Alger, Sage was able to dismiss if not forgive such behavior as an aberration: "His mind has evidently lost its balance." [43] Sage took on some aspects of the role of a patron in his relationship with Beecher. He made investments for him, provided an annuity for his wife, presented the Beechers with gifts, including each Christmas a Brooks Brothers suit of the best quality for Beecher himself. It was perhaps exactly this element of patronage which enabled Sage to dismiss the occasional aberrations of his pastor while he took comfort from the main tenor of his sermons. It was the kind of situation which occurred again and again in Sage's dealings with college professors and ministers. Of Lyman Abbott, Beecher's successor, Sage was to write:

He is a good man, a great worker, and in the right lines of thought and action except where he tries to deal with labor problems, about which he lacks education in the right schools—I sometimes come near swearing when I read some of his utterances—but for all that I like the man and have vast respect for his character and work.[44]

Repeatedly Sage was able to reject *without consideration* the opinions of educators and ministers whom he otherwise respected when

[43] Sage to Dean Sage, March 23, 1887, Nov. 1, 1884, HWS.
[44] To Mrs. Henry Ward Beecher, Dec. 22, 1892, HWS.

they suggested that the accepted course of businessmen was wrong or unworthy. These men were impractical, they did not understand the real world, they lacked "education in the right schools." Sage "fed" on doctrine that at the least reassured and usually flattered the businessman.

Neither pious nor rigid in his religious views, Sage was profoundly committed to the church as an institution and sincerely responsive to that aspect of Christianity which was concerned with personal salvation. Sage's correspondence abounds with phrases which suggest that he accepted literally the universe of the Scriptures. Perhaps it was due to the influence of Kirk and Beecher that he referred more often to the rewards of heaven than the torments of "the other place." He gave generously to churches of all denominations, recognizing them not only as religious organizations but also as stabilizing forces in the social scene. The values which he cherished he expected the churches to propagate. By and large his expectations were confirmed. His expectations were also those of his contemporaries. Indeed when on one occasion Sage refused to donate to a church in West Bay City, one of its leading citizens rebuked him, "You are one of those who defend their property in every way, and this is one of the defences, in the maintenance and support of this church." [45]

This was after all the successful businessman's century, and Sage in the decades after the Civil War was experiencing success on success. His patronage and therefore his opinion were sought. As a stockholder in Beecher's *Christian Union* he came to know figures of the publishing world; as trustee and benefactor of Cornell University educators and professors consulted with him; through the lecture impresario, James Pond, and through his old friend Anne Lynch, now "Mrs. Profr. Botta," he became friendly with the literary and artistic circles of his day. He sat for a bust of himself by Mrs. Botta, advanced the Bottas cash on their securities and advised them about investments, negotiated the sale to Ezra Cornell of an album "of some interesting things in history & art

[45] S. O. Fisher to Sage, Nov. 12, 1895, HWS.

which my friend Mrs. Botta has." [46] He entertained Mark Twain at dinner and evidently spent much of the evening discussing the economics of the lecture tour. Sage's summary—"Its hard work and I should think the endless repetition of substantially the same things would muddle the brains and make them useless for anything else" [47]—expresses a sound if prosaic view of the lecture tour as an institution.

In the eighties Sage had his portrait painted twice, once by Daniel Huntington, once by Eastman Johnson. In each case he felt the painting lacked sufficient strength. Huntington's portrait lacked, thought Sage, "some evidences of Soul in it," [48] while to Johnson Sage wrote, "It is the unanimous verdict of my Family and friends that a few touches giving more character to the face would be a very great improvement." [49] Sage saw himself as a forceful, strongly defined personality, and it was that picture he was determined to leave to posterity.

In the last three decades of his life Sage established his reputation as a generous philanthropist. Beyond his substantial contributions to Cornell University, he gave an impressive number of gifts and loans to individuals and institutions. The Sages' contribution to Yale University, Will's alma mater, was an endowed lectureship, named in honor of Lyman Beecher.

There were an exhausting number of calls and claims upon Sage; in acknowledging some and disregarding others Sage appears to have followed no rigid line. His sisters were provided for and occasionally other Sages in difficult circumstances who could claim some relationship. Ex-employees incapacitated by age or illness often tried to establish a claim on Sage's purse. This claim on himself as an employer Sage was reluctant to acknowledge. His responsibility for his workers ended, he believed, with the pay-

[46] Sage to Ezra Cornell, Jan. 2, 1873, HWS.

[47] To W. H. Sage, Dec. 4, 1884, HWS.

[48] To Dean Sage, July 23, 1887, HWS.

[49] June 20, 1885, HWS. This portrait and one of Susan Linn Sage by Johnson have been presented to the White Art Museum, Cornell University, by Mrs. Henry Manning Sage.

ment of their wages. Indeed on one occasion when a man was hurt while on the job Sage contended that "we cannot see that because a man works for us for pay, and gets it we are forever bound to take care of him if by accident or otherwise he is disabled." [50] At the same time he did provide for a number of old employees whose needs he had satisfied himself were genuine. Such gifts were probably prompted more by personal feeling for the recipient than by a sense of responsibility. Occasional impromptu gifts of money—"I remember the $10, you put in my Hand on Main St." [51] —were probably more frequent than the Sage correspondence reveals. Sage provided for a few old employees by regular contributions to their support.

Loans at low rates of interest on personal notes were a type of philanthropy that Sage employed particularly in his dealings with college students, professors, and Negroes. There may have been some feeling on his part that these groups especially needed training in business principles. The independence and the integrity of the recipient were tested, he believed, by his or her—Sage was especially open to appeals for financial aid from Sage College women—efforts to meet the interest and repay the loan.

Sage's commitment to Negro charities probably had its origins in the fervor of pre–Civil War and Civil War times. He contributed repeatedly to Negro causes: "I know none better than lifting that colored race, beginning at the bottom—They need everything of education & culture and are anxious to receive." [52] Sage urged individual Negroes to whom he occasionally made loans to regard repayment or nonpayment as a reflection on all Negroes.

The philosophy behind Sage's philanthropy was very generally in line with that given currency by Andrew Carnegie as the Gospel of Wealth: "I am in full sympathy with all movements to better the condition of the poor through measures & instrumentalities which shall help to give them a foot hold in life where they can

[50] To Hartingh and Nesbitt, April 14, 1891, HWS.
[51] Philip Case to Sage, Dec. 6, 1877, HWS.
[52] Sage to Lyman Abbott, May 10, 1884, HWS.

help themselves." [53] Therefore the large percentage of his gifts went
to educational institutions: libraries, universities, churches. When
successful businessmen gave to help others, Sage wrote, they were
giving over and over again symbolically their first hard-earned one
hundred dollars.[54] Those first dollars Sage obviously associated
with self-sacrifice, application, ambition, respect for property. It
is not unreasonable then that he expected these virtues to be
revered by the institutions he supported.

There was an element of self-justification in Sage's philanthropy.
His gifts, particularly those to Cornell University, were the evidence that he had worked for more than material goals.

My gifts have been so large that we have less, all told, than we had—
but I think the giving has been wise—and the investment you and yours
can always *see* and its value will never be less—They will show that
my life has not been spent in vain & that it has some value.[55]

This was not to imply that Sage felt guilty in any sense about the
acquisition of wealth. His philanthropy rounded out the picture
of the businessman as he had painted it. It was Sage's way of
proving that by self-interest the general good would indeed be
served.

Sage's contribution to politics in the post–Civil War decades
was largely financial. Sage was uninterested in political office for
himself or his sons. That was, he thought, an honor too dearly
bought.

Yours asking advice about accepting nomination to Assembly recd. . . .
The experience would broaden you—the associations would *harm you*
—The needful attention to your duties would greatly injure our business interests—More than this—it would unsettle you—and take you
years—as it did me—to get your head clear from Political ideas & associations.[56]

Clearly Sage did not contemplate politics as a permanent career
for his son. There was a suggestion of contempt in his attitude to-

[53] Sage to Courtlandt Palmer, April 23, 1879, HWS.
[54] To W. J. Young, Sept. 22, 1891, HWS.
[55] To Dean Sage, April 20, 1892, HWS.   [56] *Ibid.*, 1871.

ward politicians—"the associations would *harm you.*" And again when he wrote to one who had recently been defeated for office, his reaction was: "The good Lord was kind to permit your defeat. . . . When you have saved from your profession enough to keep you *three years* you may afford the Luxury of a Senatorship and forget to do anything else." [57]

Sage preferred to influence political decisions by participation in lobbying activities, through personal contact with legislators, by aiding in the election of the "right" man. He contributed regularly to the campaign expenses of the Republican party and to the expenses of individual politicians, particularly members of the New York and Michigan legislatures. That he expected active aid for his own projects in return for financial contributions is clear. Sage also received the privilege of suggesting candidates for a few patronage offices and at least a limited voice in the party councils in New York State. The importance of having "friends" in the legislature had been demonstrated from the earliest period of his career, when he was interested in canal appropriations. Sage's maxim was: "*Stand by our friends*—We always need them." [58] In the nineties evidence of more effective farmer-labor discontent movements intensified Sage's concern with government as a protector as well as a promoter of propertied interests.

Sage was vehemently partisan in his political adherence. To Dean, in danger of "apostasy" in the 1884 elections, Sage wrote: "As to Blaine I have not had a doubt of his fitness. . . . If I had and *knew* that all the charges made were true I would rather help, by voting for him, to perpetuate the Republican party than by voting for Cleveland to help place the Democratic party in power." [59] Sage recognized the validity of the charges of corruption made against some of the Republican leaders but made excuses for them:

[57] To Fremont Cole, Nov. 19, 1894, HWS.

[58] Sage to Dean Sage, urging him to vote for **Alonzo B. Cornell,** Oct. 25, 1879, HWS.

[59] Nov. 1, 1884, HWS.

271

I have known Platt always—He is not made after your plan—nor my model, but does as well as he knows how the duties of leadership which he has earned by being able & willing to do more work for the party than any other man. . . . I am inclined to stand by the Ticket, and his acts in creating it.[60]

The blatant corruption in government in the seventies and eighties which occasionally moved his sons toward "Democratic or Mugwump associations" left Sage unshaken. His partisanship was not cynical so much as it was the logical result of interpreting government action as response to pressure from the most powerful interest groups. His staunch adherence to the Republican party was based fundamentally on that party's support of "sound" currency and a tariff on lumber. Occasionally he brought himself to admit that "the Democratic party in power will quite likely be conservative and wise—They wont make any violent changes in Tariff. . . . The currency I cannot believe will be managed radically wrong." [61] But with the Democratic party in power one could not be *as* certain of support for protection and sound money as with the Republicans.

In the nineties, when new pressure groups representing labor and the debtor classes were beginning to be effective, Sage's working definition of democratic government broke down, and even his loyalty to the Republican party was temporarily shaken: "Both parties pander to silver & all its underlying interests." [62] His philosophy did not embrace a situation in which labor unions could challenge "corporate interests" or debtors affect inflation. In the seventies the danger had been less apparent to him, and he was content to leave the ultimate resolution to God: "The Cinncinnatti Inquirer say 'Universal Suffrage can make *soap* legal tender if it wishes'—An extreme view I think, but it excites reflection upon the possible evil which may attend this great advance of Liberty—May God guide us in the right way." [63] In the nineties

[60] To J. D. F. Slee, Sept. 7, 1891, HWS.
[61] To Dean Sage, Nov. 9, 1892, HWS.　　　　[62] *Ibid.*, June 29, 1894.
[63] To A. D. White, Jan. 13, 1878, ADW.

Sage was suffering losses not only on his securities investments but as well on western bonds and mortgage loans. The danger was all too apparent. He feared and blamed the "hordes of Southern & Western anarchists . . . with their Northern sympathizers." [64] Tentatively he suggested the necessity for an authoritarian political figure, "the Man on Horseback":

All these interests are to be arrayed against conservative legislation and possible alliances with Labor may defeat legislation necessary to the very existence of our Government, and may introduce as a prime necessity "the Man on Horseback" to settle existing difficulties and make new platform! [65]

If Sage's understanding of the workings of democratic government was limited to responsiveness to pressure groups, his understanding of the primary function of all government was limited to the protection of property. Interest groups which challenged those property rights he recognized were no longer interest groups but anarchists subversive of all government.

Sage was usually able to maintain his optimism and partisanship, however. In his lifetime neither the rights nor the privileges of the capitalist were permanently shaken. The portrait of the successful businessman which he had drawn and which he lived up to was still widely if not universally applauded. He died in his home in Ithaca on September 18, 1897, and was buried in Sage Chapel.

[64] To Dean Sage, Nov. 8, 1894, HWS.   [65] *Ibid.*, June 29.

Index